UK Register of Expert Witnesses

Expert Witness
Year Book
2010

CW01496389

UK Register of Expert Witnesses

Expert Witness
Year Book
2010

Dr Chris Pamplin, Editor
UK Register of Expert Witnesses

© 2010

UK Register of Expert Witnesses
J S Publications
11 Kings Court
Newmarket
Suffolk
CB8 7SG

ISBN 978-1-905926 08 4

Published: January 2010

Contents in Brief

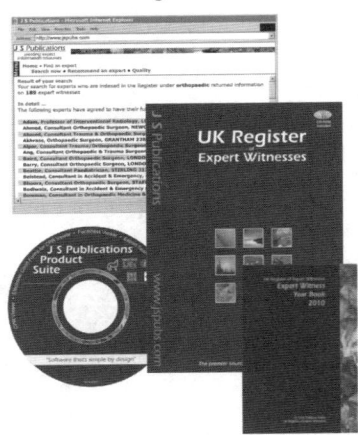

Contents in Detail

1

Rules in Civil Litigation

Civil Procedure Rules Part 1 – Overriding objective

The following is taken from the 50th update of the CPR dated October 2009. Source: www.justice.gov.uk

1.1 The overriding objective

(1)   These Rules are a new procedural code with the overriding objective of enabling the court to deal with cases justly.

(2)   Dealing with a case justly includes, so far as is practicable –

    (a)   ensuring that the parties are on an equal footing;

    (b)   saving expense;

    (c)   dealing with the case in ways which are proportionate –

        (i)   to the amount of money involved;

        (ii)   to the importance of the case;

        (iii)   to the complexity of the issues; and

        (iv)   to the financial position of each party;

    (d)   ensuring that it is dealt with expeditiously and fairly; and

    (e)   allotting to it an appropriate share of the court's resources, while taking into account the need to allot resources to other cases.

1.2 Application by the court of the overriding objective

The court must seek to give effect to the overriding objective when it –

(a)   exercises any power given to it by the Rules; or

(b)   interprets any rule subject to rules 76.2 and 79.2.

1.3 Duty of the parties

The parties are required to help the court to further the overriding objective.

1.4 Court's duty to manage cases

(1)   The court must further the overriding objective by actively managing cases.

(2)   Active case management includes –

    (a)   encouraging the parties to co-operate with each other in the conduct of the proceedings;

    (b)   identifying the issues at an early stage;

    (c)   deciding promptly which issues need full investigation and trial and accordingly disposing summarily of the others;

    (d)   deciding the order in which issues are to be resolved;

    (e)   encouraging the parties to use an alternative dispute resolution procedure if the court considers that appropriate and facilitating the use of such procedure;

    (f)   helping the parties to settle the whole or part of the case;

(g) fixing timetables or otherwise controlling the progress of the case;

(h) considering whether the likely benefits of taking a particular step justify the cost of taking it;

(i) dealing with as many aspects of the case as it can on the same occasion;

(j) dealing with the case without the parties needing to attend at court;

(k) making use of technology; and

(l) giving directions to ensure that the trial of a case proceeds quickly and efficiently.

Civil Procedure Rules Part 2.1 – Application of the Rules

The following is taken from the 50th update of the CPR dated October 2009. Source: www.justice.gov.uk

2.1 Application of the Rules

(1) Subject to paragraph (2), these Rules apply to all proceedings in –

    (a) county courts;

    (b) the High Court; and

    (c) the Civil Division of the Court of Appeal.

(2) These Rules do not apply to proceedings of the kinds specified in the first column of the following table (proceedings for which rules may be made under the enactments specified in the second column) except to the extent that they are applied to those proceedings by another enactment –

	Proceedings	Enactments
1	Insolvency proceedings	Insolvency Act 1986, ss.411 and 412
2	Non-contentious or common form probate proceedings	Supreme Court Act 1981, s.127
3	Proceedings in the High Court when acting as a Prize Court	Prize Courts Act 1894, s.3
4	Proceedings before the Court of Protection	Mental Capacity Act 2005, s.51
5	Family proceedings	Matrimonial and Family Proceedings Act 1984, s.40
6	Adoption proceedings	Adoption Act 1976, s.66 or Adoption and Children Act 2002, s.141(c)
7	Election petitions in the High Court	Representation of the People Act 1983, s.182

Civil Procedure Rules Part 35 – Experts and Assessors

The following is taken from the 50th update of the CPR dated
October 2009. Source: www.justice.gov.uk

35.1 Duty to restrict expert evidence

Expert evidence shall be restricted to that which is reasonably required to resolve the proceedings.

35.2 Interpretation and definitions

(1) A reference to an 'expert' in this Part is a reference to a person who has been instructed to give or prepare expert evidence for the purpose of proceedings.

(2) 'Single joint expert' means an expert instructed to prepare a report for the court on behalf of two or more of the parties (including the claimant) to the proceedings.

35.3 Experts – overriding duty to the court

(1) It is the duty of experts to help the court on matters within their expertise.

(2) This duty overrides any obligation to the person from whom experts have received instructions or by whom they are paid.

35.4 Court's power to restrict expert evidence

(1) No party may call an expert or put in evidence an expert's report without the court's permission.

(2) When parties apply for permission they must identify –

(a) the field in which expert evidence is required; and

(b) where practicable, the name of the proposed expert.

(3) If permission is granted it shall be in relation only to the expert named or the field identified under paragraph (2).

(3A) Where a claim has been allocated to the small claims track or the fast track, if permission is given for expert evidence, it will normally be given for evidence from only one expert on a particular issue.

(Paragraph 7 of practice direction 35 sets out some of the circumstances the court will consider when deciding whether expert evidence should be given by a single joint expert.)

(4) The court may limit the amount of a party's expert's fees and expenses that may be recovered from any other party.

35.5 General requirement for expert evidence to be given in a written report

(1) Expert evidence is to be given in a written report unless the court directs otherwise.

(2)   If a claim is on the small claims track or the fast track, the court will not direct an expert to attend a hearing unless it is necessary to do so in the interests of justice.

35.6 Written questions to experts

(1)   A party may put written questions about an expert's report (which must be proportionate) to –

    (a)   an expert instructed by another party; or

    (b)   a single joint expert appointed under rule 35.7

(2)   Written questions under paragraph (1) –

    (a)   may be put once only;

    (b)   must be put within 28 days of service of the expert's report; and,

    (c)   must be for the purpose only of clarification of the report,

    unless in any case –

        (i)   the court gives permission; or

        (ii)   the other party agrees.

(3)   An expert's answers to questions put in accordance with paragraph (1) shall be treated as part of the expert's report.

(4)   Where –

    (a)   a party has put a written question to an expert instructed by another party; and

    (b)   the expert does not answer that question,

    the court may make one or both of the following orders in relation to the party who instructed the expert –

        (i)   that the party may not rely on the evidence of that expert; or

        (ii)   that the party may not recover the fees and expenses of that expert from any other party.

35.7 Court's power to direct that evidence is to be given by a single joint expert

(1)   Where two or more parties wish to submit expert evidence on a particular issue, the court may direct that the evidence on that issue is to be given by a single joint expert.

(2)   Where the parties who wish to submit the evidence ('the relevant parties') cannot agree who should be the single joint expert, the court may –

    (a)   select the expert from a list prepared or identified by the relevant parties; or

    (b)   direct that the expert be selected in such other manner as the court may direct.

35.8 Instructions to a single joint expert

(1)   Where the court gives a direction under rule 35.7 for a single joint expert to be used, any relevant party may give instructions to the expert.

(2)   When a party gives instructions to the expert that party must, at the same time, send a copy to the other relevant parties.

(3)   The court may give directions about –

   (a)   the payment of the expert's fees and expenses; and

   (b)   any inspection, examination or experiments which the expert wishes to carry out.

(4)   The court may, before an expert is instructed –

   (a)   limit the amount that can be paid by way of fees and expenses to the expert; and

   (b)   direct that some or all of the relevant parties pay that amount into court.

(5)   Unless the court otherwise directs, the relevant parties are jointly and severally liable for the payment of the expert's fees and expenses.

35.9 Power of court to direct a party to provide information

(1)   Where a party has access to information which is not reasonably available to another party, the court may direct the party who has access to the information to –

   (a)   prepare and file a document recording the information; and

   (b)   serve a copy of that document on the other party.

35.10 Contents of report

(1)   An expert's report must comply with the requirements set out in practice direction 35.

(2)   At the end of an expert's report there must be a statement that the expert understands and has complied with their duty to the court.

(3)   The expert's report must state the substance of all material instructions, whether written or oral, on the basis of which the report was written.

(4)   The instructions referred to in paragraph (3) shall not be privileged against disclosure but the court will not, in relation to those instructions –

   (a)   order disclosure of any specific document; or

   (b)   permit any questioning in court, other than by the party who instructed the expert,

unless it is satisfied that there are reasonable grounds to consider the statement of instructions given under paragraph (3) to be inaccurate or incomplete.

35.11 Use by one party of expert's report disclosed by another

(1)   Where a party has disclosed an expert's report, any party may use that expert's report as evidence at the trial.

35.12 Discussions between experts

(1)   The court may, at any stage, direct a discussion between experts for the purpose of requiring the experts to –

    (a)   identify and discuss the expert issues in the proceedings; and

    (b)   where possible, reach an agreed opinion on those issues.

(2)   The court may specify the issues which the experts must discuss.

(3)   The court may direct that following a discussion between the experts they must prepare a statement for the court setting out those issues on which –

    (a)   they agree; and

    (b)   they disagree, with a summary of their reasons for disagreeing.

(4)   The content of the discussion between the experts shall not be referred to at the trial unless the parties agree.

(5)   Where experts reach agreement on an issue during their discussions, the agreement shall not bind the parties unless the parties expressly agree to be bound by the agreement.

35.13 Consequence of failure to disclose expert's report

(1)   A party who fails to disclose an expert's report may not use the report at the trial or call the expert to give evidence orally unless the court gives permission.

35.14 Expert's right to ask court for directions

(1)   Experts may file written requests for directions for the purpose of assisting them in carrying out their functions.

(2)   Experts must, unless the court orders otherwise, provide copies of the proposed requests for directions under paragraph (1) –

    (a)   to the party instructing them, at least 7 days before they file the requests; and

    (b)   to all other parties, at least 4 days before they file them.

(3)   The court, when it gives directions, may also direct that a party be served with a copy of the directions.

35.15 Assessors

(1)   This rule applies where the court appoints one or more persons under section 70 of the Senior Courts Act 1981 or section 63 of the County Courts Act 1984 as an assessor.

(2)   An assessor will assist the court in dealing with a matter in which the assessor has skill and experience.

(3) An assessor will take such part in the proceedings as the court may direct and in particular the court may direct an assessor to –

    (a) prepare a report for the court on any matter at issue in the proceedings; and

    (b) attend the whole or any part of the trial to advise the court on any such matter.

(4) If an assessor prepares a report for the court before the trial has begun –

    (a) the court will send a copy to each of the parties; and

    (b) the parties may use it at trial.

(5) The remuneration to be paid to an assessor is to be determined by the court and will form part of the costs of the proceedings.

(6) The court may order any party to deposit in the court office a specified sum in respect of an assessor's fees and, where it does so, the assessor will not be asked to act until the sum has been deposited.

(7) Paragraphs (5) and (6) do not apply where the remuneration of the assessor is to be paid out of money provided by Parliament.

Civil Procedure Rules Part 35 Practice Direction

The following is taken from the 50th update of the Rules dated October 2009. Source: www.justice.gov.uk

Introduction

1   Part 35 is intended to limit the use of oral expert evidence to that which is reasonably required. In addition, where possible, matters requiring expert evidence should be dealt with by only one expert. Experts and those instructing them are expected to have regard to the guidance contained in the Protocol for the Instruction of Experts to give Evidence in Civil Claims annexed to this practice direction. (Further guidance on experts is contained in Annex C to the Practice Direction (Pre-Action Conduct)).

Expert Evidence – General Requirements

2.1   Expert evidence should be the independent product of the expert uninfluenced by the pressures of litigation.

2.2   Experts should assist the court by providing objective, unbiased opinions on matters within their expertise, and should not assume the role of an advocate.

2.3   Experts should consider all material facts, including those which might detract from their opinions.

2.4   Experts should make it clear –

(a)   when a question or issue falls outside their expertise; and

(b)   when they are not able to reach a definite opinion, for example because they have insufficient information.

2.5   If, after producing a report, an expert's view changes on any material matter, such change of view should be communicated to all the parties without delay, and when appropriate to the court.

Form and Content of an Expert's Report

3.1   An expert's report should be addressed to the court and not to the party from whom the expert has received instructions.

3.2   An expert's report must:

(1)   give details of the expert's qualifications;

(2)   give details of any literature or other material which has been relied on in making the report;

(3)   contain a statement setting out the substance of all facts and instructions which are material to the opinions expressed in the report or upon which those opinions are based;

(4)   make clear which of the facts stated in the report are within the expert's own knowledge;

(5) say who carried out any examination, measurement, test or experiment which the expert has used for the report, give the qualifications of that person, and say whether or not the test or experiment has been carried out under the expert's supervision;

(6) where there is a range of opinion on the matters dealt with in the report –

    (a) summarise the range of opinions; and

    (b) give reasons for the expert's own opinion;

(7) contain a summary of the conclusions reached;

(8) if the expert is not able to give an opinion without qualification, state the qualification; and

(9) contain a statement that the expert –

    (a) understands their duty to the court, and has complied with that duty; and

    (b) is aware of the requirements of Part 35, this practice direction and the Protocol for Instruction of Experts to give Evidence in Civil Claims.

3.3 An expert's report must be verified by a statement of truth in the following form –

I confirm that I have made clear which facts and matters referred to in this report are within my own knowledge and which are not. Those that are within my own knowledge I confirm to be true. The opinions I have expressed represent my true and complete professional opinions on the matters to which they refer.

(Part 22 deals with statements of truth. Rule 32.14 sets out the consequences of verifying a document containing a false statement without an honest belief in its truth.)

Information

4 Under rule 35.9 the court may direct a party with access to information, which is not reasonably available to another party to serve on that other party a document, which records the information. The document served must include sufficient details of all the facts, tests, experiments and assumptions which underlie any part of the information to enable the party on whom it is served to make, or to obtain, a proper interpretation of the information and an assessment of its significance.

Instructions

5 Cross-examination of experts on the contents of their instructions will not be allowed unless the court permits it (or unless the party who gave the instructions consents). Before it gives permission the court

must be satisfied that there are reasonable grounds to consider that the statement in the report of the substance of the instructions is inaccurate or incomplete. If the court is so satisfied, it will allow the cross-examination where it appears to be in the interests of justice.

Questions to Experts

6.1 Where a party sends a written question or questions under rule 35.6 direct to an expert, a copy of the questions must, at the same time, be sent to the other party or parties.

6.2 The party or parties instructing the expert must pay any fees charged by that expert for answering questions put under rule 35.6. This does not affect any decision of the court as to the party who is ultimately to bear the expert's fees.

Single joint expert

7 When considering whether to give permission for the parties to rely on expert evidence and whether that evidence should be from a single joint expert the court will take into account all the circumstances in particular, whether:

(a) it is proportionate to have separate experts for each party on a particular issue with reference to –

    (i) the amount in dispute;

    (ii) the importance to the parties; and

    (iii) the complexity of the issue;

(b) the instruction of a single joint expert is likely to assist the parties and the court to resolve the issue more speedily and in a more cost-effective way than separately instructed experts;

(c) expert evidence is to be given on the issue of liability, causation or quantum;

(d) the expert evidence falls within a substantially established area of knowledge which is unlikely to be in dispute or there is likely to be a range of expert opinion;

(e) a party has already instructed an expert on the issue in question and whether or not that was done in compliance with any practice direction or relevant pre-action protocol;

(f) questions put in accordance with rule 35.6 are likely to remove the need for the other party to instruct an expert if one party has already instructed an expert;

(g) questions put to a single joint expert may not conclusively deal with all issues that may require testing prior to trial;

(h) a conference may be required with the legal representatives, experts and other witnesses which may make instruction of a single joint expert impractical; and

> (i) a claim to privilege makes the instruction of any expert as a single joint expert inappropriate.

Orders

8 Where an order requires an act to be done by an expert, or otherwise affects an expert, the party instructing that expert must serve a copy of the order on the expert. The claimant must serve the order on a single joint expert.

Discussions between experts

9.1 Unless directed by the court discussions between experts are not mandatory. Parties must consider, with their experts, at an early stage, whether there is likely to be any useful purpose in holding an experts' discussion and if so when.

9.2 The purpose of discussions between experts is not for experts to settle cases but to agree and narrow issues and in particular to identify:

(i) the extent of the agreement between them;

(ii) the points of and short reasons for any disagreement;

(iii) action, if any, which may be taken to resolve any outstanding points of disagreement; and

(iv) any further material issues not raised and the extent to which these issues are agreed.

9.3 Where the experts are to meet, the parties must discuss and if possible agree whether an agenda is necessary, and if so attempt to agree one that helps the experts to focus on the issues which need to be discussed. The agenda must not be in the form of leading questions or hostile in tone.

9.4 Unless ordered by the court, or agreed by all parties, and the experts, neither the parties nor their legal representatives may attend experts discussions.

9.5 If the legal representatives do attend –

(i) they should not normally intervene in the discussion, except to answer questions put to them by the experts or to advise on the law; and

(ii) the experts may if they so wish hold part of their discussions in the absence of the legal representatives.

9.6 A statement must be prepared by the experts dealing with paragraphs 9.2(i) - (iv) above. Individual copies of the statements must be signed by the experts at the conclusion of the discussion, or as soon thereafter as practicable, and in any event within 7 days. Copies of the statements must be provided to the parties no later than 14 days after signing.

9.7 Experts must give their own opinions to assist the court and do not require the authority of the parties to sign a joint statement.

9.8   If an expert significantly alters an opinion, the joint statement must include a note or addendum by that expert explaining the change of opinion.

Assessors

10.1   An assessor may be appointed to assist the court under rule 35.15. Not less than 21 days before making any such appointment, the court will notify each party in writing of the name of the proposed assessor, of the matter in respect of which the assistance of the assessor will be sought and of the qualifications of the assessor to give that assistance.

10.2   Where any person has been proposed for appointment as an assessor, any party may object to that person either personally or in respect of that person's qualification.

10.3   Any such objection must be made in writing and filed with the court within 7 days of receipt of the notification referred to in paragraph 10.1 and will be taken into account by the court in deciding whether or not to make the appointment.

10.4   Copies of any report prepared by the assessor will be sent to each of the parties but the assessor will not give oral evidence or be open to cross-examination or questioning.

Annotated CJC Experts Protocol

Source: www.jspubs.com

The text of the Experts Protocol is taken from the 50th update of the CPR dated October 2009. Source: www.justice.gov.uk

The *UK Register of Expert Witnesses* is delighted that the CJC has taken the initiative – cutting through the confusion created by the regrettable inability of the Academy of Experts and Expert Witness Institute to work together – to establish a single, authoritative *Experts Protocol*. The expert witness community should welcome this development.

Having worked through the Protocol in some detail, we have identified a number of areas where further guidance may assist expert witnesses. This assertion is based upon the evidence we have gathered from our helpline, i.e. what actually troubles expert witnesses enough that they contact us. We are told, by its authors, that the Protocol cannot be modified (which seems a shame since any protocol ought to be capable of reflecting the developing needs of its constituency). We have been forced, therefore, to publish below an annotated version of the Protocol that includes these additional points of guidance. It clearly differentiates the official text from our annotations (shown in boxes).

1. Introduction

1.1   Expert witnesses perform a vital role in civil litigation. It is essential that both those who instruct experts and experts themselves are given clear guidance as to what they are expected to do in civil proceedings. The purpose of this Protocol is to provide such guidance. It has been drafted by the Civil Justice Council and reflects the rules and practice directions current [in June 2005], replacing the Code of Guidance on Expert Evidence. The authors of the Protocol wish to acknowledge the valuable assistance they obtained by drawing on earlier documents produced by the Academy of Experts and the Expert Witness Institute, as well as suggestions made by the Clinical Dispute Forum. The Protocol has been approved by the Master of the Rolls.

2. Aims of Protocol

2.1   This Protocol offers guidance to experts and to those instructing them in the interpretation of and compliance with Part 35 of the Civil Procedure Rules (CPR 35) and its associated Practice Direction (PD 35) and to further the objectives of the Civil Procedure Rules in general. It is intended to assist in the interpretation of those provisions in the interests of good practice but it does not replace them. It sets out standards for the use of experts and the conduct of experts and those who instruct them. The existence of this Protocol does not remove the need for experts and those who instruct them to be familiar with CPR35 and PD35.

2.2 Experts and those who instruct them should also bear in mind para 1.4 of the Practice Direction on Protocols which contains the following objectives, namely to:

(a) encourage the exchange of early and full information about the expert issues involved in a prospective legal claim;

(b) enable the parties to avoid or reduce the scope of litigation by agreeing the whole or part of an expert issue before commencement of proceedings; and

(c) support the efficient management of proceedings where litigation cannot be avoided.

3. Application

3.1 This Protocol applies to any steps taken for the purpose of civil proceedings by experts or those who instruct them on or after 5th September 2005.

3.2 It applies to all experts who are, or who may be, governed by CPR Part 35 and to those who instruct them. Experts are governed by Part 35 if they are or have been instructed to give or prepare evidence for the purpose of civil proceedings in a court in England and Wales (CPR 35.2).

3.3 Experts, and those instructing them, should be aware that some cases may be "specialist proceedings" (CPR 49) where there are modifications to the Civil Procedure Rules. Proceedings may also be governed by other Protocols. Further, some courts have published their own Guides which supplement the Civil Procedure Rules for proceedings in those courts. They contain provisions affecting expert evidence. Expert witnesses and those instructing them should be familiar with them when they are relevant.

3.4 Courts may take into account any failure to comply with this Protocol when making orders in relation to costs, interest, time limits, the stay of proceedings and whether to order a party to pay a sum of money into court.

Limitation

3.5 If, as a result of complying with any part of this Protocol, claims would or might be time barred under any provision in the Limitation Act 1980, or any other legislation that imposes a time limit for the bringing of an action, claimants may commence proceedings without complying with this Protocol. In such circumstances, claimants who commence proceedings without complying with all, or any part, of this Protocol must apply, giving notice to all other parties, to the court for directions as to the timetable and form of procedure to be adopted, at the same time as they request the court to issue proceedings. The court may consider whether to order a stay of the whole or part of the proceedings pending compliance with this Protocol and may make orders in relation to costs.

Privilege and Disclosure: Assume no privilege would be claimed

An expert must not be given any information that is legally privileged unless it has been decided that privilege should be waived. An expert should therefore assume that his instructions do not contain any information for which privilege would be claimed.

4. Duties of Experts

4.1 Experts always owe a duty to exercise reasonable skill and care to those instructing them, and to comply with any relevant professional code of ethics. However when they are instructed to give or prepare evidence for the purpose of civil proceedings in England and Wales they have an overriding duty to help the court on matters within their expertise (CPR 35.3). This duty overrides any obligation to the person instructing or paying them. Experts must not serve the exclusive interest of those who retain them.

4.2 Experts should be aware of the overriding objective that courts deal with cases justly. This includes dealing with cases proportionately, expeditiously and fairly (CPR 1.1). Experts are under an obligation to assist the court so as to enable them to deal with cases in accordance with the overriding objective. However the overriding objective does not impose on experts any duty to act as mediators between the parties or require them to trespass on the role of the court in deciding facts.

4.3 Experts should provide opinions which are independent, regardless of the pressures of litigation. In this context, a useful test of 'independence' is that the expert would express the same opinion if given the same instructions by an opposing party. Experts should not take it upon themselves to promote the point of view of the party instructing them or engage in the role of advocates.

4.4 Experts should confine their opinions to matters which are material to the disputes between the parties and provide opinions only in relation to matters which lie within their expertise. Experts should indicate without delay where particular questions or issues fall outside their expertise.

4.5 Experts should take into account all material facts before them at the time that they give their opinion. Their reports should set out those facts and any literature or any other material on which they have relied in forming their opinions. They should indicate if an opinion is provisional, or qualified, or where they consider that further information is required or if, for any other reason, they are not satisfied that an opinion can be expressed finally and without qualification.

4.6 Experts should inform those instructing them without delay of any change in their opinions on any material matter and the reason for it.

4.7 Experts should be aware that any failure by them to comply with the Civil Procedure Rules or court orders or any excessive delay for which they are responsible may result in the parties who instructed them being penalised in costs and even, in extreme cases, being debarred from placing the experts' evidence before the court. In Phillips v Symes[1] Peter Smith J held that courts may also make orders for costs (under section 51 of the Supreme Court Act 1981) directly against expert witnesses who by their evidence cause significant expense to be incurred, and do so in flagrant and reckless disregard of their duties to the Court.

5. Conduct of Experts instructed only to Advise

5.1 Part 35 only applies where experts are instructed to give opinions which are relied on for the purposes of court proceedings. Advice which the parties do not intend to adduce in litigation is likely to be confidential; the Protocol does not apply in these circumstances.[2] [3]

5.2 The same applies where, after the commencement of proceedings, experts are instructed only to advise (e.g. to comment upon a single joint expert's report) and not to give or prepare evidence for use in the proceedings.

5.3 However this Protocol does apply if experts who were formerly instructed only to advise are later instructed to give or prepare evidence for the purpose of civil proceedings.

6. The Need for Experts

6.1 Those intending to instruct experts to give or prepare evidence for the purpose of civil proceedings should consider whether expert evidence is appropriate, taking account of the principles set out in CPR Parts 1 and 35, and in particular whether:

(a) it is relevant to a matter which is in dispute between the parties;

(b) it is reasonably required to resolve the proceedings (CPR 35.1);

(c) the expert has expertise relevant to the issue on which an opinion is sought;

(d) the expert has the experience, expertise and training appropriate to the value, complexity and importance of the case; and whether

(e) these objects can be achieved by the appointment of a single joint expert (see section 17 below).

---

1 *Phillips -v- Symes* [2004] EWHC 2330 (Ch).
2 *Carlson -v- Townsend* [2001] 1 WLR 2415.
3 *Jackson -v- Marley Davenport* [2004] 1 WLR 2926.

6.2   Although the court's permission is not generally required to instruct an expert, the court's permission is required before experts can be called to give evidence or their evidence can be put in (CPR 35.4).

7. The Appointment of Experts

7.1   Before experts are formally instructed or the court's permission to appoint named experts is sought, the following should be established:

(a)   that they have the appropriate expertise and experience;

(b)   that they are familiar with the general duties of an expert;

(c)   that they can produce a report, deal with questions and have discussions with other experts within a reasonable time and at a cost proportionate to the matters in issue;

(d)   a description of the work required;

(e)   whether they are available to attend the trial, if attendance is required; and

(f)   there is no potential conflict of interest.

7.2   Terms of appointment should be agreed at the outset and should normally include:

(a)   the capacity in which the expert is to be appointed (e.g. party appointed expert, single joint expert or expert advisor);

(b)   the services required of the expert (e.g. provision of expert's report, answering questions in writing, attendance at meetings and attendance at court);

(c)   time for delivery of the report;

(d)   the basis of the expert's charges (either daily or hourly rates and an estimate of the time likely to be required, or a total fee for the services);

(e)   travelling expenses and disbursements;

(f)   cancellation charges;

(g)   any fees for attending court;

(h)   time for making the payment;

(i)   whether fees are to be paid by a third party; and

(j)   if a party is publicly funded, whether or not the expert's charges will be subject to assessment by a costs officer.

7.3   As to the appointment of single joint experts, see section 17 below.

7.4   When necessary, arrangements should be made for dealing with questions to experts and discussions between experts, including any directions given by the court, and provision should be made for the cost of this work.

7.5   Experts should be informed regularly about deadlines for all matters concerning them. Those instructing experts should promptly send them copies of all court orders and directions which may affect the preparation of their reports or any other matters concerning their obligations.

Conditional and contingency fees

7.6   Payments contingent upon the nature of the expert evidence given in legal proceedings, or upon the outcome of a case, must not be offered or accepted. To do so would contravene the experts' overriding duty to the court and compromise their duty of independence.

Solicitors should not offer such terms anyway

It should be remembered that the Law Society's Guide to the Professional Conduct of Solicitors specifically states at 21.11 that 'A solicitor must not make or offer to make payments to a witness contingent upon the nature of the evidence given or upon the outcome of a case'.

7.7   Agreement to delay payment of experts' fees until after the conclusion of cases is permissible as long as the amount of the fee does not depend on the outcome of the case.

8. Instructions

8.1   Those instructing experts should ensure that they give clear instructions, including the following:

(a)   basic information, such as names, addresses, telephone numbers, dates of birth and dates of incidents;

(b)   the nature and extent of the expertise which is called for;

(c)   the purpose of requesting the advice or report, a description of the matter(s) to be investigated, the principal known issues and the identity of all parties;

(d)   the statement(s) of case (if any), those documents which form part of standard disclosure and witness statements which are relevant to the advice or report;

(e)   where proceedings have not been started, whether proceedings are being contemplated and, if so, whether the expert is asked only for advice;

(f)   an outline programme, consistent with good case management and the expert's availability, for the completion and delivery of each stage of the expert's work; and

(g)   where proceedings have been started, the dates of any hearings (including any Case Management Conferences and/or Pre-Trial Reviews), the name of the court, the claim number and the track to which the claim has been allocated.

8.2   Experts who do not receive clear instructions should request clarification and may indicate that they are not prepared to act unless and until such clear instructions are received.

8.3   As to the instruction of single joint experts, see section 17 below.

9. Experts' Acceptance of Instructions

9.1   Experts should confirm without delay whether or not they accept instructions. They should also inform those instructing them (whether on initial instruction or at any later stage) without delay if:

    (a)   instructions are not acceptable because, for example, they require work that falls outside their expertise, impose unrealistic deadlines, or are insufficiently clear;

    (b)   they consider that instructions are or have become insufficient to complete the work;

    (c)   they become aware that they may not be able to fulfil any of the terms of appointment;

    (d)   the instructions and/or work have, for any reason, placed them in conflict with their duties as an expert; or

    (e)   they are not satisfied that they can comply with any orders that have been made.

Obtain all relevant material

Once he has accepted instructions, the expert should request any material relevant to his consideration of the case that has not already been provided. If a time limit has been imposed for delivery of the report, an expert's task can be made more difficult if he accepts instructions but then has to wait for a party to furnish him with missing material. For this reason, an expert may prefer to only formally accept the instruction once all the material relevant to his consideration has been delivered.

9.2   Experts must neither express an opinion outside the scope of their field of expertise, nor accept any instructions to do so.

10. Withdrawal

10.1   Where experts' instructions remain incompatible with their duties, whether through incompleteness, a conflict between their duty to the court and their instructions, or for any other substantial and significant reason, they may consider withdrawing from the case. However, experts should not withdraw without first discussing the position fully with those who instruct them and considering carefully whether it would be more appropriate to make a written request for directions from the court. If experts do withdraw, they must give formal written notice to those instructing them.

11. Experts' Right to ask Court for Directions

11.1   Experts may request directions from the court to assist them in carrying out their functions as experts. Experts should normally discuss such matters with those who instruct them before making any such request. Unless the court otherwise orders, any proposed request for directions should be copied to the party instructing the expert at least seven days before filing any request to the court, and to all other parties at least four days before filing it (CPR 35.14).

11.2 Requests to the court for directions should be made by letter, containing:

(a) the title of the claim;

(b) the claim number of the case;

(c) the name of the expert;

(d) full details of why directions are sought; and

(e) copies of any relevant documentation.

In extremis

In very exceptional circumstances, experts may file with the court a written request for directions to assist them in carrying out their function as experts. It is difficult to see circumstances where this course of action would be either justified or desirable from the expert's perspective. The expert works under instruction. If he has any difficulty with his instructions, he should stop working and seek clarification from those who instruct him. If they cannot resolve the problem, it is for the instructing party or parties to seek directions from the court.

12. Power of the Court to Direct a Party to Provide Information

12.1 If experts consider that those instructing them have not provided information which they require, they may, after discussion with those instructing them and giving notice, write to the court to seek directions (CPR 35.14).

12.2 Experts and those who instruct them should also be aware of CPR 35.9. This provides that where one party has access to information which is not readily available to the other party, the court may direct the party who has access to the information to prepare, file and copy to the other party a document recording the information. If experts require such information which has not been disclosed, they should discuss the position with those instructing them without delay, so that a request for the information can be made, and, if not forthcoming, an application can be made to the court. Unless a document appears to be essential, experts should assess the cost and time involved in the production of a document and whether its provision would be proportionate in the context of the case.

13. Contents of Experts' Reports

13.1 The content and extent of experts' reports should be governed by the scope of their instructions and general obligations, the contents of CPR 35 and PD35 and their overriding duty to the court.

13.2 In preparing reports, experts should maintain professional objectivity and impartiality at all times.

13.3   PD 35, para 3 provides that experts' reports should be addressed to the court and gives detailed directions about the form and content of such reports. All experts and those who instruct them should ensure that they are familiar with these requirements.

13.4   Model forms of Experts' Reports are available from bodies such as the Academy of Experts or the Expert Witness Institute.

13.5   Experts' reports must contain statements that they –

(i)   understand their duty to the court and have complied and will continue to comply with it; and

(ii)   are aware of the requirements of Part 35 and practice direction 35, this protocol and the practice direction on pre-action conduct.

Experts' reports must also be verified by a statement of truth. The form of the statement of truth is as follows-

"I confirm that I have made clear which facts and matters referred to in this report are within my own knowledge and which are not. Those that are within my own knowledge I confirm to be true. The opinions I have expressed represent my true and complete professional opinions on the matters to which they refer."

This wording is mandatory and must not be modified.

Qualifications

13.6   The details of experts' qualifications to be given in reports should be commensurate with the nature and complexity of the case. It may be sufficient merely to state academic and professional qualifications. However, where highly specialised expertise is called for, experts should include the detail of particular training and/or experience that qualifies them to provide that highly specialised evidence.

Tests

13.7   Where tests of a scientific or technical nature have been carried out, experts should state:

(a)   the methodology used; and

(b)   by whom the tests were undertaken and under whose supervision, summarising their respective qualifications and experience.

Reliance on the work of others

13.8   Where experts rely in their reports on literature or other material and cite the opinions of others without having verified them, they must give details of those opinions relied on. It is likely to assist the court if the qualifications of the originator(s) are also stated.

Facts

13.9   When addressing questions of fact and opinion, experts should keep the two separate and discrete.

13.10 Experts must state those facts (whether assumed or otherwise) upon which their opinions are based. They must distinguish clearly between those facts which experts know to be true and those facts which they assume.

13.11 Where there are material facts in dispute experts should express separate opinions on each hypothesis put forward. They should not express a view in favour of one or other disputed version of the facts unless, as a result of particular expertise and experience, they consider one set of facts as being improbable or less probable, in which case they may express that view, and should give reasons for holding it.

Range of opinion

13.12 If the mandatory summary of the range of opinion is based on published sources, experts should explain those sources and, where appropriate, state the qualifications of the originator(s) of the opinions from which they differ, particularly if such opinions represent a well-established school of thought.

13.13 Where there is no available source for the range of opinion, experts may need to express opinions on what they believe to be the range which other experts would arrive at if asked. In those circumstances, experts should make it clear that the range that they summarise is based on their own judgement and explain the basis of that judgement.

Conclusions

13.14 A summary of conclusions is mandatory. The summary should be at the end of the report after all the reasoning. There may be cases, however, where the benefit to the court is heightened by placing a short summary at the beginning of the report whilst giving the full conclusions at the end. For example, it can assist with the comprehension of the analysis and with the absorption of the detailed facts if the court is told at the outset of the direction in which the report's logic will flow in cases involving highly complex matters which fall outside the general knowledge of the court.

Basis of report: material instructions

13.15 The mandatory statement of the substance of all material instructions should not be incomplete or otherwise tend to mislead. The imperative is transparency. The term "instructions" includes all material which solicitors place in front of experts in order to gain advice. The omission from the statement of 'off-the-record' oral instructions is not permitted. Courts may allow cross-examination about the instructions if there are reasonable grounds to consider that the statement may be inaccurate or incomplete.

14. After Receipt of Experts' Reports

14.1 Following the receipt of experts' reports, those instructing them should advise the experts as soon as reasonably practicable whether, and if so when, the report will be disclosed to other parties; and, if so disclosed, the date of actual disclosure.

14.2 If experts' reports are to be relied upon, and if experts are to give oral evidence, those instructing them should give the experts the opportunity to consider and comment upon other reports within their area of expertise and which deal with relevant issues at the earliest opportunity.

14.3 Those instructing experts should keep experts informed of the progress of cases, including amendments to statements of case relevant to experts' opinion.

14.4 If those instructing experts become aware of material changes in circumstances or that relevant information within their control was not previously provided to experts, they should without delay instruct experts to review, and if necessary update, the contents of their reports.

15. Amendment of Reports

15.1 It may become necessary for experts to amend their reports:
- (a) as a result of an exchange of questions and answers;
- (b) following agreements reached at meetings between experts; or
- (c) where further evidence or documentation is disclosed.

15.2 Experts should not be asked to, and should not, amend, expand or alter any parts of reports in a manner which distorts their true opinion, but may be invited to amend or expand reports to ensure accuracy, internal consistency, completeness and relevance to the issues and clarity. Although experts should generally follow the recommendations of solicitors with regard to the form of reports, they should form their own independent views as to the opinions and contents expressed in their reports and exclude any suggestions which do not accord with their views.

15.3 Where experts change their opinion following a meeting of experts, a simple signed and dated addendum or memorandum to that effect is generally sufficient. In some cases, however, the benefit to the court of having an amended report may justify the cost of making the amendment.

15.4 Where experts significantly alter their opinion, as a result of new evidence or because evidence on which they relied has become unreliable, or for any other reason, they should amend their reports to reflect that fact. Amended reports should include reasons for amendments. In such circumstances those instructing experts should inform other parties as soon as possible of any change of opinion.

15.5 When experts intend to amend their reports, they should inform those instructing them without delay and give reasons. They should provide the amended version (or an addendum or memorandum) clearly marked as such as quickly as possible.

16. Written Questions to Experts

16.1 The procedure for putting written questions to experts (CPR 35.6) is intended to facilitate the clarification of opinions and issues after experts' reports have been served. Experts have a duty to provide answers to questions properly put. Where they fail to do so, the court may impose sanctions against the party instructing the expert, and, if, there is continued non-compliance, debar a party from relying on the report. Experts should copy their answers to those instructing them.

16.2 Experts' answers to questions automatically become part of their reports. They are covered by the statement of truth and form part of the expert evidence.

16.3 Where experts believe that questions put are not properly directed to the clarification of the report, or are disproportionate, or have been asked out of time, they should discuss the questions with those instructing them and, if appropriate, those asking the questions. Attempts should be made to resolve such problems without the need for an application to the court for directions.

Written requests for directions in relation to questions

16.4 If those instructing experts do not apply to the court in respect of questions, but experts still believe that questions are improper or out of time, experts may file written requests with the court for directions to assist in carrying out their functions as experts (CPR 35.14). See Section 11 above.

Ensuring questions have been 'properly put'

For a question to be properly put, it must conform to the requirements of Rule 35.6(2). Generally, it is for lawyers to decide whether a question meets the requirements, not experts. However, experts can avoid all possibility of censure for answering questions they ought not to have answered by relying on Rule 35.6(2)(ii). This permits any questions to be put (regardless of frequency, timing or purpose), providing all the parties agree.

If instructed by one party, an expert should send any questions he receives from another party to his instructing party and ask for permission to answer them. If permission is given, he will be covered by Rule 35.6(2)(ii).

A jointly instructed expert should only receive questions that have already been circulated to all parties, but he should nonetheless ensure all the parties agree to his answering any questions put to him.

17. Single Joint Experts

17.1 CPR 35 and PD35 deal extensively with the instruction and use of joint experts by the parties and the powers of the court to order their use (see CPR 35.7 and 35.8, PD35, para 5).

17.2 The Civil Procedure Rules encourage the use of joint experts. Wherever possible a joint report should be obtained. Consideration should therefore be given by all parties to the appointment of single joint experts in all cases where a court might direct such an appointment. Single joint experts are the norm in cases allocated to the small claims track and the fast track.

17.3 Where, in the early stages of a dispute, examinations, investigations, tests, site inspections, experiments, preparation of photographs, plans or other similar preliminary expert tasks are necessary, consideration should be given to the instruction of a single joint expert, especially where such matters are not, at that stage, expected to be contentious as between the parties. The objective of such an appointment should be to agree or to narrow issues.

17.5 Experts who have previously advised a party (whether in the same case or otherwise) should only be proposed as single joint experts if other parties are given all relevant information about the previous involvement.

17.6 The appointment of a single joint expert does not prevent parties from instructing their own experts to advise (but the costs of such expert advisers may not be recoverable in the case).

Joint instructions

17.7 The parties should try to agree joint instructions to single joint experts, but, in default of agreement, each party may give instructions. In particular, all parties should try to agree what documents should be included with instructions and what assumptions single joint experts should make.

17.8 Where the parties fail to agree joint instructions, they should try to agree where the areas of disagreement lie and their instructions should make this clear. If separate instructions are given, they should be copied at the same time to the other instructing parties.

17.9 Where experts are instructed by two or more parties, the terms of appointment should, unless the court has directed otherwise, or the parties have agreed otherwise, include:

   (a) a statement that all the instructing parties are jointly and severally liable to pay the experts' fees and, accordingly, that experts' invoices should be sent simultaneously to all instructing parties or their solicitors (as appropriate); and

   (b) a statement as to whether any order has been made limiting the amount of experts' fees and expenses (CPR 35.8(4)(a)).

17.10 Where instructions have not been received by the expert from one or more of the instructing parties the expert should give notice (normally at least 7 days) of a deadline to all instructing parties for the receipt by the expert of such instructions. Unless the instructions are received within the deadline the expert may begin work. In the event that instructions are received after the deadline but before the signing off of the report the expert should consider whether it is practicable to comply with those instructions without adversely affecting the timetable set for delivery of the report and in such a manner as to comply with the proportionality principle. An expert who decides to issue a report without taking into account instructions received after the deadline should inform the parties who may apply to the court for directions. In either event the report must show clearly that the expert did not receive instructions within the deadline, or, as the case may be, at all.

Conduct of the single joint expert

17.11 Single joint experts should keep all instructing parties informed of any material steps that they may be taking by, for example, copying all correspondence to those instructing them.

Avoid the telephone

If a jointly appointed expert is to avoid all possibility of censure, he would be wise to avoid all telephone contact with the parties, as the telephone tends to be bilateral in nature. Rely instead on written communication that can easily be copied to all parties simultaneously.

17.12 Single joint experts are Part 35 experts and so have an overriding duty to the court. They are the parties' appointed experts and therefore owe an equal duty to all parties. They should maintain independence, impartiality and transparency at all times.

17.13 Single joint experts should not attend any meeting or conference which is not a joint one, unless all the parties have agreed in writing or the court has directed that such a meeting may be held[4] and who is to pay the experts' fees for the meeting.

17.14 Single joint experts may request directions from the court – see Section 11 above.

17.15 Single joint experts should serve their reports simultaneously on all instructing parties. They should provide a single report even though they may have received instructions which contain areas of conflicting fact or allegation. If conflicting instructions lead to different opinions (for example, because the instructions require experts to make different assumptions of fact), reports may need to contain more than one set of opinions on any issue. It is for the court to determine the facts.

---

4 *Peet -v- Mid Kent Area Healthcare NHS Trust* [2002] 1 WLR 210.

Cross-examination

17.16 Single joint experts do not normally give oral evidence at trial but if they do, all parties may cross-examine them. In general written questions (CPR 35.6) should be put to single joint experts before requests are made for them to attend court for the purpose of cross-examination.[5]

18. Discussions between Experts

18.1 The court has powers to direct discussions between experts for the purposes set out in the Rules (CPR 35.12). Parties may also agree that discussions take place between their experts.

18.2 Where single joint experts have been instructed but parties have, with the permission of the court, instructed their own additional Part 35 experts, there may, if the court so orders or the parties agree, be discussions between the single joint experts and the additional Part 35 experts. Such discussions should be confined to those matters within the remit of the additional Part 35 experts or as ordered by the court.

18.3 The purpose of discussions between experts should be, wherever possible, to:

   (a)   identify and discuss the expert issues in the proceedings;

   (b)   reach agreed opinions on those issues, and, if that is not possible, to narrow the issues in the case;

   (c)   identify those issues on which they agree and disagree and summarise their reasons for disagreement on any issue; and

   (d)   identify what action, if any, may be taken to resolve any of the outstanding issues between the parties.

The purpose is not negotiation

The purpose of discussions between experts is to identify, discuss and, where possible, agree opinion on expert issues. Experts should also seek to identify areas where their opinions differ, and give reasons for their disagreement. Experts should not treat the discussion as a negotiation. It is never acceptable for an expert to shift his opinion purely to obtain a concession from the other expert.

Arrangements for discussions between experts

18.4 Arrangements for discussions between experts should be proportionate to the value of cases. In small claims and fast-track cases there should not normally be meetings between experts. Where discussion is justified in such cases, telephone discussion or an exchange of letters should, in the interests of proportionality, usually suffice. In multi-track cases, discussion may be face to face, but the

---

5 *Daniels -v- Walker* [2000] 1 WLR 1382.

practicalities or the proportionality principle may require discussions to be by telephone or video conference.

18.5 The parties, their lawyers and experts should co-operate to produce the agenda for any discussion between experts, although primary responsibility for preparation of the agenda should normally lie with the parties' solicitors.

18.6 The agenda should indicate what matters have been agreed and summarise concisely those which are in issue. It is often helpful for it to include questions to be answered by the experts. If agreement cannot be reached promptly or a party is unrepresented, the court may give directions for the drawing up of the agenda. The agenda should be circulated to experts and those instructing them to allow sufficient time for the experts to prepare for the discussion.

18.7 Those instructing experts must not instruct experts to avoid reaching agreement (or to defer doing so) on any matter within the experts' competence. Experts are not permitted to accept such instructions.

18.8 The parties' lawyers may only be present at discussions between experts if all the parties agree or the court so orders. If lawyers do attend, they should not normally intervene except to answer questions put to them by the experts or to advise about the law.[6]

18.9 The content of discussions between experts should not be referred to at trial unless the parties agree (CPR 35.12(4)). It is good practice for any such agreement to be in writing.

18.10 At the conclusion of any discussion between experts, a statement should be prepared setting out:

(a) a list of issues that have been agreed, including, in each instance, the basis of agreement;

(b) a list of issues that have not been agreed, including, in each instance, the basis of disagreement;

(c) a list of any further issues that have arisen that were not included in the original agenda for discussion;

(d) a record of further action, if any, to be taken or recommended, including as appropriate the holding of further discussions between experts.

18.11 The statement should be agreed and signed by all the parties to the discussion as soon as may be practicable.

18.12 Agreements between experts during discussions do not bind the parties unless the parties expressly agree to be bound by the agreement (CPR 35.12(5)). However, in view of the overriding objective, parties should give careful consideration before refusing to be bound by such an agreement and be able to explain their refusal should it become relevant to the issue of costs.

---

6 *Hubbard -v- Lambeth, Southwark and Lewisham HA* [2001] EWCA 1455.

19. Attendance of Experts at Court

19.1 Experts instructed in cases have an obligation to attend court if called upon to do so and accordingly should ensure that those instructing them are always aware of their dates to be avoided and take all reasonable steps to be available.

19.2 Those instructing experts should:

 (a) ascertain the availability of experts before trial dates are fixed;

 (b) keep experts updated with timetables (including the dates and times experts are to attend) and the location of the court;

 (c) give consideration, where appropriate, to experts giving evidence via a video-link;

 (d) inform experts immediately if trial dates are vacated.

19.3 Experts should normally attend court without the need for the service of witness summonses, but on occasion they may be served to require attendance (CPR 34). The use of witness summonses does not affect the contractual or other obligations of the parties to pay experts' fees.

Pre-Action Protocol for Personal Injury Claims

The following is taken from the 50th update of the CPR dated October 2009. Source: www.justice.gov.uk

1 Introduction

1.1   Lord Woolf in his final Access to Justice Report of July 1996 recommended the development of pre-action protocols:
To build on and increase the benefits of early but well informed settlement which genuinely satisfy both parties to dispute.

1.2   The aims of pre-action protocols are:

- more pre-action contact between the parties
- better and earlier exchange of information
- better pre-action investigation by both sides
- to put the parties in a position where they may be able to settle cases fairly and early without litigation
- to enable proceedings to run to the court's timetable and efficiently, if litigation does become necessary
- to promote the provision of medical or rehabilitation treatment (not just in high value cases) to address the needs of the claimant

1.3   The concept of protocols is relevant to a range of initiatives for good litigation and pre-litigation practice, especially:

- predictability in the time needed for steps pre-proceedings
- standardisation of relevant information, including documents to be disclosed.

1.4   The Courts will be able to treat the standards set in protocols as the normal reasonable approach to pre-action conduct. If proceedings are issued, it will be for the court to decide whether non-compliance with a protocol should merit adverse consequences. Guidance on the court's likely approach will be given from time to time in practice directions.

1.5   If the court has to consider the question of compliance after proceedings have begun, it will not be concerned with minor infringements, e.g. failure by a short period to provide relevant information. One minor breach will not exempt the 'innocent' party from following the protocol. The court will look at the effect of non-compliance on the other party when deciding whether to impose sanctions.

2 Notes of Guidance

2.1   The protocol has been kept deliberately simple to promote ease of use and general acceptability. The notes of guidance which follows relate particularly to issues which arose during the piloting of the protocol.

Scope of the Protocol

2.2   This protocol is intended to apply to all claims which include a claim for personal injury (except those claims covered by the Clinical Disputes and Disease and Illness Protocols) and to the entirety of those claims: not only to the personal injury element of a claim which also includes, for instance, property damage.

2.3   This protocol is primarily designed for those road traffic, tripping and slipping and accident at work cases which include an element of personal injury with a value of less than the fast track limit and which are likely to be allocated to that track. This is because time will be of the essence, after proceedings are issued, especially for the defendant, if a case is to be ready for trial within 30 weeks of allocation. Also, proportionality of work and costs to the value of what is in dispute is particularly important in lower value claims. For some claims within the value 'scope' of the fast track some flexibility in the timescale of the protocol may be necessary, see also paragraph 3.8.

2.4   However, the 'cards on the table' approach advocated by the protocol is equally appropriate to higher value claims. The spirit, if not the letter of the protocol, should still be followed for multi-track type claims. In accordance with the sense of the civil justice reforms, the court will expect to see the spirit of reasonable pre-action behaviour applied in all cases, regardless of the existence of a specific protocol. In particular with regard to personal injury cases with a value of more than the fast track limit, to avoid the necessity of proceedings parties are expected to comply with the protocol as far as possible e.g. in respect of letters before action, exchanging information and documents and agreeing experts.

2.5   The timetable and the arrangements for disclosing documents and obtaining expert evidence may need to be varied to suit the circumstances of the case. Where one or both parties consider the detail of the protocol is not appropriate to the case, and proceedings are subsequently issued, the court will expect an explanation as to why the protocol has not been followed, or has been varied.

Early Notification

2.6   The claimant's legal representative may wish to notify the defendant and/or his insurer as soon as they know a claim is likely to be made, but before they are able to send a detailed letter of claim, particularly for instance, when the defendant has no or limited knowledge of the incident giving rise to the claim or where the claimant is incurring significant expenditure as a result of the accident which he hopes the defendant might pay for, in whole or in part. If the claimant's representative chooses to do this, it will not start the timetable for responding.

The Letter of Claim

2.7   The specimen letter of claim at Annex A will usually be sent to the
       individual defendant. In practice, he/she may have no personal
       financial interest in the financial outcome of the claim/dispute because
       he/she is insured. Court imposed sanctions for non-compliance with
       the protocol may be ineffective against an insured. This is why the
       protocol emphasises the importance of passing the letter of claim
       to the insurer and the possibility that the insurance cover might be
       affected. If an insurer receives the letter of claim only after some delay
       by the insured, it would not be unreasonable for the insurer to ask the
       claimant for additional time to respond.

2.8   In road traffic cases, the letter of claim should always contain the
       name and address of the hospital where the claimant was treated and,
       where available, the claimant's hospital reference number.

2.9   The priority at letter of claim stage is for the claimant to provide
       sufficient information for the defendant to assess liability. Sufficient
       information should also be provided to enable the defendant to
       estimate the likely size of the claim.

2.10   Once the claimant has sent the letter of claim no further investigation
       on liability should normally be carried out until a response is received
       from the defendant indicating whether liability is disputed.

Reasons for Early Issue

2.11   The protocol recommends that a defendant be given three months
       to investigate and respond to a claim before proceedings are issued.
       This may not always be possible, particularly where a claimant only
       consults a solicitor close to the end of any relevant limitation period.
       In these circumstances, the claimant's solicitor should give as much
       notice of the intention to issue proceedings as is practicable and the
       parties should consider whether the court might be invited to extend
       time for service of the claimant's supporting documents and for service
       of any defence, or alternatively, to stay the proceedings while the
       recommended steps in the protocol are followed.

Status of Letters of Claim and Response

2.12   Letters of claim and response are not intended to have the same
       status as a statement of case in proceedings. Matters may come to
       light as a result of investigation after the letter of claim has been sent,
       or after the defendant has responded, particularly if disclosure of
       documents takes place outside the recommended three-month period.
       These circumstances could mean that the 'pleaded' case of one or
       both parties is presented slightly differently than in the letter of claim
       and response. It would not be consistent with the spirit of the protocol
       for a party to 'take a point' on this in the proceedings, provided that

there was no obvious intention by the party who changed their position to mislead the other party.

Disclosure of Documents

2.13   The aim of the early disclosure of documents by the defendant is not to encourage 'fishing expeditions' by the claimant, but to promote an early exchange of relevant information to help in clarifying or resolving issues in dispute. The claimant's solicitor can assist by identifying in the letter of claim or in a subsequent letter the particular categories of documents which they consider are relevant.

Experts

2.14   The protocol encourages joint selection of, and access to, experts. The report produced is not a joint report for the purposes of CPR Part 35. Most frequently this will apply to the medical expert, but on occasions also to liability experts, e.g. engineers. The protocol promotes the practice of the claimant obtaining a medical report, disclosing it to the defendant who then asks questions and/or agrees it and does not obtain his own report. The Protocol provides for nomination of the expert by the claimant in personal injury claims because of the early stage of the proceedings and the particular nature of such claims. If proceedings have to be issued, a medical report must be attached to these proceedings. However, if necessary after proceedings have commenced and with the permission of the court, the parties may obtain further expert reports. It would be for the court to decide whether the costs of more than one expert's report should be recoverable.

2.15   Some solicitors choose to obtain medical reports through medical agencies, rather than directly from a specific doctor or hospital. The defendant's prior consent to the action should be sought and, if the defendant so requests, the agency should be asked to provide in advance the names of the doctor(s) whom they are considering instructing.

Alternative Dispute Resolution

2.16   The parties should consider whether some form of alternative dispute resolution procedure would be more suitable than litigation, and if so, endeavour to agree which form to adopt. Both the Claimant and Defendant may be required by the Court to provide evidence that alternative means of resolving their dispute were considered. The Courts take the view that litigation should be a last resort, and that claims should not be issued prematurely when a settlement is still actively being explored. Parties are warned that if the protocol is not followed (including this paragraph) then the Court must have regard to such conduct when determining costs.

2.17 It is not practicable in this protocol to address in detail how the parties might decide which method to adopt to resolve their particular dispute. However, summarised below are some of the options for resolving disputes without litigation:

- Discussion and negotiation.
- Early neutral evaluation by an independent third party (for example, a lawyer experienced in the field of personal injury or an individual experienced in the subject matter of the claim).
- Mediation – a form of facilitated negotiation assisted by an independent neutral party.

2.18 The Legal Services Commission has published a booklet on 'Alternatives to Court', CLS Direct Information Leaflet 23 (*www. clsdirect.org.uk/legalhelp/leaflet23.jsp*), which lists a number of organisations that provide alternative dispute resolution services.

2.19 It is expressly recognised that no party can or should be forced to mediate or enter into any form of ADR.

Stocktake

2.20 Where a claim is not resolved when the protocol has been followed, the parties might wish to carry out a 'stocktake' of the issues in dispute, and the evidence that the court is likely to need to decide those issues, before proceedings are started. Where the defendant is insured and the pre-action steps have been conducted by the insurer, the insurer would normally be expected to nominate solicitors to act in the proceedings and the claimant's solicitor is recommended to invite the insurer to nominate solicitors to act in the proceedings and do so 7–14 days before the intended issue date.

3 The Protocol

Letter of claim

3.1 The claimant shall send to the proposed defendant two copies of a letter of claim, immediately sufficient information is available to substantiate a realistic claim and before issues of quantum are addressed in detail. One copy of the letter is for the defendant, the second for passing on to his insurers.

3.2 The letter shall contain a clear summary of the facts on which the claim is based together with an indication of the nature of any injuries suffered and of any financial loss incurred. In cases of road traffic accidents, the letter should provide the name and address of the hospital where treatment has been obtained and the claimant's hospital reference number. Where the case is funded by a conditional fee agreement (or collective conditional fee agreement), notification should be given of the existence of the agreement and where appropriate, that there is a success fee and/or insurance premium, although not the level of the success fee or premium.

3.3 Solicitors are recommended to use a standard format for such a letter – an example is at Annex A: this can be amended to suit the particular case.

3.4 The letter should ask for details of the insurer and that a copy should be sent by the proposed defendant to the insurer where appropriate. If the insurer is known, a copy shall be sent directly to the insurer. Details of the claimant's National Insurance number and date of birth should be supplied to the defendant's insurer once the defendant has responded to the letter of claim and confirmed the identity of the insurer. This information should not be supplied in the letter of claim.

3.5 Sufficient information should be given in order to enable the defendant's insurer/solicitor to commence investigations and at least put a broad valuation on the 'risk'.

3.6 The defendant should reply within 21 calendar days of the date of posting of the letter identifying the insurer (if any) and, if necessary, identifying specifically any significant omissions from the letter of claim. If there has been no reply by the defendant or insurer within 21 days, the claimant will be entitled to issue proceedings.

3.7 The defendant('s insurers) will have a maximum of three months from the date of acknowledgment of the claim to investigate. No later than the end of that period the defendant (insurer) shall reply, stating whether liability is denied and, if so, giving reasons for their denial of liability including any alternative version of events relied upon.

3.8 Where the accident occurred outside England and Wales and/or where the defendant is outside the jurisdiction, the time periods of 21 days and three months should normally be extended up to 42 days and six months.

3.9 Where the claimant's investigation indicates that the value of the claim has increased to more than the value of the fast track limit since the letter of claim, the claimant should notify the defendant as soon as possible.

Documents

3.10 If the defendant denies liability, he should enclose with the letter of reply, documents in his possession which are material to the issues between the parties, and which would be likely to be ordered to be disclosed by the court, either on an application for pre-action disclosure, or on disclosure during proceedings.

3.11 Attached at Annex B are specimen, but non-exhaustive, lists of documents likely to be material in different types of claim. Where the claimant's investigation of the case is well advanced, the letter of claim could indicate which classes of documents are considered relevant for early disclosure. Alternatively these could be identified at a later stage.

3.12 Where the defendant admits primary liability, but alleges contributory negligence by the claimant, the defendant should give reasons supporting those allegations and disclose those documents from Annex B which are relevant to the issues in dispute. The claimant should respond to the allegations of contributory negligence before proceedings are issued.

3.13 No charge will be made for providing copy documents under the Protocol.

Special damages

3.14 The claimant will send to the defendant as soon as practicable a Schedule of Special Damages with supporting documents, particularly where the defendant has admitted liability.

Experts

3.15 Before any party instructs an expert he should give the other party a list of the name(s) of one or more experts in the relevant speciality whom he considers are suitable to instruct.

3.16 Where a medical expert is to be instructed the claimant's solicitor will organise access to relevant medical records – see specimen letter of instruction at Annex C.

3.17 Within 14 days the other party may indicate an objection to one or more of the named experts. The first party should then instruct a mutually acceptable expert (which is not the same as a joint expert). It must be emphasised that if the Claimant nominates an expert in the original letter of claim, the defendant has 14 days to object to one or more of the named experts after expiration of the period of 21 days within which he has to reply to the letter of claim, as set out in paragraph 3.6.

3.18 If the second party objects to all the listed experts, the parties may then instruct experts of their own choice. It would be for the court to decide subsequently, if proceedings are issued, whether either party had acted unreasonably.

3.19 If the second party does not object to an expert nominated, he shall not be entitled to rely on his own expert evidence within that particular speciality unless:

(a)   the first party agrees,

(b)   the court so directs, or

(c) the first party's expert report has been amended and the first party is not prepared to disclose the original report.

3.20 Either party may send to an agreed expert written questions on the report, relevant to the issues, via the first party's solicitors. The expert should send answers to the questions separately and directly to each party.

3.21 The cost of a report from an agreed expert will usually be paid by the instructing first party: the costs of the expert replying to questions will usually be borne by the party which asks the questions.

4 Rehabilitation

4.1 The claimant or the defendant or both shall consider as early as possible whether the claimant has reasonable needs that could be met by rehabilitation treatment or other measures.

4.2 The parties shall consider, in such cases, how those needs might be addressed. The Rehabilitation Code (which is attached at Annex D) may be helpful in considering how to identify the claimant's needs and how to address the cost of providing for those needs.

4.3 The time limit set out in paragraph 3.7 of this Protocol shall not be shortened, except by consent to allow these issues to be addressed.

4.4 The provision of any report obtained for the purposes of assessment of provision of a party's rehabilitation needs shall not be used in any litigation arising out of the accident, the subject of the claim, save by consent and shall in any event be exempt from the provisions of paragraphs 3.15 to 3.21 inclusive of this protocol.

5 Resolution of Issues

5.1 Where the defendant admits liability in whole or in part, before proceedings are issued, any medical reports obtained under this protocol on which a party relies should be disclosed to the other party. The claimant should delay issuing proceedings for 21 days from disclosure of the report (unless such delay would cause his claim to become time-barred), to enable the parties to consider whether the claim is capable of settlement.

5.2 The Civil Procedure Rules Part 36 permit claimants and defendants to make offers to settle pre-proceedings. Parties should always consider before issuing if it is appropriate to make Part 36 Offer. If such an offer is made, the party making the offer must always supply sufficient evidence and/or information to enable the offer to be properly considered.

5.3 Where the defendant has admitted liability, the claimant should send to the defendant schedules of special damages and loss at least 21 days before proceedings are issued (unless that would cause the claimant's claim to become time-barred).

Appendix A
See *www.justice.gov.uk/civil/procrules_fin/contents/protocols/prot_pic.htm*

Appendix B
See *www.justice.gov.uk/civil/procrules_fin/contents/protocols/prot_pic.htm*

Appendix C Letter of Instruction to Medical Expert
Dear Sir,

Re: (Name and Address)

D.O.B. –

Telephone No. –

Date of Accident –

We are acting for the above named in connection with injuries received in an accident which occurred on the above date. The main injuries appear to have been (main injuries).

We should be obliged if you would examine our Client and let us have a full and detailed report dealing with any relevant pre-accident medical history, the injuries sustained, treatment received and present condition, dealing in particular with the capacity for work and giving a prognosis.

It is central to our assessment of the extent of our Client's injuries to establish the extent and duration of any continuing disability. Accordingly, in the prognosis section we would ask you to specifically comment on any areas of continuing complaint or disability or impact on daily living. If there is such continuing disability you should comment upon the level of suffering or inconvenience caused and, if you are able, give your view as to when or if the complaint or disability is likely to resolve.

Please send our Client an appointment direct for this purpose. Should you be able to offer a cancellation appointment please contact our Client direct. We confirm we will be responsible for your reasonable fees.

We are obtaining the notes and records from our Client's GP and Hospitals attended and will forward them to you when they are to hand/or please request the GP and Hospital records direct and advise that any invoice for the provision of these records should be forwarded to us.

In order to comply with Court Rules we would be grateful if you would insert above your signature a statement that the contents are true to the best of your knowledge and belief.

In order to avoid further correspondence we can confirm that on the evidence we have there is no reason to suspect we may be pursuing a claim against the hospital or its staff.

We look forward to receiving your report within _____ weeks. If you will not be able to prepare your report within this period please telephone us upon receipt of these instructions.

When acknowledging these instructions it would assist if you could give an estimate as to the likely time scale for the provision of your report and also an indication as to your fee.

Yours faithfully

Annex C to the CPR Practice Direction on Pre-Action Conduct

The aims of the CPR Practice Direction on Pre-Action Conduct are to enable parties to settle the issue between them without the need to start proceedings (that is, a court claim); and support the efficient management by the court and the parties of proceedings that cannot be avoided.

These aims are to be achieved by encouraging the parties to exchange information about the issue, and consider using a form of Alternative Dispute Resolution.

We reproduce here just Annex C dealing with the instruction of expert witnesses.

The following is taken from the 50th update of the Rules dated October 2009. Source: www.justice.gov.uk

Guidance on instructing experts

1. The CPR contain extensive provisions which strictly control the use of experts both before and after proceedings are started. These provisions are contained in –
   (1) CPR Part 35;
   (2) the Practice Direction supplementing Part 35; and
   (3) the Protocol for the 'Instruction of Experts to give Evidence in Civil Claims' which is annexed to that Practice Direction.

2. Parties should be aware that once proceedings have been started –
   (1) expert evidence may not be used in court without the permission of the court;
   (2) a party who instructs an expert will not necessarily be able to recover the cost from another party; and
   (3) it is the duty of an expert to help the court on the matters within the expert's scope of expertise and this duty overrides any obligation to the person instructing or paying the expert.

3. Many matters can and should be resolved without the need for advice or evidence from an expert. If an expert is needed, the parties should consider how best to minimise the expense for example by agreeing to instruct –
   (1) a single joint expert (i.e. engaged and paid jointly by the parties whether instructed jointly or separately); or
   (2) an agreed expert (i.e. the parties agree the identity of the expert but only one party instructs the expert and pays the expert's costs).

4. If the parties do not agree that the nomination of a single joint expert is appropriate, then the party seeking the expert evidence (the first party)

should give the other party (the second party) a list of one or more experts in the relevant field of expertise whom the first party would like to instruct.

5. Within 14 days of receipt of the list of experts, the second party may indicate in writing an objection to one or more of the experts listed. If there remains on the list one or more experts who are acceptable, then the first party should instruct an expert from the list.

6. If the second party objects to all the listed experts, the first party may then instruct an expert of the first party's own choice. Both parties should bear in mind that if proceedings are started the court will consider whether a party has acted reasonably when instructing (or rejecting) an expert.

2

Rules in Criminal Litigation

Criminal Procedure Rules Part 1 – The overriding objective

The following is taken from the 8th update of the Rules dated October 2009. Source: www.justice.gov.uk

1.1 The overriding objective

(1)   The overriding objective of this new code is that criminal cases be dealt with justly.

(2)   Dealing with a criminal case justly includes—

    (a)   acquitting the innocent and convicting the guilty;

    (b)   dealing with the prosecution and the defence fairly;

    (c)   recognising the rights of a defendant, particularly those under Article 6 of the European Convention on Human Rights;

    (d)   respecting the interests of witnesses, victims and jurors and keeping them informed of the progress of the case;

    (e)   dealing with the case efficiently and expeditiously;

    (f)   ensuring that appropriate information is available to the court when bail and sentence are considered; and

    (g)   dealing with the case in ways that take into account—

        (i)   the gravity of the offence alleged,

        (ii)   the complexity of what is in issue,

        (iii)   the severity of the consequences for the defendant and others affected, and

        (iv)   the needs of other cases.

1.2 The duty of the participants in a criminal case

(1)   Each participant, in the conduct of each case, must—

    (a)   prepare and conduct the case in accordance with the overriding objective;

    (b)   comply with these Rules, practice directions and directions made by the court; and

    (c)   at once inform the court and all parties of any significant failure (whether or not that participant is responsible for that failure) to take any procedural step required by these Rules, any practice direction or any direction of the court. A failure is significant if it might hinder the court in furthering the overriding objective.

(2)   Anyone involved in any way with a criminal case is a participant in its conduct for the purposes of this rule.

1.3 The application by the court of the overriding objective

The court must further the overriding objective in particular when—

(a) exercising any power given to it by legislation (including these Rules);

(b) applying any practice direction; or

(c) interpreting any rule or practice direction.

Criminal Procedure Rules Part 2 – Understanding and applying the Rules

The following is taken from the 8th update of the Rules dated October 2009. Source: www.justice.gov.uk

2.1 When the Rules apply

(1) In general, the Criminal Procedure Rules apply –

    (a) in all criminal cases in magistrates' courts and in the Crown Court; and

    (b) in all cases in the criminal division of the Court of Appeal.

(2) If a rule applies only in one or two of those courts, the rule makes that clear.

(3) The Rules apply on and after 4 th April, 2005, but do not affect any right or duty existing under the rules of court revoked by the coming into force of these Rules.

(4) The rules in Part 33 apply in all cases in which the defendant is charged on or after 6th November 2006 and in other cases if the court so orders.

(5) The rules in Part 14 apply in cases in which one of the events listed in sub-paragraphs (a) to (d) of rule 14.1(1) takes place on or after 2nd April 2007. In other cases the rules of court replaced by those rules apply.

(6) The rules in Part 28 apply in cases in which an application under rule 28.3 is made on or after 2nd April 2007. In other cases the rules replaced by those rules apply.

(7) The rules in Parts 65, 66, 67, 68, 69 and 70 apply where an appeal, application or reference, to which one of those Parts applies, is made on or after 1st October 2007. In other cases the rules replaced by those rules apply.

(8) The rules in Parts 57 – 62 apply in proceedings to which one of those Parts applies that begin on or after 1st April 2008. In such proceedings beginning before that date the rules in those Parts apply as if –

    (a) the amendments made to them by The Criminal Procedure (Amendment No. 3) Rules 2007 had not been made; and

    (b) references to the Director of the Assets Recovery Agency or to that Agency were references to the Serious Organised Crime Agency.

(9) The rules in Part 50 apply in cases in which the defendant is charged on or after 7th April 2008 and in other cases if the court so orders. Otherwise, the rules replaced by those rules apply.

(10)   The rules in Part 74 apply where an appeal, application or reference, to which Part 74 applies, is made on or after 7th April 2008. In other cases the rules replaced by those rules apply.

(11)   The rules in Part 7 apply in cases in which on or after 6th October 2008 –

    (a)   a prosecutor serves an information on the court officer or presents it to a magistrates' court;

    (b)   a public prosecutor issues a written charge; or

    (c)   a person who is in custody is charged with an offence.

In other cases the rules replaced by those rules apply.

(12)   The rules in Part 63 apply in cases in which the decision that is the subject of the appeal, or reference, to which that Part applies is made on or after 6th October 2008. In other cases the rules replaced by those rules apply.

(13)   The rules in Part 21 apply unless the court otherwise directs under rule 21.1(2). If it does so, the rules replaced by those rules apply.

(14)   The rules in Part 37 apply in cases in which on or after 6th April 2009 –

    (a)   the court tries a case; or

    (b)   the defendant pleads guilty.

In other cases, the rules in Parts 37 and 38 apply as if The Criminal Procedure (Amendment No. 2) Rules 2008 had not been made.

(15)   The rules in Part 44 apply in cases in which an application to which that Part applies is made on or after 6th April 2009. In other cases, the rules in Parts 38 and 44 apply as if The Criminal Procedure (Amendment No. 2) Rules 2008 had not been made.

(16)   The rules in Part 6 apply in cases in which an application to which that Part applies is made on or after 5th October, 2009, and in other cases if the court so orders. Otherwise, the rules in Part 62 (Proceeds of Crime Act 2002 - rules applicable to investigations) apply as if The Criminal Procedure (Amendment) Rules 2009 had not been made.

(17)   The rules in Part 22 apply in cases in which a step or an application to which that Part applies is taken or made on or after 5th October, 2009, and in other cases if the court so orders. Otherwise, the rules in Parts 25 (Applications for public interest immunity and specific disclosure) and 26 (Confidential material) apply as if The Criminal Procedure (Amendment) Rules 2009 had not been made.

(18)   The rules in Part 62 apply in cases in which an application to which that Part applies is made on or after 5th October, 2009, and in other cases if the court so orders. Otherwise, the rules replaced by those rules apply as if The Criminal Procedure (Amendment) Rules 2009 had not been made.

(19)   The rules in Part 76 apply in cases in which the court makes an order about costs on or after 5th October, 2009, and in other cases if the

court so orders. Otherwise, the rules in Part 78 (Costs orders against the parties) apply as if The Criminal Procedure (Amendment) Rules 2009 had not been made.

Note. The rules replaced by the first Criminal Procedure Rules (The Criminal Procedure Rules 2005) were revoked when those Rules came into force by provisions of the Courts Act 2003, The Courts Act 2003 (Consequential Amendments) Order 2004 and The Courts Act 2003 (Commencement No. 6 and Savings) Order 2004. The first Criminal Procedure Rules reproduced the substance of all the rules they replaced.

2.2 Definitions

(1)   In these Rules, unless the context makes it clear that something different is meant:

"business day" means any day except Saturday, Sunday, Christmas Day, Boxing Day, Good Friday, Easter Monday or a bank holiday;

"court" means a tribunal with jurisdiction over criminal cases. It includes a judge, recorder, District Judge (Magistrates' Courts), lay justice and, when exercising their judicial powers, the Registrar of Criminal Appeals, a justices' clerk or assistant clerk;

"court officer" means the appropriate member of the staff of a court;

'justices' legal adviser' means a justices' clerk or an assistant to a justices' clerk;

"live link" means an arrangement by which a person can see and hear, and be seen and heard by, the court when that person is not in court;

"Practice Direction" means the Lord Chief Justice's Consolidated Criminal Practice Direction, as amended; and

"public interest ruling" means a ruling about whether it is in the public interest to disclose prosecution material under sections 3(6), 7A(8) or 8(5) of the Criminal Procedure and Investigations Act 1996.

(2)   Definitions of some other expressions are in the rules in which they apply.

2.3 References to Acts of Parliament and to Statutory Instruments

In these Rules, where a rule refers to an Act of Parliament or to subordinate legislation by title and year, subsequent references to that Act or to that legislation in the rule are shortened: so, for example, after a reference to the Criminal Procedure and Investigations Act 1996 that Act is called "the 1996 Act"; and after a reference to the Criminal Procedure and Investigations Act 1996 (Defence Disclosure Time Limits) Regulations 1997 those Regulations are called "the 1997 Regulations".

2.4 The glossary

The glossary at the end of the Rules is a guide to the meaning of certain legal expressions used in them.

2.5 Representatives

(1)   Under these Rules, unless the context makes it clear that something different is meant, anything that a party may or must do may be done –

    (a)   by a legal representative on that party's behalf;

    (b)   by a person with the corporation's written authority, where that party is a corporation;

    (c)   with the help of a parent, guardian or other suitable supporting adult where that party is a defendant –

        (i)   who is under 18, or

        (ii)   whose understanding of what the case involves is limited.

(2)   Anyone with a prosecutor's authority to do so may, on that prosecutor's behalf –

    (a)   serve on the magistrates' court officer, or present to a magistrates' court, an information under section 1 of the Magistrates' Courts Act 1980; or

    (b)   issue a written charge and requisition under section 29 of the Criminal Justice Act 2003.

Note. See also section 122 of the Magistrates' Courts Act 1980. A party's legal representative must be entitled to act as such under section 27 or 28 of the Courts and Legal Services Act 1990.

Section 33(6) of the Criminal Justice Act 1925, section 46 of the Magistrates' Courts Act 1980 and Schedule 3 to that Act provide for the representation of a corporation.

Part 7 contains rules about starting a prosecution.

Criminal Procedure Rules Part 33 – Expert evidence

The following is taken from the 8th update of the Rules dated October 2009. Source: www.justice.gov.uk

Note. For the use of an expert report as evidence, see section 30 of the Criminal Justice Act 1988.

33.1 Reference to expert

A reference to an 'expert' in this Part is a reference to a person who is required to give or prepare expert evidence for the purpose of criminal proceedings, including evidence required to determine fitness to plead or for the purpose of sentencing.

Note. Expert medical evidence may be required to determine fitness to plead under section 4 of the Criminal Procedure (Insanity) Act 1964. It may be required also under section 11 of the Powers of Criminal Courts (Sentencing) Act 2000, under Part III of the Mental Health Act 1983 or under Part 12 of the Criminal Justice Act 2003. Those Acts contain requirements about the qualification of medical experts.

33.2 Expert's duty to the court

(1) An expert must help the court to achieve the overriding objective by giving objective, unbiased opinion on matters within his expertise.

(2) This duty overrides any obligation to the person from whom he receives instructions or by whom he is paid.

(3) This duty includes an obligation to inform all parties and the court if the expert's opinion changes from that contained in a report served as evidence or given in a statement.

33.3 Content of expert's report

(1) An expert's report must -

    (a) give details of the expert's qualifications, relevant experience and accreditation;

    (b) give details of any literature or other information which the expert has relied on in making the report;

    (c) contain a statement setting out the substance of all facts given to the expert which are material to the opinions expressed in the report or upon which those opinions are based;

    (d) make clear which of the facts stated in the report are within the expert's own knowledge;

    (e) say who carried out any examination, measurement, test or experiment which the expert has used for the report and,

       (i)   give the qualifications, relevant experience and accreditation of that person;

       (ii)   say whether or not the examination, measurement, test or experiment was carried out under the expert's supervision; and

       (iii)   summarise the findings on which the expert relies;

   (f)   where there is a range of opinion on the matters dealt with in the report -

       (i)   summarise the range of opinion, and

       (ii)   give reasons for his own opinion;

   (g)   if the expert is not able to give his opinion without qualification, state the qualification;

   (h)   contain a summary of the conclusions reached;

   (i)   contain a statement that the expert understands his duty to the court, and has complied and will continue to comply with that duty; and

   (j)   contain the same declaration of truth as a witness statement.

(2)   Only sub-paragraphs (i) and (j) of rule 33.3(1) apply to a summary by an expert of his conclusions served in advance of that expert's report.

Note: Part 27 contains rules about witness statements. Declarations of truth in witness statements are required by section 9 of the Criminal Justice Act 1967 and section 5B of the Magistrates' Courts Act 1980. A party who accepts another party's expert's conclusions may admit them as facts under section 10 of the Criminal Justice Act 1967. Evidence of examinations, etc., on which an expert relies may be admissible under section 127 of the Criminal Justice Act 2003.

33.4 Service of expert evidence

(1)   A party who wants to introduce expert evidence must –

   (a)   serve it on –

       (i)   the court officer, and

       (ii)   each other party;

   (b)   serve it –

       (i)   as soon as practicable, and in any event

       (ii)   with any application in support of which that party relies on that evidence; and

   (c)   if another party so requires, give that party a copy of, or a reasonable opportunity to inspect –

       (i)   a record of any examination, measurement, test or experiment on which the expert's findings and opinion are based, or that were carried out in the course of reaching those findings and opinion, and

(ii)   anything on which any such examination, measurement, test or experiment was carried out.

(2)   A party may not introduce expert evidence if that party has not complied with this rule, unless –

(a)   every other party agrees; or

(b)   the court gives permission.

Note. Under section 81 of the Police and Criminal Evidence Act 1984 and under section 20(3) of the Criminal Procedure and Investigations Act 1996 rules may –

(a)   require the disclosure of expert evidence before it is introduced as part of a party's case; and

(b)   prohibit its introduction without the court's permission, if it was not disclosed as required.

33.5 Expert to be informed of service of report

A party who serves on another party or on the court a report by an expert must, at once, so inform that expert of that fact.

33.6 Pre-hearing discussion of expert evidence

(1)   This rule applies where more than one party wants to introduce expert evidence.

(2)   The court may direct the experts to -

(a)   discuss the expert issues in the proceedings; and

(b)   prepare a statement for the court of the matters on which they agree and disagree, giving their reasons.

(3)   Except for that statement the content of that discussion must not be referred to without the court's permission.

(4)   A party may not introduce expert evidence without the court's permission if the expert has not complied with a direction under this rule.

Note. At a pre-trial hearing a court may make binding rulings about the admissibility of evidence and about questions of law under section 7 of the Criminal Justice Act 1987; sections 31 and 40 of the Criminal Procedure and Investigations Act 1996; and section 45 of the Courts Act 2003.

33.7 Court's power to direct that evidence is to be given by a single joint expert

(1) Where more than one defendant wants to introduce expert evidence on an issue at trial, the court may direct that the evidence on that issue is to be given by one expert only.

(2) Where the co-defendants cannot agree who should be the expert, the court may –

    (a) select the expert from a list prepared or identified by them; or

    (b) direct that the expert be selected in such other manner as the court may direct.

33.8 Instructions to a single joint expert

(1) Where the court gives a direction under rule 33.7 for a single joint expert to be used, each of the co-defendants may give instructions to the expert.

(2) When a co-defendant gives instructions to the expert he must, at the same time, send a copy of the instructions to the other co-defendant(s).

(3) The court may give directions about –

    (a) the payment of the expert's fees and expenses; and

    (b) any examination, measurement, test or experiment which the expert wishes to carry out.

(4) The court may, before an expert is instructed, limit the amount that can be paid by way of fees and expenses to the expert.

(5) Unless the court otherwise directs, the instructing co-defendants are jointly and severally liable for the payment of the expert's fees and expenses.

33.9 Court's power to vary requirements under this Part

(1) The court may –

    (a) extend (even after it has expired) a time limit under this Part;

    (b) allow the introduction of expert evidence which omits a detail required by this Part.

(2) A party who wants an extension of time must –

    (a) apply when serving the expert evidence for which it is required; and

    (b) explain the delay.

Criminal Regulations

Source: www.justice.gov.uk

Extracted from the Prosecution of Offences Act 1985, the Costs in Criminal Cases (General) Regulations 1986 and the Criminal Defence Service (Funding) Order 2007 made under the Access to Justice Act 1999

Prosecution of Offences Act 1985

Section 19

(3)   The Lord Chancellor may by regulations make provision for the payment out of central funds, in such circumstances and in relation to such criminal proceedings as may be specified, of such sums as appear to the court to be reasonably necessary:

(a)   to compensate any witness in the proceedings... for the expense, trouble or loss of time properly incurred in or incidental to his attendance...

Costs in Criminal Cases (General) Regulations 1986[1]

Reg 16

(1)   Where, in any proceedings in a criminal cause or matter in a magistrates' court, the Crown Court, a Divisional Court of the Queen's Bench Division, the Court of Appeal or the House of Lords:

(a)   a witness attends at the instance of the accused, a private prosecutor or the court...

... the expenses properly incurred by that witness... shall be allowed out of central funds..., unless the court directs otherwise.

(2)   ... any entitlement to an allowance... shall be the same whether the witness... attends on the same day in one case or more than one case.

Reg 17

The Lord Chancellor shall, with the consent of the Treasury, determine the rates or scales of allowances payable out of central funds to witnesses...[2]

Reg 20

(1)   The court may make an allowance in respect of an expert witness for attending to give expert evidence and for work in connection with its preparation of such an amount as it may consider reasonable having

---

1 These regulations were made pursuant to Section 19(3) of the 1985 Act.
2 For details of the current rates for expert witnesses, see MoJ Guidance to Determining Officers on page 56.

regard to the nature and difficulty of the case and the work necessarily involved.

Reg 21

(1)   [An] expert witness who is necessarily absent from his place of residence overnight may be allowed a night allowance not exceeding the relevant amount.[3]

Reg 24

(1)   Subject to paragraphs (2) and (3), a witness who travels to or from court by public transport (including by air) may be allowed the fare actually paid.

(2)   Unless the court otherwise directs, only the second class fare shall be allowed under paragraph (1) for travel by railway by witnesses.[4]

(3)   A witness who travels to or from court by air may be allowed the fare actually paid only if:

(a)   there is no reasonable alternative to travel by air and the class of fare paid was reasonable in all the circumstances; or

(b)   travel by air was more economical... taking into account any savings of time... and [their] consequent effect in reducing the amount of allowances payable under the other provisions of this Part of these Regulations and, where the air fare is not allowed, there may be allowed such amount as the court considers reasonable.

(4)   A witness who travels to or from court by hired vehicle may be allowed:

(a)   the fare actually paid and any reasonable gratuity so paid in a case of urgency or where public transport is not reasonably available; or

(b)   in any other case, the amount of fare for travel by public transport.

(5)   A witness who travels to or from court by private vehicle may be allowed an appropriate private vehicle allowance not exceeding the relevant amount.

(6)   Where:

(a)   a witness is in the opinion of the court suffering from a serious illness; or

(b)   heavy exhibits have to be taken to court,

the court may allow reasonable additional sums in excess of those allowed under paragraphs (1) to (5).

---

3 'Relevant amount' means an amount calculated in accordance with the rates or scales fixed under Reg 17.
4 Note, however, that determining officers have been advised by the MoJ that first-class travel would normally be appropriate for expert witnesses.

The Criminal Defence Service (Funding) Order 2007

Section 11 – Payments from other sources

Where a representation order has been made in respect of any proceedings, the representative, whether acting under a representation order or otherwise, must not receive or be a party to the making of any payment for work done in connection with those proceedings, except such payments as may be made –

(a)   by the Lord Chancellor or the Commission; or

(b)   in respect of any expenses or fees incurred in –

    (i)   preparing, obtaining or considering any report, opinion or further evidence, whether provided by an expert witness or otherwise; or

    (ii)   obtaining any transcripts or recordings,

where an application under CDS Regulations for an authority to incur such fees or expenses has been refused by a committee appointed under arrangements made by the Commission to deal with, amongst other things, appeals of, or review of, assessment of costs.

MoJ Guidance to Determining Officers

Source: www.hmcourts-service.gov.uk

Reg 24, Travelling allowances

Guidance on allowances payable under Regulation 24 of *Part V of the Costs in Criminal Cases (General) Regulations 1986* published by the MoJ in the *Guide to Allowances, June 2007.*

(a) Public Transport Rate
> Rate per mile with effect from 1.8.2001
> Motor-cycles: 25p
> Motor cars: 25p

(b) Standard Rate
> Rate per mile with effect from 1.8.2001
> Motor-cycles: 45p
> Motor cars: 45p

(c) Passenger Supplement
> First passenger: 2p
> Each additional passenger: 1p

(d) Parking Fees – fees actually and reasonably incurred

(e) Pedal-cycle 20p with effect from 1.6.2005

Appendix 2: Guidance for Taxing/Determining Officers when assessing Expert Witness and other Allowances

Extracted from Appendix 2 of the Guide to Allowances under Part V of the Costs in Criminal Cases (General) Regulations 1986, as revised by the Lord Chancellor Department's Legal Aid Division in April 2003, published by the Public Legal Services Division, Department for Constitutional Affairs, in June 2005, and republished by the MoJ in June 2007.

1. As there are no prescribed scales for the remuneration of expert witnesses... [this] guidance is issued to assist taxing/determining officers by providing a point of reference on **quantum** for use when exercising their discretion in determining [claims from expert witnesses].

2. The figures are based upon allowances made throughout England and Wales. It is intended that the information will be revised annually.

3. The rate bands cover a wide [range] of skill and, in some cases, a number of different kinds of skill. They provide neither a minimum nor a maximum limit, merely a guide to the level of allowances in normal circumstances. It may be appropriate, having regard to the particular circumstances of the

case, to depart from the guidance scales. Such occasions will, however, arise exceptionally.

4. In exercising their discretion, taxing/determining officers are to bear in mind that each case must be considered individually. They are to take into account all relevant circumstances surrounding the claim, including such things as the work done, the status or experience of the person doing the work, and the availability of such persons in the area of the country concerned.

5. In cases of difficulty, taxing/determining officers should seek advice from the Circuit Taxing Co-ordinator.

Schedule of Rates from 6 May 2003

1. **Consultant medical practitioner, psychiatrist, pathologist**
   Preparation (examination/report): ....£70–£100 per hour
   Attendance at court (full day) ....£346–£500

2. **Fire (assessor) and/or explosives expert**
   Preparation: ....£50–£75 per hour
   Attendance at court (full day) ....£255–£365

3. **Forensic scientist (including questioned document examiner), surveyor, accountant, engineer, medical practitioner, architect, veterinary surgeon, meteorologist**
   Preparation ....£47–£100 per hour
   Attendance at court (full day) ....£226–£490

4. **Fingerprint [expert]**
   Preparation ....£32–£52 per hour
   Attendance at court (full day) ....£153–£256

Disclosure: Experts' evidence and unused material – Guidance Booklet for Experts

Source: CPS Disclosure Manual – Annex K, www.cps.gov.uk

1 Introduction

You are instructed by the Prosecution Team, which comprises the Police and Crown Prosecution Service, as an expert in this investigation. It is important that you understand the obligations placed upon you by this status. As an expert witness you have an overriding duty to assist the court and, in this respect, your duty is to the court and not to the Prosecuting Team instructing you. This will include obligations relating to disclosure.

The obligations which apply to you as an expert are to assist in ensuring that the Prosecution Team can comply fully with their statutory disclosure obligations. These obligations take precedence over any internal codes of practice or other standards set by any professional organisations to which you may belong. Your obligations are set out in part 3 of this booklet, but can be summarised in the key actions of **retain, record and reveal**.

A failure to comply with the guidelines in this booklet may have a number of adverse consequences which could include:

- A prosecution being halted or delayed;
- The appellate courts finding that a conviction is unsafe;
- The tribunal making an adverse judicial comment about you as an expert. Such an adverse judicial comment could seriously undermine your credibility as an expert and consequently your fitness to be instructed in future cases;
- Professional embarrassment, including possible action by a professional body, loss of accreditation and the potential for civil action by an accused.

Conversely, your credibility as an expert will be enhanced by the considered application of this guidance and your appropriate management of the materials within the investigation.

An expert employed by the police is not a third party and is already required to comply with the Criminal Procedure and Investigations Act and should comply with the detailed guidance in the Disclosure Manual (see below).

2. Disclosure obligations under the criminal law

2.1. Aims of disclosure

The regime for disclosure is set out in the Act and the Code, issued under it. This is designed to ensure that there is a fair system for the disclosure of unused material which assists the defence in the timely preparation of its case, does not overburden the parties and enables the court to focus on all the important issues in the trial.

2.2.The meaning of unused material

During the course of any investigation material is generated. Some of it is used as evidence and other material is not used. The material that is not used as evidence is known as unused material, to which the disclosure regime applies.

Unused material is material that is relevant to the investigation but which does not actually form part of the case for the prosecution against the accused. Even though the material may not be used as evidence, it is important that for the purposes of disclosure this material is retained.

It is not for you to determine whether the material generated in the course of an investigation is relevant to the investigation.

2.3.The Disclosure Manual/Attorney General's Guidelines

The Disclosure Manual (The Manual) contains the operational instructions on disclosure which have been agreed by the CPS and the Association of Chief Police Officers. It explains how the Prosecution Team have agreed to fulfil their duties to disclose unused material to the defence. These duties arise under statute and at common law.

The Manual contains practical guidance to the police and CPS practitioners which supplements the framework of the Act, the Code and the Attorney General's Guidelines. The Manual is available on this website.

The Attorney General's Guidelines build on existing law to help ensure that the legislation is operated consistently and fairly by the Prosecution Team. They can be found at: http://www.lslo.gov.uk/guidelines.htm.

3.Discharging your obligations

There are three key obligations arising for you, as an expert, as the investigation progresses. Your understanding of these obligations and delivering them is the key to you adequately fulfilling your disclosure obligations. The relevant steps are to retain, to record, and to reveal. The flowchart attached at appendix D to this guidance illustrates this process.

3.1.Retain

3.1.1.What to retain

You should retain everything, including physical, written and electronically captured material, until otherwise instructed and the investigator has indicated the appropriate action to take.

3.1.2. How long to retain

The period of time for which materials are required to be retained will vary from case to case and will depend on a number of factors. Examples include the nature of the offence; the stage and status of any legal proceedings; whether the case is of special interest. It must also be remembered that the retention requirement may alter as a result of a change of circumstances during the course of the investigation.

You should, therefore, obtain advice from the investigator for the retention period hat applies to this particular investigation and always before contemplating destruction of any material.

3.2.Record

3.2.1.When to record

The requirement for you to commence making records begins at the time you receive instructions and continues for the whole of the time you are involved.

Circumstances may exist, however, where practitioners should commence making records, in accordance with this guidance, prior to any instructions from the police. Examples of this would be:

- where as a pathologist the outcome of a 'routine' post-mortem suggests to you that death has been caused under suspicious circumstances;
- as a medical practitioner you find injuries that are not consistent with the alleged cause;
- as a fire scene examiner you believe a fire to have been started deliberately.

In all these examples the criminal investigation will start after the practitioner's original involvement but the results of the previous examinations will almost certainly be material to any investigation and subsequent prosecution. The list is not intended to be exhaustive.

This practitioner could be you. If you have any doubts start recording.

3.2.2.What to record

You should keep records of all the work you have carried out and any findings you make in relation to the investigation. The guidance provided below reflects best practice and your records, as a minimum, should contain information relating to:

the collection and movement of items, including

the date on which you take or receive material (physical items and information) and the date of subsequent movement of the material to another party

from who or where and to whom or where material is moved

the means by which you receive or pass material from/to another party

the examination of materials

your notes, and those of any assistant should be signed, dated, attributable to the individual and produced contemporaneously, whenever practicable

the notes should be sufficiently detailed and expressed in such a manner that another expert, in your field, can follow the nature of the work undertaken, any assumptions made and the inferences you have drawn from the work

verbal and other communications

you should keep your own notes of all meetings you attend

you should keep your own notes of telephone conversations and it is important that points of agreement, or disagreement and agreed actions are recorded

you should ensure that a record of all e-mails and other electronic transmissions (e.g. images), sent or received, is kept

you should keep clear notes of any witness accounts or explanations that you have been provided with, or any other information received

3.2.3. How to record

The media you use for making your records should be capable of meeting all the requirements given above, be durable and provide a means of retrieval.

Your notes, in whatever form, should also be structured in a manner that facilitates review. Any updates, alterations or comments should be clear. It is important that your notes are clear and comprehensive. This will allow another person who may subsequently review them to have a full understanding of the position at any given time.

3.3.Reveal

3.3.1.What to reveal

You are required to reveal everything you have recorded.

It is a necessary and important part of your disclosure obligations to make the Prosecution Team aware of all the material you have in your possession in relation to the investigation. This will then enable them to make informed decisions, as to what material is relevant, and then what material satisfies the disclosure test.

3.3.2.How to reveal

There are three ways in which you will reveal material to the Prosecution Team.

The Report

Your report(s) should contain information relating to the following:

- details of your qualifications, experience or accreditation relevant to the work performed
- the range and extent of your expertise
- details of any information upon which you have relied in arriving at your opinion
- details of any statements of fact upon which you have relied in reaching your opinion
- clarification of which of the facts are within your own knowledge
- information relating to who has carried out measurements, examinations, tests etc and if under your supervision
- your opinion(s) and a justification for these
- where you have provided qualified opinions details of the qualifications
- a summary of all your conclusions

Statements

In addition to all of the above you may be required to make a formal statement. The statement should contain all of the above and the following:

- the declaration which confirms that you understand your duty to the court in respect of disclosure
- an acknowledgement that you will inform all parties and, where appropriate the court, in the event that your view changes on any material issue.

When compiling your report/statement you should ensure that due regard is given to any information that points away from, as well as towards, the defendant(s).

You must not give expert opinion beyond your area of expertise.

The Index of Unused Material

In order to reveal material to the Prosecution Team, it is necessary that you to complete an index of unused material, (the Index) describing all the unused material in your possession. All the material not identified in your report/statement should be placed on the Index.

The Index is designed to enable you to provide to the Prosecution Team a description of all the unused material in your possession in a structured, comprehensive and informative manner.

An example of a specimen Index is given in Appendix A. You will need to tailor the descriptions of the materials to meet your specific case requirements. Your descriptions, however, must be full enough for others to clearly understand the nature of the material. Please note that this example is neither exhaustive nor exclusive.

You should not attempt to make judgements on the significance of material when producing the Index. Where you believe material may be confidential or sensitive, for example for commercial reasons, then this should be placed on a separate schedule and discussed with the Prosecution Team.

Revelation to the Prosecution Team does not necessarily mean disclosure to the defence.

4. Declaration of Understanding
You are required to confirm your understanding of your disclosure obligations to the court, as set out in the guidance given in this booklet, by signing a declaration (the Declaration) of understanding. This Declaration will be incorporated into your statement and the required form of words is given in Appendix B.

An expert employed by the police is obliged to comply with the disclosure regime as set out in the Act. All non-police experts will be expected to sign the Declaration that they have done so.

5. The Experts Self-Certificate
Upon receipt of instructions you are required to complete a self-certificate (the Certificate) in every case that you are instructed as an expert witness for the Prosecution. The completed Certificate should be sent to the disclosure officer or investigating officer. The Certificate can be found at Appendix C.

6. The Experts Revelation Process Flowchart
A flowchart summarising your obligations can be found at Appendix D.

7. Queries
If you have any queries relating to the contents of this guidance, please contact the investigating officer, the disclosure officer or the prosecutor.

Appendix A: Expert's Index of unused material

The following is a suggested list of all the unused material in the possession of the above named expert in this case (Note, the material should be considered to be NON-SENSITIVE, unless a specific flag exists to suggest it might be SENSITIVE). The list is provided in accordance with the guidance given in 'Disclosure: Experts' evidence and unused material: Guidance Booklet for Experts.

This list is an example and is not designed to be exhaustive or exclusive

No.	Description of material	Location	Insert C, I or CND	Comment
1	**FORMS** detailing : Receipt and Dispatch of items to laboratory; movement of items within and between sites; Submission forms detailing nature of offence, work required and details of suspects, victims etc	Case file		
2	**CASE NOTES** made at the time of the examination of the items: provide details of dates of examinations; details of packaging and integrity of items; records of work performed on the items, who was involved and dates; analytical and test results; details of quality checks	Case file		
3	**DRAFT REPORTS** electronic and/ or hard copy drafts of reports or statements sent out to police and CPS	Case file/ IT		
4	**ADMINISTRATIVE DOCUMENTS** time recording sheets; case costings; delivery notes; invoices; records of enquiries with customer relating to costs etc	Case file		
5	**MINUTES** of conversations with and instructions to other staff; [records of conversations with the OIC and other police personnel]; [records of conversations with Prosecutor and other CPS personnel]	Case file		

6	RECORDS of material submitted but not examined; of material examined but relating to suspects not included in reports or statements; of work carried out by others, including the results; of procedures and techniques used during the examinations	Case file		
7	RETAINED MATERIALS material from Items.....	Stores		
8	SCENE OF CRIME related material: written notes, [voice recorded notes], diagrams, photographs/images taken at the time of the scene attendance	Case file/ IT Media		
9	POST MORTEM related material: written notes, [voice recorded notes], diagrams, photographs/images taken during the post mortem examination of [name]	Case file/ IT Media		
10	WITNESS STATEMENTS from the following people: [name, .]	Case file		
11	ADDITIONAL INFORMATION in the form of : maps, plans, photographs, videos relating to the scene of the offence; details of modus operandi; details of related offences	Case file/ Stores		
12	DATABASES material from the following databases have been used: [name of database] [source]			
13	OTHER			

Completed by:

Signed:

Dated:

Reviewing Lawyer Signature:

Date:

Appendix B: Declaration

I am an expert in [field of expertise] and I have been requested to provide a statement. I confirm that I have read guidance contained in a booklet known as Disclosure: Expert's evidence and unused material which details my role and documents my responsibilities, in relation to revelation as an expert witness. I have followed the guidance and recognise the continuing nature of my responsibilities of revelation. In accordance with my duties of revelation, as documented in the guidance booklet, I

a   confirm that I have complied with my duties to record, retain and reveal material in accordance with the Criminal Procedure and Investigations Act 1996, as amended;

b   have compiled an Index of all material. I will ensure that the Index is updated in the event I am provided with or generate additional material;

c   that in the event my opinion changes on any material issue, I will inform the investigating officer, as soon as reasonably practicable and give reasons.

Signed _____

Dated _____

Appendix C: Expert Witnesses Self-Certificate

Expert Witnesses

Self-Certificate

Revelation of information

(Criminal Procedure and Investigations Act 1996)

Name of Expert Witness:

Date of birth:

Business Address:

Defendant (if known):

I have been instructed to provide expert evidence in relation to the prosecution of the above-named, or an investigation into the following criminal offence:

I confirm that I have read the booklet known as Disclosure: Experts evidence and unused material, that has been given to me with this form, and that I am aware of my responsibilities as an expert witness to reveal to the Prosecution Team any information that might undermine my evidence.

1	Have you ever been convicted of, cautioned for, or received a penalty notice for, any criminal offence (other than minor traffic offences)?	YES	NO
2	Are there any proceedings pending against you in any criminal or civil court?	YES	NO
3	Are you aware of any adverse finding by a judge, magistrate or coroner about your professional competence or credibility as a witness?	YES	NO
4	Have you ever been the subject of any adverse findings by a professional or regulatory body?	YES	NO
5	Are there any proceedings, referrals or investigations pending against you that have been brought by a professional or regulatory body?	YES	NO
6	Are you aware of any other information that you think may adversely affect your professional competence and credibility as an expert witness?	YES	NO

Should you have any queries in relation to your answers to any of the above, please contact the investigator.

Please note that the questions above apply to any proceedings, findings or other relevant information in this or any other jurisdiction.

If you have answered YES to any of the questions numbered 1-6, please give details below:

DECLARATION

All the information I have given in this certificate is true to the best of my knowledge and belief.

I will notify those instructing me of any change in this information.

I am aware that any false or misleading information I have given in this document, or any deliberate omission of relevant information may lead to disciplinary or criminal proceedings.

Signed: ....

Name (in block capitals): ....

Date: ....

Appendix D: Experts Revelation Process Flowchart

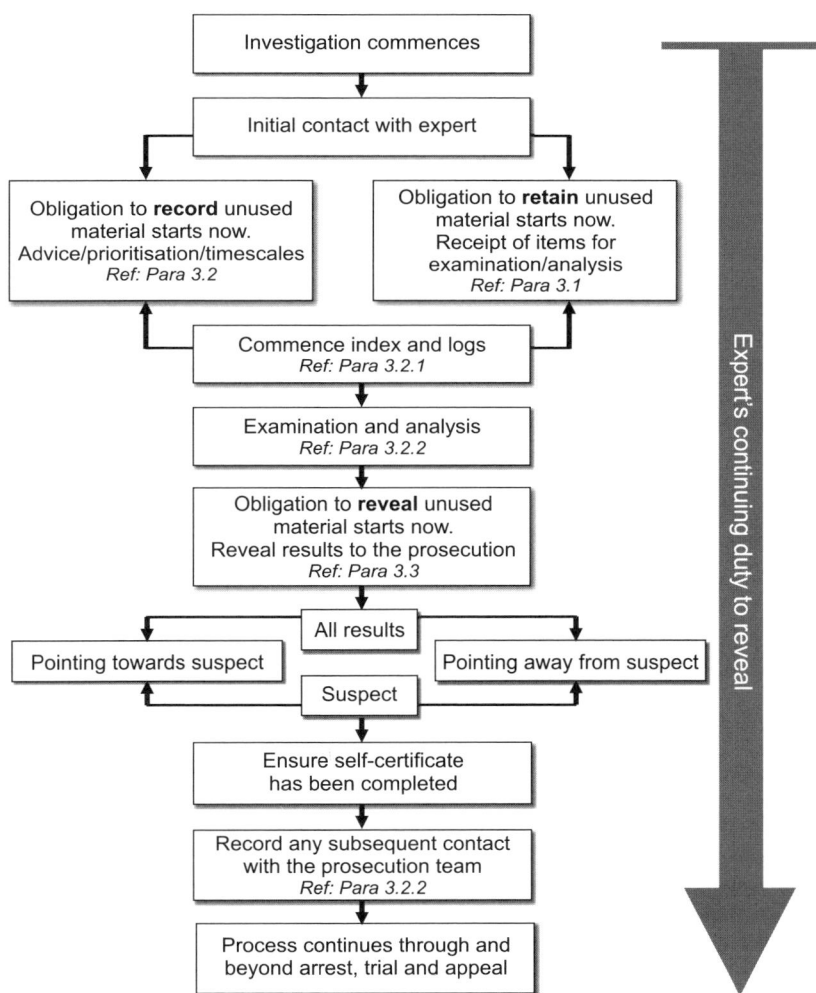

CPS Witness expenses

Source: www.cps.gov.uk

Legal Guidance – Witness expenses and allowances

'Expert Witnesses

These will receive a fee. The fee should, wherever possible, be agreed in advance. The fee is discretionary but scales of guidance exist.

Subsistence allowance is not payable, except when an overnight stay is necessary. Travelling expenses are payable.'

NFR EFC 1A(8/05) – Expert Witness Expenses

Rates from 15 September 2008

This gives the current rates of allowances payable by the Crown Prosecution Service to expert witnesses for travel and subsistence.

Subsistence Allowances

Overnight allowances

Where it is necessary to stay overnight a fixed allowance is paid towards the cost of meals and accommodation. The allowance is:

Attendance overnight in London, Birmingham, Manchester, Leeds, Liverpool and Newcastle upon Tyne city centres	£85.25
Attendance overnight elsewhere	£55.25

Both figures are exclusive of VAT according to the Criminal Bills Assessment Manual, section 4.13.5

Travel expenses

Public transport
Bus, coach, tram and tube fares will be reimbursed in full. Rail travel will be reimbursed at standard class unless it was necessary to undertake preparation for court on the train when first class may be paid.

Motor car
If you use your own motor car, you will be paid 25p for each mile. Exceptionally, if you can show that you had to use your own car instead of public transport (for example, because there was no public transport, or there was a considerable saving of time and money, or because you are disabled or infirm), then a higher rate of 45p per mile may be paid. You will need to justify using your own motor car to be eligible for the higher rate.

Motorcycles

Similar rules apply if you use your own motorcycle. The rate per mile that will be paid is 23.8p. Exceptionally the higher rate of 25.4p per mile may also be paid if you can show it was necessary to use your own vehicle instead of public transport.

Car parking

Car parking charges will normally be paid if it was necessary to use your own motor vehicle.

Congestion Charge

Congestion Charges will normally be reimbursed in full.

Taxis

The cost of taxi fares or other hired vehicles (including any reasonable tips) will only be paid in cases of emergency, illness, infirmity or where no other reasonable means of transport was available.

Other transport

If you intend to use some other form of transport (e.g. aeroplane or ship), you are advised to consult the CPS instructing office for advice as to whether the cost will be allowed. The cost of travel by air or sea will be reimbursed at economy class fare only.

Travel and subsistence costs, in accordance with the above rates, should be included on your invoice for fees.

3

Rules in Family Litigation

Practice Direction – Experts in Family Proceedings relating to Children

The following is taken from the final text dated 14 Jan 2008.
Source: www.hmcourts-service.gov.uk

The Practice Direction below is made by the President of the Family Division under the powers delegated to him by the Lord Chief Justice under Schedule 2, Part 1, paragraph 2(2) of the Constitutional Reform Act 2005, and is approved by the Lord Chancellor.

1. Introduction

1.1   This Practice Direction deals with the use of expert evidence and the instruction of experts in family proceedings relating to children, and comes into force on 1 April 2008. The guidance supersedes, for such proceedings, that contained in Appendix C (the Code of Guidance for Expert Witnesses in Family Proceedings) to the Protocol of June 2003 (Judicial Case Management in Public Law Children Act Cases) and in the Practice Direction to Part 17 (Experts) of the Family Procedure (Adoption) Rules 2005 ('FP(AR) 2005') with effect on and from 1 April 2008.

Where the guidance refers to 'an expert' or 'the expert', this includes a reference to an expert team.

1.2   For the purposes of this guidance, the phrase 'family proceedings relating to children' is a convenient description. It is not a legal term of art and has no statutory force. In this guidance it means:

- placement and adoption proceedings, or
- family proceedings held in private which:
    - relate to the exercise of the inherent jurisdiction of the High Court with respect to children,
    - are brought under the Children Act 1989 in any family court, or
    - are brought in the High Court and county courts and 'otherwise relate wholly or mainly to the maintenance or upbringing of a minor'.

Aims of the guidance

1.3   The guidance aims to provide the court in family proceedings relating to children with early information to determine whether an expert or expert evidence will assist the court to:

- identify, narrow and where possible agree the issues between the parties;
- provide an opinion about a question that is not within the skill and experience of the court;

- encourage the early identification of questions that need to be answered by an expert; and

- encourage disclosure of full and frank information between the parties, the court and any expert instructed.

1.4 The guidance does not aim to cover all possible eventualities. Thus it should be complied with so far as consistent in all the circumstances with the just disposal of the matter in accordance with the rules and guidance applying to the procedure in question.

Permission to instruct an expert or to use expert evidence

1.5 In family proceedings relating to children, the court's permission is required to instruct an expert. Such proceedings are confidential and, in the absence of the court's permission, disclosure of information and documents relating to such proceedings risks contravening the law of contempt of court or the various statutory provisions protecting this confidentiality. Thus, for the purposes of the law of contempt of court, information relating to such proceedings (whether or not contained in a document filed with the court or recorded in any form) may be communicated only to an expert whose instruction by a party has been permitted by the court. Additionally, in proceedings under the Children Act 1989, the court's permission is required to cause the child to be medically or psychiatrically examined or otherwise assessed for the purpose of the preparation of expert evidence for use in the proceedings; and, where the court's permission has not been given, no evidence arising out of such an examination or assessment may be adduced without the court's permission.

1.6 In practice, the need to have the court's permission to disclose information or documents to an expert – and, in Children Act 1989 proceedings, to have the child examined or assessed – means that in proceedings relating to children the court strictly controls the number, fields of expertise and identity of the experts who may be first instructed and then called.

1.7 Before permission is obtained from the court to instruct an expert in family proceedings relating to children, it will be necessary for the party wishing to instruct an expert to make enquiries designed so as to provide the court with information about that expert which will enable the court to decide whether or not to give permission. In practice, enquiries may need to be made of more than one expert for this purpose. This will in turn require each expert to be given sufficient information about the case to enable that expert to decide whether or not he or she is in a position to accept instructions. Such preliminary enquiries, and the disclosure of anonymised information about the case which is a necessary part of such enquiries, will not require the court's permission and will not amount to a contempt of court: see sections 4.1 and 4.2 (Preliminary Enquiries of the Expert and Expert's Response to Preliminary Enquiries).

1.8   Section 4 (Preparation for the relevant hearing) gives guidance on applying for the court's permission to instruct an expert, and on instructing the expert, in family proceedings relating to children. The court, when granting permission to instruct an expert, will also give directions for the expert to be called to give evidence, or for the expert's report to be put in evidence: see section 4.4 (Draft Order for the relevant hearing).

When should the court be asked for permission?

1.9   The key event is 'the relevant hearing', which is any hearing at which the court's permission is sought to instruct an expert or to use expert evidence. Both expert issues should be raised with the court – and, where appropriate, with the other parties – as early as possible. This means:

-      in public law proceedings under the Children Act 1989, by or at the Case Management Conference: see the Practice Direction: Guide to Case Management in Public Law Proceedings, paragraphs 13.7, 14.3 and 25(29) which contains the definition of public law proceedings for the purposes of that practice direction;

-      in private law proceedings under the Children Act 1989, by or at the First Hearing Dispute Resolution Appointment: see the Private Law Programme (9 November 2004), section 4 (Process);

-      in placement and adoption proceedings, by or at the First Directions Hearing: see FP(A)R 2005 rule 26 and the President's Guidance: Adoption: the New Law and Procedure (March 2006), paragraph 23.

2. General matters

Scope of the Guidance

2.1   This guidance does not apply to cases issued before 1 April 2008, but in such a case the court may direct that this guidance will apply either wholly or partly. This is subject to the overriding objective for the type of proceedings, and to the proviso that such a direction will neither cause further delay nor involve repetition of steps already taken or of decisions already made in the case.

2.2   This guidance applies to all experts who are or have been instructed to give or prepare evidence for the purpose of family proceedings relating to children in a court in England and Wales.

Pre-application instruction of experts

2.3   When experts' reports are commissioned before the commencement of proceedings, it should be made clear to the expert that he or she may in due course be reporting to the court and should therefore consider himself or herself bound by this guidance. A prospective party to family proceedings relating to children (for example, a local authority) should always write a letter of instruction when asking a potential witness for a report or an opinion, whether that request is within proceedings or pre-proceedings (for example, when commissioning specialist assessment materials, reports from a treating expert or other evidential materials); and the letter of instruction should conform to the principles set out in this guidance.

Emergency and urgent cases

2.4   In emergency or urgent cases – for example, where, before formal issue of proceedings, a without-notice application is made to the court during or out of business hours; or where, after proceedings have been issued, a previously unforeseen need for (further) expert evidence arises at short notice - a party may wish to call expert evidence without having complied with all or any part of this guidance. In such circumstances, the party wishing to call the expert evidence must apply forthwith to the court – where possible or appropriate, on notice to the other parties – for directions as to the future steps to be taken in respect of the expert evidence in question.

Orders

2.5   Where an order or direction requires an act to be done by an expert, or otherwise affects an expert, the party instructing that expert – or, in the case of a jointly instructed expert, the lead solicitor – must serve a copy of the order or direction on the expert forthwith upon receiving it.

Adults who may be protected parties

2.6   The court will investigate as soon as possible any issue as to whether an adult party or intended party to family proceedings relating to children lacks capacity (within the meaning of the Mental Capacity Act 2005) to conduct the proceedings. An adult who lacks capacity to act as a party to the proceedings is a protected party and must have a representative (a litigation friend, next friend or guardian ad litem) to conduct the proceedings on his or her behalf.

2.7   Any issue as to the capacity of an adult to conduct the proceedings must be determined before the court gives any directions relevant to that adult's role in the proceedings.

2.8   Where the adult is a protected party, his or her representative should be involved in any instruction of an expert, including the instruction of an expert to assess whether the adult, although a protected party, is competent to give evidence. The instruction of an expert is a significant step in the proceedings. The representative will wish to consider (and ask the expert to consider), if the protected party is competent to give evidence, their best interests in this regard. The representative may wish to seek advice about 'special measures'. The representative may put forward an argument on behalf of the protected party that the protected party should not give evidence.

2.9   If at any time during the proceedings there is reason to believe that a party may lack capacity to conduct the proceedings, then the court must be notified and directions sought to ensure that this issue is investigated without delay.

Child likely to lack capacity to conduct the proceedings on when he or she reaches 18

2.10   Where it appears that a child is:

-       a party to the proceedings and not the subject of them;
-       nearing his or her 18th birthday, and
-       considered likely to lack capacity to conduct the proceedings when he or she attains the age of 18,

the court will consider giving directions for the child's capacity in this respect to be investigated.

3. The Duties of Experts

Overriding Duty

3.1   An expert in family proceedings relating to children has an overriding duty to the court that takes precedence over any obligation to the person from whom the expert has received instructions or by whom the expert is paid.

Particular Duties

3.2   Among any other duties an expert may have, an expert shall have regard to the following duties:

1)   to assist the court in accordance with the overriding duty;

2)   to provide advice to the court that conforms to the best practice of the expert's profession;

3)   to provide an opinion that is independent of the party or parties instructing the expert;

4)   to confine the opinion to matters material to the issues between the parties and in relation only to questions that are within the expert's expertise (skill and experience);

5)   where a question has been put which falls outside the expert's expertise, to state this at the earliest opportunity and to volunteer an opinion as to whether another expert is required to bring expertise not possessed by those already involved or, in the rare case, as to whether a second opinion is required on a key issue and, if possible, what questions should be asked of the second expert;

6) in expressing an opinion, to take into consideration all of the material facts including any relevant factors arising from ethnic, cultural, religious or linguistic contexts at the time the opinion is expressed;

7) to inform those instructing the expert without delay of any change in the opinion and of the reason for the change.

Content of the Expert's Report

3.3 The expert's report shall be addressed to the court and prepared and filed in accordance with the court's timetable and shall:

1) give details of the expert's qualifications and experience;

2) contain a statement setting out the substance of all material instructions (whether written or oral) summarising the facts stated and instructions given to the expert which are material to the conclusions and opinions expressed in the report;

3) identify materials that have not been produced either as original medical or other professional records or in response to an instruction from a party, as such materials may contain an assumption as to the standard of proof, the admissibility or otherwise of hearsay evidence, and other important procedural and substantive questions relating to the different purposes of other enquiries (for example, criminal or disciplinary proceedings);

4) identify all requests to third parties for disclosure and their responses in order to avoid partial disclosure which tends only to prove a case rather than give full and frank information;

5) make clear which of the facts stated in the report are within the expert's own knowledge;

6) state who carried out any test, examination or interview which the expert has used for the report and whether or not the test, examination or interview has been carried out under the expert's supervision;

7) give details of the qualifications of any person who carried out the test, examination or interview;

8) in expressing an opinion to the court:

(a) take into consideration all of the material facts including any relevant factors arising from ethnic, cultural, religious or linguistic contexts at the time the opinion is expressed, identifying the facts, literature and any other material including research material that the expert has relied upon in forming an opinion;

(b) describe their own professional risk assessment process and process of differential diagnosis, highlighting factual assumptions, deductions from the factual assumptions, and any unusual, contradictory or inconsistent features of the case;

   (c)   highlight whether a proposition is an hypothesis (in particular a controversial hypothesis), or an opinion deduced in accordance with peer-reviewed and -tested technique, research and experience accepted as a consensus in the scientific community;

   (d)   indicate whether the opinion is provisional (or qualified, as the case may be), stating the qualification and the reason for it, and identifying what further information is required to give an opinion without qualification;

9)   where there is a range of opinion on any question to be answered by the expert:

   (a)   summarise the range of opinion;

   (b)   highlight and analyse within the range of opinion an 'unknown cause', whether on the facts of the case (for example, there is too little information to form a scientific opinion) or because of limited experience, lack of research, peer review or support in the field of expertise which the expert professes;

   (c)   give reasons for any opinion expressed: the use of a balance sheet approach to the factors that support or undermine an opinion can be of great assistance to the court;

10)   contain a summary of the expert's conclusions and opinions;

11)   contain a statement that the expert understands his or her duty to the court and has complied and will continue to comply with that duty;

12)   contain a statement that the expert:

   (a)   has no conflict of interest of any kind, other than any conflict disclosed in his or her report;

   (b)   does not consider that any interest disclosed affects his or her suitability as an expert witness on any issue on which he or she has given evidence;

   (c)   will advise the instructing party if, between the date of the expert's report and the final hearing, there is any change in circumstances which affects the expert's answers to (a) or (b) above;

13)   be verified by a statement of truth in the following form:

'I confirm that insofar as the facts stated in my report are within my own knowledge I have made clear which they are and I believe them to be true, and that the opinions I have expressed represent my true and complete professional opinion.'

4. Preparation for the relevant hearing

Preliminary Enquiries of the Expert

4.1 In good time for the information requested to be available for the relevant hearing or for the advocates' meeting or discussion where one takes place before the relevant hearing, the solicitor for the party proposing to instruct the expert (or lead solicitor or solicitor for the child if the instruction proposed is joint) shall approach the expert with the following information:

1) the nature of the proceedings and the issues likely to require determination by the court;

2) the questions about which the expert is to be asked to give an opinion (including any ethnic, cultural, religious or linguistic contexts);

3) the date when the court is to be asked to give permission for the instruction (or if - unusually - permission has already been given, the date and details of that permission);

4) whether permission is to be asked of the court for the instruction of another expert in the same or any related field (that is, to give an opinion on the same or related questions);

5) the volume of reading which the expert will need to undertake;

6) whether or not permission has been applied for or given for the expert to examine the child;

7) whether or not it will be necessary for the expert to conduct interviews - and, if so, with whom;

8) the likely timetable of legal and social work steps;

9) when the expert's report is likely to be required;

10) whether and, if so, what date has been fixed by the court for any hearing at which the expert may be required to give evidence (in particular the Final Hearing).

It is essential that there should be proper co-ordination between the court and the expert when drawing up the case management timetable: the needs of the court should be balanced with the needs of the expert whose forensic work is undertaken as an adjunct to his or her main professional duties, whether in the National Health Service or elsewhere.

The expert should be informed at this stage of the possibility of making, through his or her instructing solicitor, representations to the court about being named or otherwise identified in any public judgment given by the court.

Expert's Response to Preliminary Enquiries

4.2 In good time for the relevant hearing or for the advocates'
meeting or discussion where one takes place before the relevant
hearing, the solicitors intending to instruct the expert shall obtain
confirmation from the expert:

1) that acceptance of the proposed instructions will not involve
the expert in any conflict of interest;

2) that the work required is within the expert's expertise;

3) that the expert is available to do the relevant work within the
suggested time scale;

4) when the expert is available to give evidence, of the dates
and times to avoid and, where a hearing date has not been
fixed, of the amount of notice the expert will require to
make arrangements to come to court (or to give evidence
by video link) without undue disruption to his or her normal
professional routines;

5) of the cost, including hourly or other charging rates, and
likely hours to be spent, attending experts' meetings,
attending court and writing the report (to include any
examinations and interviews);

6) of any representations which the expert wishes to make to
the court about being named or otherwise identified in any
public judgment given by the court.

Where parties have not agreed on the appointment of a single
joint expert before the relevant hearing, they should obtain the
above confirmations in respect of all experts whom they intend to
put to the court as candidates for the appointment.

The proposal to instruct an expert

4.3 Any party who proposes to ask the court for permission to instruct
an expert shall, by 11 a.m. on the business day before the
relevant hearing, file and serve a written proposal to instruct the
expert in the following detail:

1) the name, discipline, qualifications and expertise of the
expert (by way of C.V. where possible);

2) the expert's availability to undertake the work;

3) the relevance of the expert evidence sought to be adduced
to the issues in the proceedings and the specific questions
upon which it is proposed that the expert should give an
opinion (including the relevance of any ethnic, cultural,
religious or linguistic contexts);

4) the timetable for the report;

5)   the responsibility for instruction;

6)   whether or not the expert evidence can properly be obtained by the joint instruction of the expert by two or more of the parties;

7)   whether the expert evidence can properly be obtained by only one party (for example, on behalf of the child);

8)   why the expert evidence proposed cannot be given by social services undertaking a core assessment or by the Children's Guardian in accordance with their respective statutory duties;

9)   the likely cost of the report on an hourly or other charging basis: where possible, the expert's terms of instruction should be made available to the court;

10)   the proposed apportionment (at least in the first instance) of any jointly instructed expert's fee; when it is to be paid; and, if applicable, whether public funding has been approved.

Draft Order for the relevant hearing

4.4   Any party proposing to instruct an expert shall, by 11 a.m. on the business day before the relevant hearing, submit to the court a draft order for directions dealing in particular with:

1)   the party who is to be responsible for drafting the letter of instruction and providing the documents to the expert;

2)   the issues identified by the court and the questions about which the expert is to give an opinion;

3)   the timetable within which the report is to be prepared, filed and served;

4)   the disclosure of the report to the parties and to any other expert;

5)   the organisation of, preparation for and conduct of an experts' discussion;

6)   the preparation of a statement of agreement and disagreement by the experts following an experts' discussion;

7)   making available to the court at an early opportunity the expert reports in electronic form;

8)   the attendance of the expert at court to give oral evidence (alternatively, the expert giving his or her evidence in writing or remotely by video link), whether at or for the Final Hearing or another hearing; unless agreement about the opinions given by the expert is reached at or before the Issues Resolution Hearing ('IRH') or, if no IRH is to be held,

by a specified date prior to the hearing at which the expert is to give oral evidence ('the specified date').

5. Letter of Instruction

5.1   The solicitor instructing the expert shall, within 5 business days after the relevant hearing, prepare (in agreement with the other parties where appropriate), file and serve a letter of instruction to the expert which shall:

1)   set out the context in which the expert's opinion is sought (including any ethnic, cultural, religious or linguistic contexts);

2)   set out the specific questions which the expert is required to answer, ensuring that they:

   (a)   are within the ambit of the expert's area of expertise;

   (b)   do not contain unnecessary or irrelevant detail;

   (c)   are kept to a manageable number and are clear, focused and direct; and

   (d)   reflect what the expert has been requested to do by the court.

The Annex to this guidance sets out suggested questions in letters of instruction to (1) child mental health professionals or paediatricians, and (2) adult psychiatrists and applied psychologists, in Children Act 1989 proceedings;

3)   list the documentation provided, or provide for the expert an indexed and paginated bundle which shall include:

   (a)   a copy of the order (or those parts of the order) which gives permission for the instruction of the expert, immediately the order becomes available;

   (b)   an agreed list of essential reading; and

   (c)   a copy of this guidance;

4)   identify materials that have not been produced either as original medical (or other professional) records or in response to an instruction from a party, as such materials may contain an assumption as to the standard of proof, the admissibility or otherwise of hearsay evidence, and other important procedural and substantive questions relating to the different purposes of other enquiries (for example, criminal or disciplinary proceedings);

5)   identify all requests to third parties for disclosure and their responses, to avoid partial disclosure, which tends only to prove a case rather than give full and frank information;

6)   identify the relevant people concerned with the proceedings (for example, the treating clinicians) and inform the expert of his or her right to talk to them provided that an accurate record is made of the discussions;

7) identify any other expert instructed in the proceedings and advise the expert of his or her right to talk to the other experts provided that an accurate record is made of the discussions;

8) subject to any public funding requirement for prior authority, define the contractual basis upon which the expert is retained and in particular the funding mechanism including how much the expert will be paid (an hourly rate and overall estimate should already have been obtained), when the expert will be paid, and what limitation there might be on the amount the expert can charge for the work which he or she will have to do. In cases where the parties are publicly funded, there should also be a brief explanation of the costs and expenses excluded from public funding by Funding Code criterion 1.3 and the detailed assessment process.

Asking the court to settle the letter of instruction to a joint expert

5.2 Where the court has directed that the instructions to the expert are to be contained in a jointly agreed letter and the terms of the letter cannot be agreed, any instructing party may submit to the court a written request, which must be copied to the other instructing parties, that the court settle the letter of instruction. Where possible, the written request should be set out in an e-mail to the court, preferably sent directly to the judge dealing with the proceedings (or, in the Family Proceedings Court, to the legal adviser who will forward it to the appropriate judge or justices), and be copied by e-mail to the other instructing parties. The court will settle the letter of instruction, usually without a hearing to avoid delay; and will send (where practicable, by e-mail) the settled letter to the lead solicitor for transmission forthwith to the expert, and copy it to the other instructing parties for information.

Keeping the expert up to date with new documents

5.3 As often as may be necessary, the expert should be provided promptly with a copy of any new document filed at court, together with an updated document list or bundle index.

6. The Court's control of expert evidence: consequential issues

Written Questions

6.1 Any party wishing to put written questions to an expert for the purpose of clarifying the expert's report must put the questions to the expert not later than 10 business days after receipt of the report.

The court will specify the timetable according to which the expert is to answer the written questions.

Experts' Discussion or Meeting: Purpose

6.2   By the specified date, the court may - if it has not already given such a direction - direct that the experts are to meet or communicate:

1)   to identify and narrow the issues in the case;

2)   where possible, to reach agreement on the expert issues;

3)   to identify the reasons for disagreement on any expert question and what, if any, action needs to be taken to resolve any outstanding disagreement or question;

4)   to explain or add to the evidence in order to assist the court to determine the issues;

5)   to limit, wherever possible, the need for the experts to attend court to give oral evidence.

Experts' Discussion or Meeting: Arrangements

6.3   In accordance with the directions given by the court, the solicitor or other professional who is given the responsibility by the court ('the nominated professional') shall - within 15 business days after the experts' reports have been filed and copied to the other parties – make arrangements for the experts to meet or communicate. Where applicable, the following matters should be considered:

1)   where permission has been given for the instruction of experts from different disciplines, a global discussion may be held relating to those questions that concern all or most of them;

2)   separate discussions may have to be held among experts from the same or related disciplines, but care should be taken to ensure that the discussions complement each other so that related questions are discussed by all relevant experts;

3)   5 business days prior to a discussion or meeting, the nominated professional should formulate an agenda including a list of questions for consideration. The agenda should contain only those questions which are intended to clarify areas of agreement or disagreement. Questions which repeat questions asked in the letter of instruction or which seek to rehearse cross-examination in advance of the hearing should be rejected as likely to defeat the purpose of the meeting.

The agenda may usefully take the form of a list of questions to be circulated among the other parties in advance. The agenda should comprise all questions that each party wishes the experts to consider. The agenda and list of questions should be sent to each of the experts not later than 2 clear business days before the discussion;

4)   the nominated professional may exercise his or her discretion to accept further questions after the agenda with list of questions has been circulated to the parties. Only in exceptional

circumstances should questions be added to the agenda within the 2-day period before the meeting. Under no circumstances should any question received on the day of or during the meeting be accepted. Strictness in this regard is vital, for adequate notice of the questions enables the parties to identify and isolate the issues in the case before the meeting so that the experts' discussion at the meeting can concentrate on those issues;

5) the discussion should be chaired by the nominated professional. A minute must be taken of the questions answered by the experts, and a Statement of Agreement and Disagreement must be prepared which should be agreed and signed by each of the experts who participated in the discussion. The statement should be served and filed not later than 5 business days after the discussion has taken place;

6) in each case, whether some or all of the experts participate by telephone conference or video link to ensure that minimum disruption is caused to professional schedules and that costs are minimised.

Meetings or conferences attended by a jointly instructed expert

6.4 Jointly instructed experts should not attend any meeting or conference which is not a joint one, unless all the parties have agreed in writing or the court has directed that such a meeting may be held, and it is agreed or directed who is to pay the expert's fees for the meeting or conference. Any meeting or conference attended by a jointly instructed expert should be proportionate to the case.

Court-directed meetings involving experts in public law Children Act cases

6.5 In public law Children Act proceedings, where the court gives a direction that a meeting shall take place between the local authority and any relevant named experts for the purpose of providing assistance to the local authority in the formulation of plans and proposals for the child, the meeting shall be arranged, chaired and minuted in accordance with the directions given by the court.

7. Positions of the Parties

7. Where a party refuses to be bound by an agreement that has been reached at an experts' discussion or meeting, that party must inform the court and the other parties in writing, within 10 business days after the discussion or meeting or, where an IRH is to be held, not less than 5 business days before the IRH, of his reasons for refusing to accept the agreement.

8. Arrangements for Experts to give evidence

Preparation

8.1   Where the court has directed the attendance of an expert witness, the party who is responsible for the instruction of the expert shall, by the specified date or, where an IRH is to be held, by the IRH, ensure that:

1)   a date and time (if possible, convenient to the expert) are fixed for the court to hear the expert's evidence, substantially in advance of the hearing at which the expert is to give oral evidence and no later than a specified date prior to that hearing or, where an IRH is to be held, than the IRH;

2)   if the expert's oral evidence is not required, the expert is notified as soon as possible;

3)   the witness template accurately indicates how long the expert is likely to be giving evidence, in order to avoid the inconvenience of the expert being delayed at court;

4)   consideration is given in each case to whether some or all of the experts participate by telephone conference or video link, or submit their evidence in writing, to ensure that minimum disruption is caused to professional schedules and that costs are minimised.

Experts attending Court

8.2   Where expert witnesses are to be called, all parties shall, by the specified date or, where an IRH is to be held, by the IRH, ensure that:

1)   the parties' advocates have identified (whether at an advocates' meeting or by other means) the issues which the experts are to address;

2)   wherever possible, a logical sequence to the evidence is arranged, with experts of the same discipline giving evidence on the same day;

3)   the court is informed of any circumstance where all experts agree but a party nevertheless does not accept the agreed opinion, so that directions can be given for the proper consideration of the experts' evidence and of the party's reasons for not accepting the agreed opinion;

4)   in the exceptional case the court is informed of the need for a witness summons.

9. Action after the Final Hearing

9.1   Within 10 business days after the Final Hearing, the solicitor instructing the expert shall inform the expert in writing of the outcome of the case, and of the use made by the court of the expert's opinion.

9.2   Where the court directs preparation of a transcript, it may also direct that the solicitor instructing the expert shall send a copy to the expert within 10 business days after receiving the transcript.

9.3   After a Final Hearing in the Family Proceedings Court, the (lead) solicitor instructing the expert shall send the expert a copy of the court's written reasons for its decision within 10 business days after receiving the written reasons.

Annex

Questions in letters of instruction to child mental health professional or paediatrician in Children Act 1989 proceedings

A. The Child(ren)

1   Please describe the child(ren)'s current health, development and functioning (according to your area of expertise), and identify the nature of any significant changes which have occurred

- Behavioural
- Emotional
- Attachment organisation
- Social/peer/sibling relationships
- Cognitive/educational
- Physical
  - Growth, eating, sleep
  - Non-organic physical problems (including wetting and soiling)
  - Injuries
  - Paediatric conditions

2   Please comment on the likely explanation for/aetiology of the child(ren)'s problems/difficulties/injuries

- History/experiences (including intrauterine influences, and abuse and neglect)
- Genetic/innate/developmental difficulties
- Paediatric/psychiatric disorders

3   Please provide a prognosis and risk if difficulties not addressed above.

4   Please describe the child(ren)'s needs in the light of the above

- Nature of care-giving
- Education
- Treatment

in the short and long term (subject, where appropriate, to further assessment later).

B. The parents/primary care-givers

5   Please describe the factors and mechanisms which would explain the parents' (or primary care-givers') harmful or neglectful interactions with the child(ren) (if relevant)

6   What interventions have been tried and what has been the result?

7   Please assess the ability of the parents or primary care-givers to fulfil the child(ren)'s identified needs now.

8   What other assessments of the parents or primary care-givers are indicated?

- Adult mental health assessment
- Forensic risk assessment
- Physical assessment
- Cognitive assessment

9   What, if anything, is needed to assist the parents or primary care-givers now, within the child(ren)'s time scales and what is the prognosis for change?

- Parenting work
- Support
- Treatment/therapy

C. Alternatives

10   Please consider the alternative possibilities for the fulfilment of the child(ren)'s needs.

- What sort of placement?
- Contact arrangements

Please consider the advantages, disadvantages and implications of each for the child(ren).

Questions in letters of instruction to adult psychiatrists and applied psychologists in Children Act 1989 proceedings

1   Does the parent/adult have – whether in his/her history or presentation – a mental illness/disorder (including substance abuse) or other psychological/emotional difficulty and, if so, what is the diagnosis?

2   How do any/all of the above (and their current treatment if applicable) affect his/her functioning, including interpersonal relationships?

3   If the answer to Q1 is yes, are there any features of either the mental illness or psychological/emotional difficulty or personality disorder which could be associated with risk to others, based on the available evidence base (whether published studies or evidence from clinical experience)?

4   What are the experiences/antecedents/aetiology which would explain his/her difficulties, if any, (*taking into account any available evidence base or other clinical experience*)?

5   What treatment is indicated, what is its nature and the likely duration?

6   What is his/her capacity to engage in/partake of the treatment/ therapy?

7   Are you able to indicate the prognosis for, time scales for achieving, and likely durability of, change?

8   What other factors might indicate positive change?

(It is assumed that this opinion will be based on collateral information as well as interviewing the adult).

4

Court Rules – General

Statements of Truth

Source: www.justice.gov.uk

Civil
Reports written for cases covered by the Civil Procedure Rules

Date introduced: 1 October 2009 (CPR Update 50)
Relevant rules: CPR 35 PD 3.2.9, CPR 35 PD 3.3

All that the CPR require is a statement embodying the declarations in CPR PD 3.2.9 and the mandatory wording of the Statement of Truth in CPR PD 3.3. The following two paragraphs achieve this.

> *I understand that my overriding duty is to the court and I have complied with that duty. I am aware of the requirements of CPR Part 35, its practice direction and the Protocol for Instruction of Experts to give Evidence in Civil Claims.*
>
> *I confirm that I have made clear which facts and matters referred to in this report are within my own knowledge and which are not. Those that are within my own knowledge I confirm to be true. The opinions I have expressed represent my true and complete professional opinions on the matters to which they refer.*

Family
Reports written for cases covered by the Practice Direction for Experts in Family Proceedings Relating to Children

Date introduced: 1 April 2008
Relevant rules: PD 3.11–13

The Family Practice Direction requires four declarations (PD 3.11 and PD 3.12) and the mandatory wording of a Statement of Truth. The following two paragraphs achieve this.

> *I understand that my overriding duty is to the court and I have complied with, and will continue to comply with, that duty. I have no conflict of interest of any kind.*
>
> *I confirm that insofar as the facts stated in my report are within my own knowledge I have made clear which they are and I believe them to be true, and that the opinions I have expressed represent my true and complete professional opinion.*

Obviously, if you do have a conflict of interest you need to consider the further guidance in PD 3.12 and modify the second sentence of this declaration accordingly.

Crime
Reports written for cases covered by the Criminal Procedure Rules

Date introduced: 5 October 2009 (CrimPR Update 8)
Relevant rules: CrimPR 33.3, CrimPR 27.2

CrimPr 33.3(i) and (j) require that expert reports contain:

- a statement that the expert understands his duty to the court, and has complied and will continue to comply with that duty; and
- the same declaration of truth as a witness statement.

However, in the criminal arena, unlike the civil, statute itself prescribes the equivalent of a statement of truth. So the Criminal Procedure Rules do not offer a mandatory wording.

What the expert needs to do is to declare that:

- any fact contained in the report is true, whether a fact within the expert's own knowledge or the fact that something relied upon by the expert as fact came from the source the expert identifies, and
- the expert's opinions are all true, to the best of the expert's knowledge and belief.

We believe that the following should achieve that end.

I understand that my overriding duty is to the court and I have complied with, and will continue to comply with, that duty.

This report is true to the best of my knowledge and belief, and I know that if it is introduced in evidence then it would be an offence wilfully to have stated in it anything that I knew to be false or did not believe to be true.

5

Miscellaneous

GMC guidelines: Acting as an expert witness

Source: www.gmc-uk.org

1   Our core guidance *Good Medical Practice* sets out the principles which underpin good care. When doctors act as expert witnesses, they take on a different role from that of a doctor providing treatment or advice to patients. The principles set out in *Good Medical Practice* also apply to doctors working as expert witnesses.

2   In paragraphs 63-67 of *Good Medical Practice* we say

- You must be honest and trustworthy when writing reports and when completing or signing forms, reports and other documents.

- You must always be honest about your experience, qualifications and position, particularly when applying for posts.

- You must do your best to make sure that any documents you write or sign are not false or misleading. This means that you must take reasonable steps to verify the information in the documents, and that you must not deliberately leave out relevant information.

- If you have agreed to prepare a report, complete or sign a document or provide evidence, you must do so without unreasonable delay.

- If you are asked to give evidence or act as a witness in litigation or formal inquiries, you must be honest in all your spoken and written statements. You must make clear the limits of your knowledge or competence.

3   This guidance explains how the principles set out in *Good Medical Practice* apply to the work of the medical expert witness. It also lists other sources of information and advice. If you have concerns arising from an appointment as a medical expert witness, you should consider seeking advice from the GMC, your medical defence body or professional association.

4   Serious or persistent failure to follow this guidance will put your registration at risk.

The role of the expert witness

5   The role of an expert witness is to assist the court on specialist or technical matters within their expertise[1]. The expert's duty to the court overrides any obligation to the person who is instructing or paying them[2]. This means that you have a duty to act independently and not be influenced by the party who retains you.

---

1 Doctors are not necessarily expert witnesses. They may also be witnesses of fact (testifying about events that they themselves have observed) or professional witnesses (giving evidence regarding a particular patient that they have treated).
2 Civil Procedure Rules Part 35.3, Criminal Justice Procedure Rules Part 33.2, Rule 156 of the draft Family Procedure Rules.

Giving expert advice and evidence

6   You must ensure that you understand exactly what questions you are being asked to answer. If your instructions are unclear, inadequate or conflicting, you should seek clarification from those instructing you. If you cannot obtain sufficiently clear instructions, you should not provide expert advice or opinion.

7   When giving evidence or writing reports, you must restrict your statements to areas in which you have relevant knowledge or direct experience. You should be aware of the standards and nature of practice at the time of the incident under proceedings.

8   You must only deal with matters, and express opinions, that fall within the limits of your professional competence[3]. If a particular question or issue falls outside your area of expertise, you should make this clear. In the event that you are ordered by the court to answer a question, regardless of your expertise, you should answer to the best of your ability but make clear that you consider the matter to be outside your competence.

9   You must give a balanced opinion, and be able to state the facts or assumptions on which it is based. If there is a range of opinion on the question upon which you have been asked to comment, you should summarise the range of opinion and explain how you arrived at your own view. If you do not have enough information on which to reach a conclusion on a particular point, or your opinion is otherwise qualified, you must make this clear.[4]

10   You must make sure that any report that you write, or evidence that you give, is accurate and is not misleading. This means that you must take reasonable steps to verify any information you provide, and you must not deliberately leave out relevant information.

11   Where you are asked to give advice or opinion about an individual without the opportunity to consult with or examine them, you should explain any limitations that this may place on your advice or opinion, and be able to justify the decision to proceed on such a basis.

12   Your advice and evidence will be relied upon for decision-making purposes by people who do not come from a medical background. Wherever it is possible to do so without being misleading, you should use language and terminology that will be readily understood by those for whom you are providing expert advice or opinion. You should explain any abbreviations and medical or other technical terminology that you use.

13   If, at any stage, you change your view on any material matter, you have a duty to ensure that those instructing you, the opposing party

---

3 The same principle applies where doctors act in other roles, for example as an advisor in a case.
4 See judgment of Cresswell J in The 'Ikarian Reefer' [1993] *FSR* 563.

and the judge are made aware of this without delay. Usually you need only inform your instructing solicitor who will communicate with the other parties. If the solicitor fails to disclose your change of view, you should inform the court. If you are unsure what to do, you should seek legal advice.

14   You must be honest, trustworthy, objective and impartial. You must not allow your views about any individual's age, colour, culture, disability, ethnic or national origin, gender, lifestyle, marital or parental status, race, religion or beliefs, sex, sexual orientation or social or economic status to prejudice the evidence or advice that you give.

Keeping up to date

15   You must keep up to date in your specialist area of practice. You must also ensure that you understand, and adhere to, the laws and codes of practice that affect your work as an expert witness. In particular, you should make sure that you understand

- how to construct a court-compliant report
- how to give oral evidence
- the specific framework of law and procedure within which you are working

Information security and disclosure

16   You must take all reasonable steps to access all relevant evidence materials and maintain their integrity and security whilst in your possession.

17   If you have reason to believe that appropriate consent for disclosure of information has not been obtained (from the patient or client, or from any third party to whom their medical records refer) you should return the information to the person instructing you and seek clarification.

18   You should not disclose confidential information other than to the parties to proceedings, unless

- the subject consents (and there are no other restrictions or prohibitions on disclosure)
- you are obliged to do so by law
- you are ordered to do so by a court or tribunal
- your overriding duty to the court and the administration of justice demands that you disclose information

Conflicts of interest

19   If there is any matter that gives rise to a potential conflict of interest, such as any prior involvement with one of the parties, or a personal interest, you must follow the guidance on disclosure in paragraph 13. You may continue to act as an expert witness only if the court decides that the conflict is not material to the case.

Key terms and concepts

Access to Justice: The report written by Lord Woolf in July 1996 reviewing the civil justice framework in England and Wales. It was from this work that the Civil Procedure Rules arose.

Bolam Test: In professional negligence cases, the Bolam Test states that a professional has not been negligent if his actions are accepted as proper by a responsible body of this profession.

Bolitho Test: Following on from the Bolam Test, the Bolitho Test states that the actions being accepted in the Bolam Test must have a logical basis. In effect, the Bolitho Test allows the Court to rule that even if a responsible body of fellow professionals would see the actions in question as proper, they still amount to negligence.

Civil Procedure Rules: The rules of court for civil cases that flowed from the Woolf report, *Access to Justice*. They contain specific rules and guidance for expert witnesses in Part 35.

Cresswell Principles: The principles of expert evidence that Mr Justice Cresswell laid down in his judgment in the shipping case known as *The Ikarian Reefer* ([1993] 2 *Lloyd's Rep.* 68) have become widely accepted as a classic statement of the duties and responsibilities of an expert witness. They were endorsed by the Court of Appeal, commended by Lord Woolf in his report on the civil justice system in England and Wales, and have been cited with approval in several subsequent cases.

Criminal Procedure Rules: The rules of court for criminal cases that flowed from Lord Justice Auld's *Review of the Criminal Courts of England and Wales*. These contain specific rules and guidance for expert witnesses in Part 33.

Family Procedure Rules: The rules of court that govern (for now, just in adoption cases) the court procedures in family court cases.

Pre-action Protocol: A Protocol created under the Civil Procedure Rules that seeks to govern the actions of the parties in the period before a claim becomes an action before the courts. The main protocols of interest to expert witnesses are the *Pre-Action Protocol for Construction and Engineering Disputes*, the *Pre-Action Protocol for Personal Injury Claims* and the *Pre-Action Protocol for the Resolution of Clinical Disputes*.

Single Joint Expert: An expert instructed by all parties in a civil case in accordance with the provisions contained in CPR 35.7.

Toulmin Principles: Seven years after Mr Justice Cresswell formulated the principles of expert evidence, a judge in the Technology and Construction Court, Judge John Toulmin, had occasion to update them in the light of the Woolf reforms in the case *Anglo Group plc -v- Winther Brown & Co. Ltd and BML (Office Computers) Ltd.*

Woolf Reforms: The reforms of the civil justice system in England and Wales that followed on from the *Access to Justice* report written by Lord Woolf in 1996.

Common acronyms

ADR............alternative dispute resolution

CAFCASS ..Children and Family Court Advisory Support Service

CDPA..........Copyright, Designs and Patents Act

CFA ....conditional fee arrangements

CJC ....Civil Justice Council

CPR............Civil Procedure Rules

CPS ....Crown Prosecution Service

CRFP..........Council for the Registration of Forensic Practitioners

CrimPR ......Criminal Procedure Rules

ENE ....Early Neutral Evaluation

HMRC.........Her Majesty's Revenue and Customs

LSC ....Legal Services Commission

MoJ ....Ministry of Justice; formerly the Department for Constitutional Affairs, and before that the Lord Chancellor's Department

MRO ....medical reporting organisation

SJE.............single joint expert

VAT.............value added tax

UK Register of Expert Witnesses Fee Survey data

Since 1997, the *UK Register of Expert Witnesses* has carried out a general expert witness survey once every 2 years. These snapshots of the expert witness landscape provide the most in-depth intelligence on expert witnesses, the work they do and their charging rates within the UK.

Presented on the following pages are the fee data for the surveys conducted between 1997 and 2009, broken down by broad discipline. For a more detailed discussion of the surveys and their data, see *http://www.jspubs.com/ Surveys/feesurveys.cfm*.

Court appearances

Year	Medicine		Nursing, etc.		Engineering		Accountancy and Banking	
	n	Day rate	n	Day rate	n	Day rate	n	Day rate
1997	166	£870	42	£535	116	£560	34	£821
1999	249	£890	36	£512	94	£567	49	£987
2001	200	£927	39	£718	63	£663	24	£895
2003	230	£1,041	42	£749	79	£694	26	£1,105
2005	264	£984	28	£658	84	£631	34	£1,059
2007	181	£1,163	21	£827	52	£876	21	£1,105
2009	226	£1,252	49	£1,067	65	£836	28	£1,246

Year	Science and Agriculture		Surveying and Valuing		Architecture and Building		Others	
	n	Day rate	n	Day rate	n	Day rate	n	Day rate
1997	68	£543	35	£629	28	£612	58	£525
1999	79	£577	49	£642	19	£612	96	£521
2001	53	£648	36	£787	17	£712	50	£622
2003	37	£690	24	£984	27	£744	78	£802
2005	35	£614	28	£888	33	£610	68	£657
2007	19	£720	18	£938	17	£835	85	£811
2009	32	£811	19	£1,140	31	£860	61	£760

Report writing

Year	Medicine		Nursing, etc.		Engineering		Accountancy and Banking	
	n	per hour	n	per hour	n	per hour	n	per hour
1997	166	£124	42	£76	116	£73	34	£116
1999	249	£136	36	£68	94	£71	49	£135
2001	200	£149	39	£100	63	£85	24	£133
2003	230	£153	42	£91	79	£86	26	£151
2005	264	£171	28	£104	84	£96	34	£161
2007	181	£170	21	£116	52	£112	21	£175
2009	226	£192	49	£153	65	£118	28	£192

Year	Science and Agriculture		Surveying and Valuing		Architecture and Building		Others	
	n	per hour	n	per hour	n	per hour	n	per hour
1997	68	£89	35	£77	28	£75	58	£76
1999	79	£79	49	£83	19	£77	96	£71
2001	53	£78	36	£104	17	£84	50	£127
2003	37	£82	24	£121	27	£92	78	£109
2005	35	£89	28	£122	33	£97	68	£97
2007	19	£107	18	£143	17	£103	85	£121
2009	32	£114	19	£162	31	£118	61	£120

UK Register of Expert Witnesses Factsheets

As part of its service to member expert witnesses, J S Publications (publisher of the *UK Register of Expert Witnesses*) writes, maintains and publishes a wide range of factsheets on those parts of the litigation system that affect expert witnesses. Factsheet summaries are reproduced below. Full factsheets can be accessed by members through the publisher's website at www.jspubs.com.

Factsheet 01 Civil Litigation and the Expert Witness
Explains the structure of the English civil litigation system together with the various stages a case will go through from initial claim to possible appeal. Gives a detailed analysis of the expert's involvement at each juncture.

Factsheet 02 Expert Evidence
Defines the meaning of the terms 'expert witness' and 'expert evidence' and explains when they may - and may not - be required in civil litigation. Clarifies the duties of an expert witness, together with a number of ethical considerations, and the difference between acting as an adviser and a witness.

Factsheet 03 The Woolf Report: recommendations concerning expert evidence
Gives a synopsis of Lord Woolf's recommendations concerning expert evidence – covering the use of single experts, the responsibilities of experts, expert reports and meetings of experts, amongst others.

Factsheet 04 The 'Cresswell' Principles of Expert Evidence
A summary of the key duties and responsibilities of the expert witness as provided by Mr Justice Cresswell in his judgement in the case known as *The Ikarian Reefer* (1993).

Factsheet 05 Expert Witness Survey 1995
An analysis of the results from the expert witness survey undertaken by J S Publications, covering topics such as frequency of enquiries and instruction, business practices, payment, training and membership of expert witness organisations.

Factsheet 06 Expert Resource List
Lists details of the more recent publications concerning expert evidence and expert witness skills.

Factsheet 07 Fees and Disbursements
Defines the difference between fees and disbursements and explains the nature of the contract between expert witness and solicitor plus the solicitor's duties in respect of payment of fees. Also gives practical advice on how best to secure payment.

Factsheet 08 Getting Paid in Legal Aid Cases

Delays in payment are a constant source of complaint to expert witnesses – especially so if legal aid is involved. This factsheet considers the reasons for this and what the expert can do to speed up payment.

Factsheet 09 Payment of Expert Witnesses in Criminal Cases

Highlights the differences in the way in which expert witnesses are paid for giving evidence in court in criminal as opposed to civil cases. Also defines what is allowed in terms of travelling and hotel expenses and claims for cancellation and postponement.

Factsheet 10 Regulations Governing the Payment of Expert Witnesses in Criminal Cases

Extracts from the Costs in Criminal Cases (General) Regulations 1986, the Legal Aid in Criminal and Care Proceedings (General) Regulations 1989 and the Legal Aid in Criminal and Care Proceedings (Costs) Regulations 1989.

Factsheet 11 Expert Witness Allowances in Criminal Cases

Contains an extract from Appendix 2 of the Guide to Allowances under Part V of the Costs in Criminal Cases (General) Regulations 1986, as revised by the Lord Chancellor's Department's Legal Aid Division in April 2003. Also includes the schedule of rates payable to experts for preparation of case and attendance at court.

Factsheet 12 The Legal Aid System and its Reform

Provides an overview of the system prior to April 2000 and how this has been replaced by the new scheme managed by the Legal Services Commission.

Factsheet 13 Expert Witness Organisations

Provides information on the background of the three organisations representing expert witnesses and an outline of the aims of each one. Also details the membership criteria plus services provided along with current subscription rates.

Factsheet 14 Professional Indemnity Insurance for Expert Witnesses

Addresses the issue of why professional indemnity insurance is needed and potential liability of the expert witness.

Factsheet 15 Terms of Engagement for Experts

Use of Terms of Engagement can often avoid misunderstandings as to what expert witnesses and instructing solicitors can expect from each other. This factsheet considers various matters that an expert would be well advised to include in such Terms, together with a framework that can be adapted according to individual circumstances.

Factsheet 16 Expert Witness Training

A number of organisations provide training courses for expert witnesses, and this factsheet offers the views of experts themselves on the benefits to be derived from such training. It also gives advice on how to select the most appropriate and cost-effective course for your needs, together with a list of the main players in this market.

Factsheet 17 The Middleton Report
In June 1997 the Lord Chancellor announced that he had invited Sir Peter Middleton, a former Permanent Secretary at the Treasury, to conduct a review both of Lord Woolf's recommendations for the reform of the civil justice system and of the previous government's proposals for the overhaul of the legal aid system. Sir Peter completed his report in September 1997, and in a speech at the Law Society's Annual Conference in Cardiff on 18 October 1997, Lord Irvine welcomed the recommendations it made. The full text of the report was published 2 days later. We reproduce here the 'executive summary' that prefaces the Middleton Report, together with the text of the section in Chapter 2 which relates to expert witnesses.

Factsheet 18 Civil Justice and Legal Aid Reforms
This was the keynote address by Lord Irvine of Lairg, The Lord Chancellor, to the Solicitors' Annual Conference on 19 October 1997. It covers the reasons behind the move to reform civil justice and the recommendations made by both Lord Woolf and Sir Peter Middleton. It is reproduced in its entirety.

Factsheet 19 The Society of Expert Witnesses Autumn Conference
A report on a Society of Expert Witnesses Autumn Conference.

Factsheet 20 The Bond Solon Conference
A report on an annual expert witness conference organised by Bond Solon Training Ltd.

Factsheet 21 The Small Claims Track
An increase to the upper level of claims being heard in the small claims track affects expert witnesses both as providers of expert evidence in small claims hearings and as potential claimants in disputes with solicitors over unpaid fees. This factsheet provides the background to this change and explains how a claim is allocated to this track. It also gives information on the form the hearing is likely to take and explains the importance of the 'no costs' rule.

Factsheet 22 Conditional Fees and their likely impact
The scope of Conditional Fee Agreements has been widened to plug the gap left by the withdrawal of legal aid. This factsheet explains what they are, how they work and their implication for both solicitors and expert witnesses.

Factsheet 23 Meetings of Experts
Explains how such meetings have come about and the implications of the Civil Procedure Rules in respect of these. It also lists the guidelines as contained in the Code of Guidance for Experts and gives in-depth examination of the various practicalities concerning the management of such

meetings (i.e. who should participate, when they should be held, how best to prepare for and manage them, and whether or not they are binding).

Factsheet 24 Fees Survey 1997
Provides an analysis of the responses received to the 1997 fees survey. Findings are broken down by professional category, and details supplied on workload, mean hourly rate for reports and court appearance. The question of cancellation fees is also covered.

Factsheet 25 Training Opportunities
Lists full details of the main providers of training courses, together with information on the types of course on offer. Many providers offer discounts to experts listed in the *Register*.

Factsheet 26 The Society of Expert Witnesses Spring Conference
Report a Society of Expert Witnesses Spring Conference.

Factsheet 27 Expert Reports: Requirements and Characteristics
This factsheet explains the role that an expert's report can play in court, together with its purpose and scope. It also elaborates on various procedural issues and provides useful advice concerning content, structure, style and layout. Relevant extracts from the Civil Procedure Rules and Practice Direction are included, together with the full text of the expert's declaration and statement of truth for inclusion in reports.

Factsheet 28 Expert Witness Immunity from Suit
This factsheet examines the differences between preparing a report for litigation and the various other services that an expert could be asked to perform in terms of immunity from suit. Case law relating to such circumstances is also included.

Factsheet 29 Taking Instructions
This is a helpful guide to the 'do's and don'ts' of accepting instructions from a solicitor. It details the need for clear, formal instructions from the solicitor, together with acceptance of these by the expert, and the necessity for all relevant material to be provided early on. It lists the elements a solicitor will be looking for in a report and the practicalities that should then be dealt with.

Factsheet 30 Privilege
This factsheet deals at length with the issues of privilege and disclosure in civil litigation, covering the issues of reports, instructions and discussions. It also includes a number of cautionary tales.

Factsheet 31 Taxation and the Expert Witness
Taxation of costs is a complicated issue and this factsheet explains some of the fundamental concepts as they relate to expert witnesses.

Factsheet 32 Modernising Justice: a summary of the Government's proposals
This factsheet reproduces the Lord Chancellor's Department's summary

of government proposals for modernising justice in England and Wales. Amongst other matters, it covers the government's objectives, the introduction of the Community Legal Service, changes to the civil courts and criminal justice.

Factsheet 33 The Funding Code for Civil Litigation

Legal aid *per se* has now been scrapped in favour of a new system of determining which civil and family cases are to be helped from public funds. This factsheet looks at the criteria to be used in doing this and how legal representation will be granted, with particular emphasis on personal injury cases.

Factsheet 34 The Woolf Reforms: an Overview for Expert Witnesses

Gives the background that preceded Lord Woolf's enquiry, together with the problems and solutions he highlighted in his various reports. Provides a synopsis of the various procedures that have been introduced as a result of the Woolf reforms, such as case management and the various 'claims tracks', whilst also drawing attention to some of the problems that have come to light so far.

Factsheet 35 Experts and Assessors: the New Rules and Practice Direction

Contains the text of Part 35, which is of most direct concern to expert witnesses, together with the supplementary Practice Direction and a cautionary tale underlining just how vital it is to adhere to both of these.

Factsheet 36 The Access to Justice Act 1999

Contains the official summary of the Access to Justice Act. Amongst other topics, this factsheet covers the replacement of Legal Aid by Community Legal Service and the introduction of conditional fees.

Factsheet 37 Guidance for Experts

Your Witness 27 considered the unhappy situation that arose with the circulation of two 'rival' codes of guidance for experts. A main difficulty with both codes, though, is that they attempt too much. J S Publications has extracted from both codes the guidance they offer experts, and combined it in this single document, which eschewed repeating CPR provisions that are to be found in Part 35 and its Practice Direction. Finally, some text has been added to cover issues raised by experts listed in the *UK Register of Expert Witnesses*, in the hope that this will prompt others to identify further topics relating to CPR on which they feel guidance is needed.

Factsheet 38 Pre-action Protocols

The pre-action protocol was one of the major innovations of the Woolf Reforms, and this factsheet explains the rationale behind the introduction of this new document, as well as how it is working in practice. By way of example, the personal injury protocol is included for consideration, together with comments.

Factsheet 39 Expert Witness Survey 1999

A summary of the findings of J S Publications's third survey into the views, experiences and working practices of expert witnesses. Topics covered include, amongst others, workload, experience (including work as a single joint expert), membership of organisations, reports, court appearances and fees.

Factsheet 40 The Expert Witness Institute Conference

The 2001 Expert Witness Institute (EWI) conference was held on Wednesday 26 September 2001 in the auspicious surroundings of The Royal College of Physicians, Regent's Park, London. It was attended by some 57 delegates, and its topic for this year was 'The Expert Witness - in Support of Justice'. Once again, the majority of its cast of speakers hailed from the judiciary and the legal professions (barristers and solicitors).

Factsheet 41 Marketing your Services as an Expert Witness

This factsheet contains a wealth of practical help that is relevant to both the established practitioner wishing to expand upon existing activity and the newcomer wondering how best to get started. Gives detailed coverage of the most widely used marketing tools and also suggests other avenues to explore that could benefit even the most experienced of expert witnesses.

Factsheet 42 ADR for Experts

Alternative Dispute Resolution - or ADR - is increasingly being considered as an alternative to litigation and can take many different forms. This factsheet explains each type, how ADR works in practice and the areas to which it is best suited.

Factsheet 43 The Witness Summons

The background and use of the witness summons is covered in detail, together with information on who may be summoned, the reasons an expert might be summoned and the practicalities of their use and service. Payment issues and setting aside are also discussed.

Factsheet 44 The Single Joint Expert

The background and rules governing the appointment and role of the Single Joint Expert are covered in detail, together with information on when it may, and when it may not, be reasonable to appoint an SJE. Also discussed are the practical issues of being selected, instructed and paid as an SJE, and a summary of the leading cases relating to SJE appointments is provided.

Factsheet 45 Expert Evidence in Employment Cases

Employment tribunals constitute a specialist jurisdiction within the UK's system of civil justice. Being specialist, it is easy to underestimate their importance. Yet they deal with cases brought under increasingly complex, and controversial, areas of legislation, and their workload is growing by leaps and bounds.

Factsheet 46 The Auld Report and Experts
Presents the material from the Auld Report on the criminal justice system relating to expert witnesses.

Factsheet 47 Expert Witness Survey 2001
A summary of the findings of J S Publications's fourth survey into the views, experiences and working practices of expert witnesses. Topics covered include, amongst others, workload, experience (including work as a single joint expert), membership of organisations, reports, court appearances and fees.

Factsheet 48 Answering Written Questions
The Civil Procedure Rules 1998 require that evidence shall be given in a written report 'unless the court directs otherwise'. Clearly, though, there are dangers in a court receiving a written report that has not been scrutinised for inconsistencies or ambiguities – especially when, as is often the case nowadays, there will be no opportunity to cross-examine the expert at a later stage in the proceedings. Hence, the provisions of Rule 35.6, the subject of this Factsheet, that enable parties to seek clarification of an expert's report by means of written questions, the answers to which will then form part of the report.

Factsheet 49 Expert Witness Survey 2003
A summary of the findings of J S Publications's fifth survey into the views, experiences and working practices of expert witnesses. Topics covered include, amongst others, workload, experience (including work as a single joint expert), reports, court appearances and fees.

Factsheet 50 VAT for experts
On 1 May 2007, HM Revenue & Customs (HMRC; formerly HM Customs and Excise) announced that medical experts were required to charge VAT on the supply of services that do not relate directly to medical care or intervention. Services that attract VAT (subject to the VAT registration limits) include the provision of reports in medico-legal work. For those experts not already wrestling with the complexities of VAT, we offer this simple guide.

Factsheet 51 A Practical Guide to Securing Payment from Lawyers
Late payment of fees remains one of the most frequently encountered subjects in correspondence received and is a subject guaranteed to raise the temperature at any expert witness conference. Here, we examine ways in which the risk of late payment can be minimised and look at the practical steps that can be taken for fee recovery in the worst cases.

Factsheet 52 Copyright for Experts
A guide for experts in relation to the identification and use of copyright materials belonging to another, and some pointers for those experts who might wish to identify and preserve copyright in materials of which they are the author or creator.

Factsheet 53 Protocol for the Instruction of Experts to give Evidence in Civil Claims

The Civil Justice Council eventually took the initiative – cutting through the confusion created by the regrettable inability of the Academy of Experts and Expert Witness Institute to work together – to establish a single, authoritative Experts Protocol. The Protocol is written in clear English and provides some important extensions to existing guidance.

Factsheet 54 Expert Witness Survey 2005

A summary of the findings of J S Publications's sixth survey into the views, experiences and working practices of expert witnesses. Topics covered include, amongst others, workload, experience (including work as a single joint expert), reports, court appearances and fees.

Factsheet 55 Criminal Procedure Rules

In October 2005 the Department for Constitutional Affairs (now the Ministry of Justice, MoJ) commenced its consultation process on proposed procedural rules governing expert evidence in criminal proceedings. It was intended that these rules should form part of the newly introduced Criminal Procedure Rules (CrimPR). The main body of rules came into force on 4 April 2005. However, CrimPR rule 33, which was to contain rules specifically regulating expert evidence, was left blank pending consultation.

As participants in the consultation process, we at the *UK Register of Expert Witnesses* gave keen scrutiny to the draft. The drafting of Part 33 afforded the Committee a unique opportunity to recognise and address past problems in relation to expert evidence. It was also to be welcomed that some attempt was being made to codify all the regulations governing experts in the criminal courts and to bring these under the umbrella of the Rules in the same way as CPR Part 35. So, have they got it right?

Factsheet 56 Giving Evidence in Court

Experts who provide reports will not always have to appear in court. In a great many cases their reports will have been agreed and, consequently, they will not be called upon to attend a hearing. This is particularly so in civil cases, like personal injury claims, where it is becoming more and more uncommon for experts to be examined and cross-examined on their evidence. An expert who works in the criminal justice system is, however, more likely to be called to give evidence in court. Those unfamiliar with the workings of the court should, therefore, prepare by making themselves familiar with court etiquette and the rules governing the giving of evidence.

Factsheet 57 Expert Witness Survey 2007

In 1995, J S Publications undertook a survey of the views, experiences and working practices of experts listed in the *UK Register of Expert Witnesses*. Some 2 years later, the findings of that survey were updated with a more limited investigation into the fees experts were charging. Then, in 1999, 2001, 2003 and 2005, J S Publications conducted further surveys that combined the main features of the predecessors, while adding some new topics of enquiry.

The 2007 printed questionnaire was dispatched to all expert witnesses listed in the *UK Register of Expert Witnesses* along with the June 2007 issue of *Your Witness*. Listed experts could also complete the survey on-line. There was a good response, with almost 400 forms returned or submitted on-line at www.jspubs.com, accounting for some 16% of the readership. This Factsheet presents an analysis of their replies.

Factsheet 58 Retention of Documents
The documents that are received, prepared, assessed, considered and created by an expert in the course of proceedings are papers of importance. A document which at the time of the original hearing might have been considered trifling could suddenly take on new importance. It is not inconceivable, therefore, that an expert witness might be asked for a document months or years after the case has been concluded. The expert, then, is faced with a dilemma. Which documents in a case should he retain – and for how long?

Factsheet 59 Experts in Family Proceedings
The family justice system exists to help families resolve disputes. If disputes or problems should arise, the system tries to enable them to be resolved quickly and with the minimum of pain caused to those involved. If at all possible, the parties are encouraged to resolve their disputes out of court, e.g. through mediation, because they are more likely to adhere to an agreement if they themselves have had a role in formulating it. This factsheet is offered as an introduction to family proceedings in England and Wales.

Factsheet 60 Experts in Criminal Proceedings
This factsheet takes a general look at the criminal justice system. For details of Part 33: Expert Evidence, the rules that apply to all experts working within the criminal justice system, see Factsheet 55. To learn more about appearing in court, see Factsheet 56. Factsheet 61 deals in detail with disclosure of evidence in criminal proceedings. For all the rules and regulations relating to payment of your fees and disbursements in criminal cases, see Factsheets 9, 10 and 11.

Factsheet 61 Record, retain, reveal
The Attorney General, as part of his investigation into Shaken Baby Syndrome cases, ordered a review of the legislation that controls the disclosure of evidence in criminal cases. At the same time there was a consultation carried out by the Crown Prosecution Service under the chairmanship of the Director of Public Prosecutions which dealt with procedures for instructing expert witnesses. The result of the review was the CPS Service Disclosure Manual.

Forms of judicial address

Before attending court it is worth making some effort to find out who will be presiding over the case and their title. There are correct forms of address that should be adopted, and they are detailed below.

Who	Correct form of address
Magistrate	Sir or Madam or Your Worship
District judge	Sir or Madam
Circuit judge, recorder or assistant recorder	Your Honour
Registrar	Sir or Madam
High Court Master	Master (regardless of gender)
High Court Judge	Your Lordship/Your Ladyship or My Lord/ My Lady
Lord Justice of Appeal	Your Lordship/Your Ladyship or My Lord/ My Lady
Lord Chief Justice (most senior criminal judge in England and Wales)	Your Lordship/Your Ladyship or My Lord/ My Lady

The form of address is not court-dependent. So, for example, a High Court Judge should be referred to as Your Lordship/Your Ladyship or My Lord/My Lady regardless of the court setting. If in doubt, or to be doubly sure, ask your instructing lawyer or a court usher for confirmation prior to the hearing.

You should avoid excessive use of these terms. It is probably sufficient to use them once to preface or end responses. It would be inappropriate and, frankly, laborious to use them in every sentence.

Data protection principles

Source: www.opsi.gov.uk

Data Protection Act 1998

SCHEDULE 1

1   Personal data shall be processed fairly and lawfully and, in particular, shall not be processed unless –

      (a)   at least one of the conditions in Schedule 2 is met, and

      (b)   in the case of sensitive personal data, at least one of the conditions in Schedule 3 is also met.

2   Personal data shall be obtained only for one or more specified and lawful purposes, and shall not be further processed in any manner incompatible with that purpose or those purposes.

3   Personal data shall be adequate, relevant and not excessive in relation to the purpose or purposes for which they are processed.

4   Personal data shall be accurate and, where necessary, kept up to date.

5   Personal data processed for any purpose or purposes shall not be kept for longer than is necessary for that purpose or those purposes.

6   Personal data shall be processed in accordance with the rights of data subjects under this Act.

7   Appropriate technical and organisational measures shall be taken against unauthorised or unlawful processing of personal data and against accidental loss or destruction of, or damage to, personal data.

8   Personal data shall not be transferred to a country or territory outside the European Economic Area unless that country or territory ensures an adequate level of protection for the rights and freedoms of data subjects in relation to the processing of personal data.

SCHEDULE 2

      Conditions relevant for purposes of the first principle: processing of any personal data

1   The data subject has given his consent to the processing.

2   The processing is necessary –

      (a)   for the performance of a contract to which the data subject is a party, or

      (b)   for the taking of steps at the request of the data subject with a view to entering into a contract.

3   The processing is necessary for compliance with any legal obligation to which the data controller is subject, other than an obligation imposed by contract.

4   The processing is necessary in order to protect the vital interests of the data subject.

5   The processing is necessary –

 (a)   for the administration of justice,

 (b)   for the exercise of any functions conferred on any person by or under any enactment,

 (c)   for the exercise of any functions of the Crown, a Minister of the Crown or a government department, or

 (d)   for the exercise of any other functions of a public nature exercised in the public interest by any person.

6   1) The processing is necessary for the purposes of legitimate interests pursued by the data controller or by the third party or parties to whom the data are disclosed, except where the processing is unwarranted in any particular case by reason of prejudice to the rights and freedoms or legitimate interests of the data subject.

 2) The Secretary of State may by order specify particular circumstances in which this condition is, or is not, to be taken to be satisfied.

SCHEDULE 3

Conditions relevant for purposes of the first principle: processing of sensitive personal data

1   The data subject has given his explicit consent to the processing of the personal data.

2   1) The processing is necessary for the purposes of exercising or performing any right or obligation which is conferred or imposed by law on the data controller in connection with employment.

 2) The Secretary of State may by order –

 (a)   exclude the application of sub-paragraph (1) in such cases as may be specified, or

 (b)   provide that, in such cases as may be specified, the condition in sub-paragraph (1) is not to be regarded as satisfied unless such further conditions as may be specified in the order are also satisfied.

3   The processing is necessary –

 (a)   in order to protect the vital interests of the data subject or another person, in a case where—

     (i)   consent cannot be given by or on behalf of the data subject, or

     (ii)   the data controller cannot reasonably be expected to obtain the consent of the data subject, or

  (b)   in order to protect the vital interests of another person, in a case where consent by or on behalf of the data subject has been unreasonably withheld.

4   The processing –

  (a)   is carried out in the course of its legitimate activities by any body or association which –

     (i)   is not established or conducted for profit, and

     (ii)   exists for political, philosophical, religious or trade-union purposes,

  (b)   is carried out with appropriate safeguards for the rights and freedoms of data subjects,

  (c)   relates only to individuals who either are members of the body or association or have regular contact with it in connection with its purposes, and

  (d)   does not involve disclosure of the personal data to a third party without the consent of the data subject.

5   The information contained in the personal data has been made public as a result of steps deliberately taken by the data subject.

6   The processing –

  (a)   is necessary for the purpose of, or in connection with, any legal proceedings (including prospective legal proceedings),

  (b)   is necessary for the purpose of obtaining legal advice, or

  (c)   is otherwise necessary for the purposes of establishing, exercising or defending legal rights.

7   1) The processing is necessary –

  (a)   for the administration of justice,

  (b)   for the exercise of any functions conferred on any person by or under an enactment, or

  (c)   for the exercise of any functions of the Crown, a Minister of the Crown or a government department.

  2)   The Secretary of State may by order –

  (a)   exclude the application of sub-paragraph (1) in such cases as may be specified, or

  (b)   provide that, in such cases as may be specified, the condition in sub-paragraph (1) is not to be regarded as satisfied unless such further conditions as may be specified in the order are also satisfied.

8   1) The processing is necessary for medical purposes and is undertaken by –

(a)   a health professional, or

(b)   a person who in the circumstances owes a duty of confidentiality which is equivalent to that which would arise if that person were a health professional.

2) In this paragraph "medical purposes" includes the purposes of preventative medicine, medical diagnosis, medical research, the provision of care and treatment and the management of healthcare services.

9   1) The processing –

(a)   is of sensitive personal data consisting of information as to racial or ethnic origin,

(b)   is necessary for the purpose of identifying or keeping under review the existence or absence of equality of opportunity or treatment between persons of different racial or ethnic origins, with a view to enabling such equality to be promoted or maintained, and

(c)   is carried out with appropriate safeguards for the rights and freedoms of data subjects.

2) The Secretary of State may by order specify circumstances in which processing falling within sub-paragraph (1)(a) and (b) is, or is not, to be taken for the purposes of sub-paragraph (1)(c) to be carried out with appropriate safeguards for the rights and freedoms of data subjects.

10   The personal data are processed in circumstances specified in an order made by the Secretary of State for the purposes of this paragraph.

Court structure in England and Wales

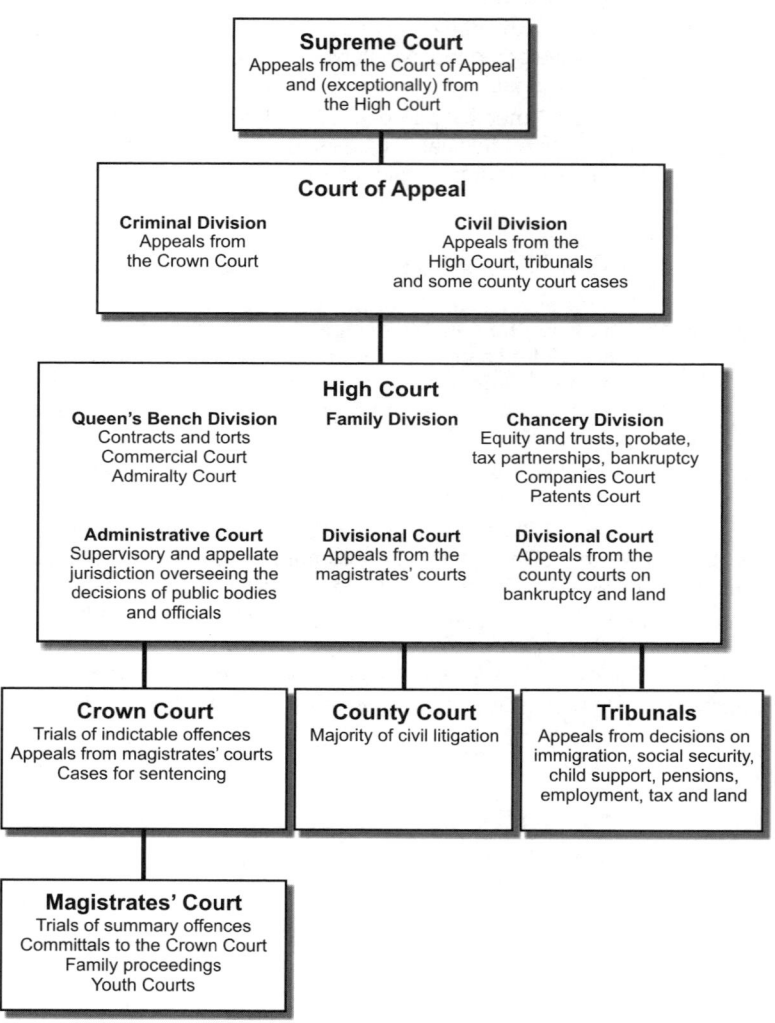

Supreme Court
Appeals from the Court of Appeal
and (exceptionally) from
the High Court

Court of Appeal

Criminal Division
Appeals from
the Crown Court

Civil Division
Appeals from the
High Court, tribunals
and some county court cases

High Court

Queen's Bench Division
Contracts and torts
Commercial Court
Admiralty Court

Family Division

Chancery Division
Equity and trusts, probate,
tax partnerships, bankruptcy
Companies Court
Patents Court

Administrative Court
Supervisory and appellate
jurisdiction overseeing the
decisions of public bodies
and officials

Divisional Court
Appeals from the
magistrates' courts

Divisional Court
Appeals from the
county courts on
bankruptcy and land

Crown Court
Trials of indictable offences
Appeals from magistrates' courts
Cases for sentencing

County Court
Majority of civil litigation

Tribunals
Appeals from decisions on
immigration, social security,
child support, pensions,
employment, tax and land

Magistrates' Court
Trials of summary offences
Committals to the Crown Court
Family proceedings
Youth Courts

Court structure in Scotland

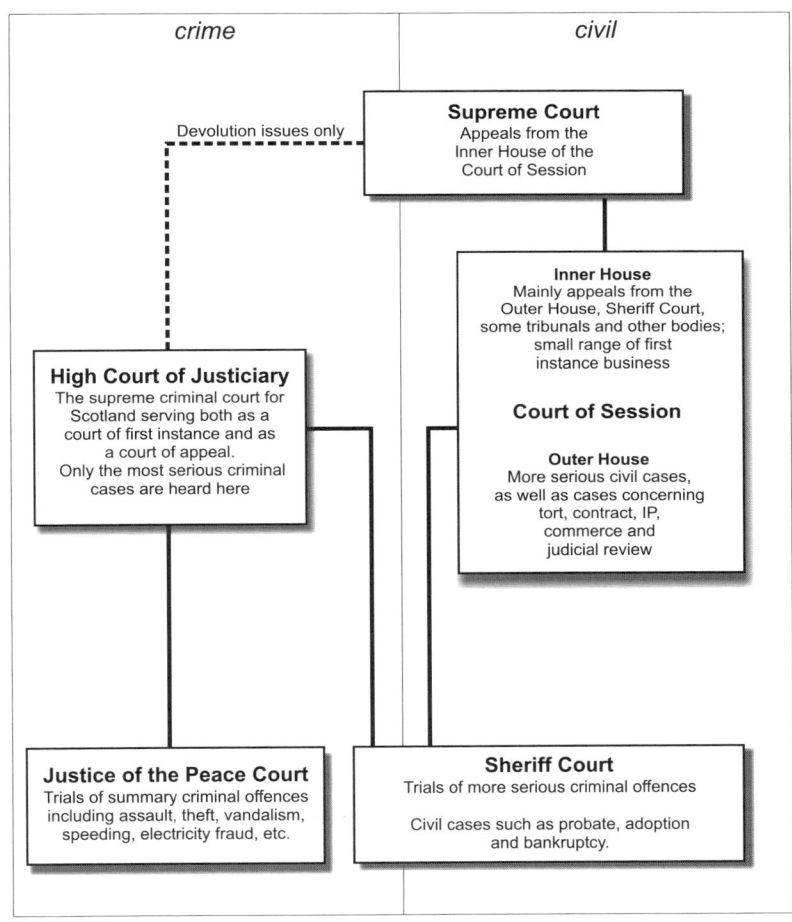

Court structure in Northern Ireland

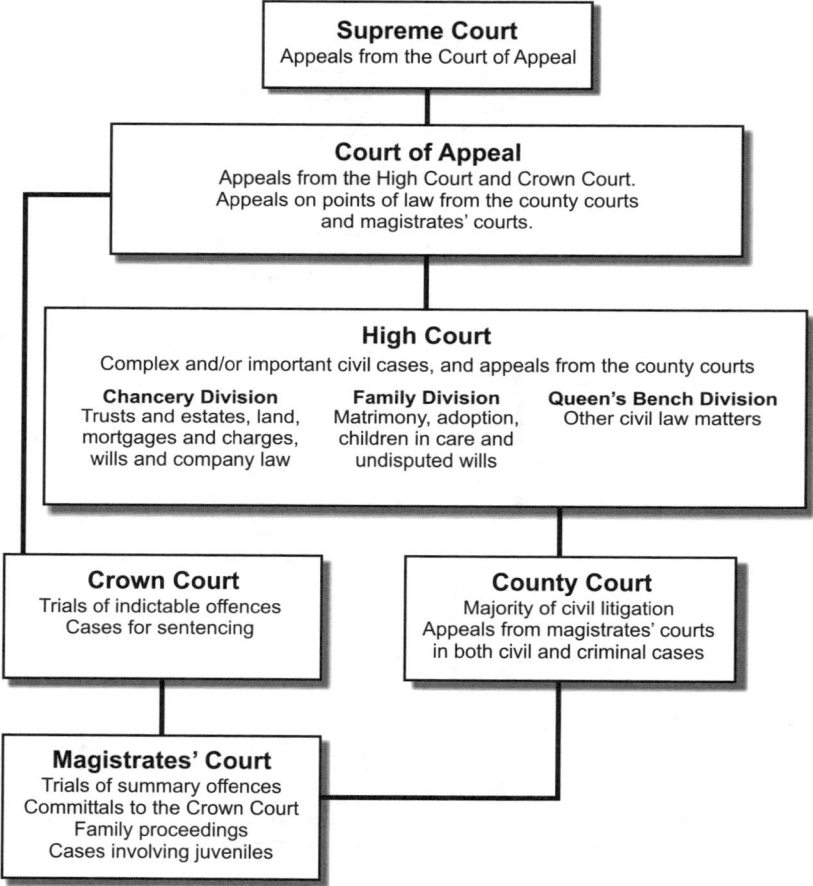

Supreme Court
Appeals from the Court of Appeal

Court of Appeal
Appeals from the High Court and Crown Court.
Appeals on points of law from the county courts
and magistrates' courts.

High Court
Complex and/or important civil cases, and appeals from the county courts

Chancery Division
Trusts and estates, land,
mortgages and charges,
wills and company law

Family Division
Matrimony, adoption,
children in care and
undisputed wills

Queen's Bench Division
Other civil law matters

Crown Court
Trials of indictable offences
Cases for sentencing

County Court
Majority of civil litigation
Appeals from magistrates' courts
in both civil and criminal cases

Magistrates' Court
Trials of summary offences
Committals to the Crown Court
Family proceedings
Cases involving juveniles

6

Addresses

Courts in England and Wales

Source: www.hmcourts-service.gov.uk

Aberdare County Court, The Court House, Cwmbach Road, Aberdare, Glamorgan, Wales, CF44 0JE
DX 99600 Aberdare 2
Switchboard: 01685 888575, General Fax: 01685 883413

Aberdare Magistrates' Court, The Court House, Cwmbach Road, Aberdare, Glamorgan, Wales, CF44 0NW
Switchboard: 01685 727600 - Administration done at Merthyr Tydfil, General Fax: 01685 727703

Abergavenny Magistrates' Court, Tudor Street, Abergavenny, Monmouthshire, Wales, NP7 5DL
DX 43665 Cwmbran
Switchboard: 01633 645000, General Fax: 01633 645177

Abertillery Magistrates' Court, Spring Bank, Abertillery, Blaenau, Gwent, Wales, NP13 1PB
Switchboard: 01633 645000, General Fax: 01633 645177

Aberystwyth County Court, Edleston House, Queens Road, Aberystwyth, Ceredigion, Wales, SY23 2HP
DX 99560 Aberystwyth 2
Switchboard: 01970 636370, General Fax: 01970 625985

Aberystwyth Magistrates' Court, Swyddfa'r Sir, Marine Terrace, Aberystwyth, Ceredigion, Wales, SY23 2DE
General Office: 01545 570886, General Fax: 01545 570295

Accrington County Court, Bradshawgate House, 1 Oak Street, Accrington, Lancashire, BB5 1EQ
DX 702645 Accrington 2
Switchboard: 01254 237490, General Fax: 01254 393869

Accrington Magistrates' Court, The Law Courts, Manchester Road, Accrington, Lancashire, BB5 2BH
Switchboard: 01254 687500, General Fax: 01254 687524

Acton Magistrates' Court, Winchester Street, Acton, London, W3 8PB
DX 5166 Ealing
Switchboard: 0845 601 3600, General Fax: 020 8993 9647

Administrative Court, Administrative Court Office, The Royal Courts of Justice, Strand, London, WC2A 2LL
DX 44450 RCJ/Strand
Switchboard: 020 7947 6000
Birmingham Administrative Court Regional Office: 0121 250 6319
Cardiff Administrative Court Regional Office: 02920 376400
Leeds Administrative Court Regional Office: 0113 306 2578
Manchester Administrative Court Regional Office: 0161 240 5313

Admiralty Court, The Royal Courts of Justice, Strand, London, WC2A 2LL
Tel: 020 7947 6112, Fax: 020 7947 6245

Aldershot & Farnham County Court, 78-82 Victoria Road, Aldershot, Hampshire, GU11 1SS
DX 98530 Aldershot 2
Switchboard: 01252 796800, General Fax: 01252 345705

Aldershot Magistrates' Court, The Court House, Civic Centre, Aldershot, Hampshire, GU11 1NY
DX 145110 Aldershot 4
Switchboard: 01252 366000, General Fax: 01252 330877

Aldridge Magistrates' Court, Rookery Lane, Aldrdige, Walsall, West Midlands, WS9 8NR
Switchboard: 01922 638222, General Fax: 01922 635657

Alnwick Magistrates' Court, The Court House, Prudhoe Street, Alnwick, Northumberland, NE66 1UJ
Switchboard: 01665 602727, General Fax: 01665 510247

Alton Magistrates' Court, The Court House, 25 Normandy Street, Alton, Hampshire, GU34 1DQ
DX 145110 Aldershot 4
Switchboard: 01252 366000, General Fax: 01252 330877

Altrincham County Court, Trafford Courthouse, Ashton Lane, Sale, Cheshire, M33 7WX
DX 708292 Sale 6
Switchboard: 0161 975 4760, General Fax: 0161 975 4761

Amersham Magistrates' Court, King George V Road, Amersham, Buckinghamshire, HP6 5AJ
Switchboard: 01296 554350, General Fax: 01296 554320

Ammanford Magistrates' Court, The Court House, Margaret Street, Ammanford, Carmarthenshire, Wales, SA18 2NP
Switchboard: 01554 757201, General Fax: 01554 759669

Andover Magistrates' Court, The Court House, West Street, Andover, Hampshire, SP10 2AB
Switchboard: 01252 366000, General Fax: 01256 811447

Ashford County Court, Ground Floor, The Court House, Tufton Street, Ashford, Kent, TN23 1QQ
DX 98060 Ashford (Kent) 3
Switchboard: 01233 632464, General Fax: 01233 612786

Ashford Magistrates' Court, The Courthouse, Tufton Street, Ashford, Kent, TN23 1QS,
Switchboard: 01304 218600, General Fax: 01304 213819

Avon & Somerset Fixed Penalty Office, PO Box 622, Taunton, Somerset, TA1 4WE
Switchboard: 01823 287080, General Fax: 01823 326021

Avon & Somerset Central Accounts Department, HMCS, Central Accounts Department, PO Box 480, Weston-Super-Mare, Avon, BS23 9BE
Accounts Teams: Bath/Taunton & Bridgwater/Weston Super Mare: 01934 528528
Accounts Teams: Bristol/Yate/Yeovil: 01934 528528
Confiscation Team: 01934 528567
Queensway Enforcement Team: 01934 528528
General Fax: 01934 528615

Aylesbury County Court, Walton Street, Aylesbury, Buckinghamshire, HP21 7QZ
DX 97820 Aylesbury 10
Switchboard: 01296 554326/554327, General Fax: 01296 554320

Aylesbury Crown Court, County Hall, Market Square, Aylesbury, Buckinghamshire, HP20 1XD
DX 97400 Aylesbury 2
Switchboard: 01296 434401, General Fax: 01296 435665

Aylesbury Magistrates' Court, Walton Street, Aylesbury, Buckinghamshire, HP21 7QZ
DX 149920 Aylesbury 10
Switchboard: 01296 554350, General Fax: 01296 554320

Balham Youth Court, 217 Balham High Road, Balham, London, SW17 7BS
DX 58559 Clapham Junction
Switchboard: 0845 601 3600

Banbury County Court, The Court House, Warwick Road, Banbury, Oxfordshire, OX16 2AW
DX 701967 Banbury 2
Switchboard: 01295 452090, General Fax: 01295 452051

Banbury Fixed Penalty Office, PO Box 429, Banbury, Oxfordshire, OX16 9PR
Switchboard: 01865 293358

Banbury Magistrates' Court, The Court House, Warwick Road, Banbury, Oxfordshire, OX16 2AW
Switchboard: 01295 452000, General Fax: 01295 452050

Bankruptcy & Companies Court, The Royal Courts of Justice, Strand, London, WC2A 2LL
Switchboard: 020 7947 6000

Barking & Dagenham Magistrates' Court, The Court House, East Street, Barking, Essex, IG11 8EW
DX 743410 Romford 15
Switchboard: 0845 601 3600, Fax: 01708 794270

Barnet Civil & Family Courts Centre, St Marys Court, Regents Park Road, Finchley Central, London, N3 1BQ
DX 122570 Finchley (Church End)
Switchboard: 020 8343 4272, General Fax: 020 8343 1324

Barnsley County Court, 12 Regent Street, Barnsley, South Yorkshire, S70 2EW
DX 702080 Barnsley 3
Switchboard: 01226 777550, General Fax: 01226 779126

Barnsley Magistrates' Court, The Court House, Westgate, Barnsley, South Yorkshire, S70 2DW
DX 12279 Barnsley 1
Switchboard: 01226 320000, General Fax: 01226 320044

Barnstaple County Court, 7th Floor, The Civic Centre, North Walk, Barnstaple, Devon, EX31 1DY
DX 98560 Barnstaple 2
General Enquiries: 01271 372252, General Fax: 01271 322968

Barnstaple Magistrates' Court, The Law Courts, The Civic Centre, Barnstaple, Devon, EX31 1DX
DX 98563 Barnstaple 2
General Enquiries: 01271 340410, General Fax: 01271 340415

Barrow-in-Furness County Court, Barrow Law Courts, Abbey Road, Barrow in Furness, Cumbria, LA14 5QX
DX 65210 Barrow in Furness 2
Switchboard: 01229 840370, General Fax: 01229 840371

Barrow-in-Furness Magistrates' Court, Abbey Road, Barrow in Furness, Cumbria, LA14 5QX
DX 63909 Barrow-in-Furness
Switchboard: 01229 820161, General Fax: 01229 870287

Barry Magistrates' Court, Thompson Street, Barry, Glamorgan, Wales, CF63 4SX
Switchboard: 01446 737491, General Fax: 01446 732743

Basildon Combined Court, The Gore, Basildon, Essex, SS14 2BU
DX 97633 Basildon 5
Switchboard: 01268 458000, General Fax: 01268 458100

Basildon Magistrates' Court, The Court House, Great Oaks, Basildon, Essex, SS14 1EH
Switchboard: 01245 313300, General Fax: 01245 313399

Basingstoke County Court, 3rd Floor, Grosvenor House, Basing View, Basingstoke, Hampshire, RG21 4HG
DX 98570 Basingstoke 3
Switchboard: 01256 318200, General Fax: 01256 318225

Basingstoke Magistrates' Court, The Court House, London Road, Basingstoke, Hampshire, RG21 4AB
DX 145110 Aldershot 4
Switchboard: 01252 366000, General Fax: 01256 811447

Bath County Court, The Law Courts, North Parade Road, Bath, Somerset, BA1 5AF
DX 98580 Bath 2
Switchboard: 01225 476730, General Fax: 01225 476724

Bath Magistrates' Court, North Parade Road, Bath, Somerset, BA1 5AF
DX 98580 Bath 2
Switchboard: 01225 463281, General Fax: 01225 420255

Batley & Dewsbury Magistrates' Court, The Court House, Grove Street, Dewsbury, West Yorkshire, WF13 1JP
Switchboard: 01924 468287, General Fax: 01924 430483

Bedford & Mid Beds Magistrates' Court, Shire Hall, 3 St Paul's Square, Bedford, Bedfordshire, MK40 1SQ
DX 729420 Bedford 10
Switchboard: 01234 319100, General Fax: 01234 319114

Bedford County Court, Shire Hall, 3 St Paul's Square, Bedford, Bedfordshire, MK40 1SQ, 97590 Bedford 11
Switchboard: 01234 319001, Fax: 01234 319026

Belmarsh Magistrates' Court, 4 Belmarsh Road, Thamesmead, London
Please make all enquiries to Greenwich Magistrates' Court

Berwick upon Tweed Magistrates' Court, 40 Church Street, Berwick upon Tweed, Northumberland, TD15 1DX
Switchboard: 01289 306885, General Fax: 01289 302735

Beverley Magistrates' Court, The Court House, Champney Road, Beverley, East Yorkshire, HU17 9EJ
Switchboard: 01482 861607, General Fax: 01482 882004

Bexley Magistrates' Court, Norwich Place, Bexleyheath, Kent, DA6 7NB
DX 156800 Bromley
Switchboard: 020 8304 5211, General Fax: 020 8303 6849

Bicester Magistrates' Court, Waverley House, Queens Avenue, Bicester, Oxfordshire, OX26 2NZ
Switchboard: 01295 452000, General Fax: 01295 452050

Bingley Magistrates' Court (incorporating Keighley Magistrates' Court), The Court House, Bradford Road, Bingley, West Yorkshire, BD16 1YA
DX 743840 Bingley 5
Switchboard: 01274 568411, General Fax: 01274 551289

Birkenhead County Court, 76 Hamilton Street, Birkenhead, Merseyside, CH41 5EN
DX 725000 Birkenhead 10
Switchboard: 0151 666 5800, General Fax: 0151 666 5873

Birmingham Civil Justice Centre, Priory Courts, 33 Bull Street, Birmingham, West Midlands, B4 6DS
DX 701987 Birmingham 7
Switchboard: 0121 681 4441, General Fax: 0121 681 3001

Birmingham Crown Court, Queen Elizabeth II Law Courts, 1 Newton Street, Birmingham, West Midlands, B4 7NA
DX 702033 Birmingham 8
Switchboard: 0121 681 3300, General Fax: 0121 681 3370

Birmingham District Probate Registry, Priory Courts, 33 Bull Street, Birmingham, West Midlands, B4 6DU
DX 701990 Birmingham 7
Switchboard: 0121 681 3400, General Fax: 0121 236 2465

Birmingham Family Courts, Priory Courts, 33 Bull Street, Birmingham, West Midlands, B4 6DS
DX 701987 Birmingham 7
General Fax: 0121 250 6183/6386

Birmingham Magistrates' Court, Victoria Law Courts, Corporation Street, Birmingham, West Midlands, B4 6QA
DX 715205 Birmingham 39
Switchboard: 0121 212 6600, General Fax: 0121 212 6771

Birmingham Youth Court, Steelhouse Lane, Birmingham, West Midlands, B4 6BJ
Switchboard: 0121 212 6600, General Fax: 0121 212 6771

Bishop Auckland County Court, Woodhouse Close, Bishop Auckland, Co. Durham, DL14 6LD
DX 65100 Bishop Auckland 2
Switchboard: 01388 660251, General Fax: 01388 660264

Bishop Auckland Magistrates' Court, Woodhouse Close, Bishop Auckland, Co. Durham, DL14 6LD
Switchboard: 01388 660250, General Fax: 01325 327697

Blackburn County Court, 64 Victoria Street, Blackburn, Lancashire, BB1 6DJ
DX 702650 Blackburn 4
General Fax: 01254 692712, Civil Section: 01254 299852, Family Section: 01254 299841

Blackburn Magistrates' Court, The Court House, Northgate, Blackburn, Lancashire, BB2 1AA
DX 742020 Blackburn 10
General Enquiries: 01254 687500, General Fax: 01254 687524

Blackfriars Crown Court, 1-15 Pocock Street, London, SE1 0BJ
DX 400800 Lambeth 3
Switchboard: 020 7922 5800, General Fax: 020 7922 5827

Blackpool County Court, The Law Courts, Chapel Street, Blackpool, Lancashire, FY1 5RJ
DX 724900 Blackpool 10
Switchboard: 01253 754020, General Fax: 01253 295255

Blackpool Magistrates' Court, PO Box 27, Civic Centre Chapel Street, Blackpool, Lancashire, FY1 5RH
Switchboard: 01253 757000, General Fax: 01253 757024

Blackwood Civil & Family Court, 8 Hall Street, Blackwood, South Wales, Wales, NP12 1NY
DX 99470 Blackwood 2
Tel: 01495 238200, Fax: 01495 238203

Blandford Forum Magistrates' Court, The Law Courts, Salisbury Road, Blandford Forum, Dorset, DT11 7HR
Switchboard: 01305 783891, General Fax: 01305 761418

Bodmin County Court, The Law Courts, Launceston Road, Bodmin, Cornwall, PL31 2AL
DX 136846 Bodmin 2
Switchboard: 01208 261580, General Fax: 01208 77255

Bodmin Magistrates' Court, Launceston Road, Bodmin, Cornwall, PL31 2AL
Switchboard: 01208 262700, General Fax: 01208 77198

Bodmin Probate Sub-Registry, Launceston Road, Bodmin, Cornwall, PL31 2AL
DX 136847 Bodmin 2
Switchboard: 01208 261581, General Fax: 01208 77542

Bolton Combined Court Centre, The Law Courts, Blackhorse Street, Bolton, Greater Manchester, BL1 1SU
DX 702610 Bolton 3
Switchboard: 01204 392881, County Court Fax: 01204 373706, Crown Court Fax: 01204 363204

Bolton Magistrates' Court, The Courts, Le Mans Crescent, Bolton, Greater Manchester, BL1 1UA
Switchboard: 01204 558200, General Fax: 01204 364373

Boston County Court, Boston Court House, 55 Norfolk Street, Boston, Lincolnshire, PE21 6PE
DX 701922 Boston 2
Switchboard: 01205 366080, General Fax: 01205 311692

Boston Magistrates' Court, Boston Court House, 55 Norfolk Street, Boston, Lincolnshire, PE21 6PE
Switchboard: 01754 898848, General Fax: 01754 767318

Bourne Magistrates' Court, Town Hall, North Street, Bourne, Lincolnshire, PE10 9AE
Switchboard: 01476 563438, General Fax: 01476 567200

Bournemouth County Court, Courts of Justice, Deansleigh Road, Bournemouth, Dorset, BH7 7DS
DX 98420 Bournemouth 4
Switchboard: 01202 502800, General Fax: 01202 502801

Bournemouth Crown Court, Courts of Justice, Deansleigh Road, Bournemouth, Dorset, BH7 7DS
DX 98420 Bournemouth 4
Switchboard: 01202 502800, General Fax: 01202 502801

Bournemouth Magistrates' Court, The Law Courts, Stafford Road, Bournemouth, Dorset, BH1 1LA
DX 98700 Poole 4
Switchboard: 01202 745309, General Fax: 01202 711999

Bow County Court, 96 Romford Road, London, E15 4EG
DX 97490 Stratford (London) 2
Switchboard: 020 8536 5200, General Fax: 020 8503 1152

Bradford Combined Court Centre, Bradford Law Courts, Exchange Square, Drake Street, Bradford, West Yorkshire, BD1 1JA
DX 702083 Bradford 2
Switchboard: 01274 840274, General Fax: 01274 840275

Bradford Magistrates' Court, The Tyrls, Bradford, West Yorkshire, BD1 1JL
Switchboard: 01274 390111, General Fax: 01274 391731

Brecon Law Courts, Brecon Law Courts, Cambrian Way, Brecon, Powys, Wales, LD3 7HR
DX 124340 Brecon 2
General Office: 01874 622993, General Fax: 01874 622441

Brent Magistrates' Court, 448 High Road, London, NW10 2DZ
DX 110850 Willesden 2
Switchboard: 020 8955 0555, General Fax: 020 8955 0543

Brentford County Court, Alexandra Road, High Street, Brentford, Middlesex, TW8 0JJ
DX 97840 Brentford 2
Switchboard: 020 8231 8940, General Fax: 020 8568 2401

Brentford Magistrates' Court, Market Place, Brentford, Middlesex, TW8 8EN
DX 133823 Feltham 3
Switchboard: 020 8917 3400, General Fax: 020 8917 3448

Bridgend Law Courts, The Law Courts, Sunnyside, Bridgend, South Wales, Wales, CF31 4AJ
DX 99750 Bridgend 2
Magistrates' Court: Switchboard: 01656 673800, Fax: 01656 668981
County Court: Switchboard: 01656 673833, Fax: 01656 647124

Bridgwater Magistrates' Court, The Court House, Northgate, Bridgwater, Somerset, TA6 3YL
Switchboard: 01823 257084, General Fax: 01823 335195

Bridlington Magistrates' Court, The Court House, Quay Road, Bridlington, East Yorkshire, YO16 4EJ
Switchboard: 01482 861607, General Fax: 01482 882004

Bridport Magistrates' Court, The Court House, Mountfield, Bridport, Dorset, DT6 3JP
Switchboard: 01305 783891, General Fax: 01305 761418

Brighton County & Family Proceedings Court, 1 Edward Street, Brighton, East Sussex, BN2 0JD
DX 142600 Brighton 12
Switchboard: 01273 811333, General Fax: 01273 607638

Brighton County Court, William Street, Brighton, East Sussex, BN2 0RF
DX 98070 Brighton 3
Switchboard: 01273 674421, General Fax: 01273 602138

Brighton District Probate Registry, William Street, Brighton, East Sussex, BN2 0RF
DX 98073 Brighton 3
Switchboard: 01273 573510, General Fax: 01273 625845

Brighton Magistrates' Court, The Law Courts, Edward Street, Brighton, East Sussex, BN2 0LG
Switchboard: 01273 670888, General Fax: 01273 811770

Bristol County Court, Lewins Place, Lewins Mead, Bristol, BS1 2NR
DX 95903 Bristol 3
Switchboard: 0117 910 6700

Bristol Crown Court, The Law Courts, Small Street, Bristol, BS1 1DA
DX 78128 Bristol
Switchboard: 0117 976 3030, General Fax: 0117 976 3026

Bristol District Probate Registry, Ground Floor, The Crescent Centre, Temple Back, Bristol, BS1 6EP
DX 94400 Bristol 5
Switchboard: 0117 927 3915, General Fax: 0117 925 3549

Bristol Magistrates' Court, Marlborough Street, Bristol, BS1 3NU
DX 78126 Bristol
Switchboard: 0117 930 2400, General Fax: 0117 930 2486

Bromley County Court, Court House, College Road, Bromley, Kent, BR1 3PX
DX 98080 Bromley 2
Switchboard: 020 8290 9620, General Fax: 020 8313 9624

Bromley Magistrates' Court, The Court House, London Road, Bromley, Kent, BR1 1RA
DX 156800 Bromley
Switchboard: 0845 601 3600, General Fax: 020 8437 3506

Bromsgrove & Redditch Magistrates' Court, Redditch, Worcestershire
Please refer to Kidderminster Magistrates' Court

Burnley Combined Court Centre, The Law Courts, Hammerton Street, Burnley, Lancashire, BB11 1XD
DX 724940 Burnley 4
Switchboard: 01282 855300, General Fax: 01282 414911

Burnley Magistrates' Court, The Court House, Parker Lane, Burnley, Lancashire, BB11 2BS
DX 741470 Burnley 7
Switchboard: 01282 610000, General Fax: 01282 610034

Burton-upon-Trent County Court, 165 Station Street, Burton-upon-Trent, Staffordshire, DE14 1BP
DX 702044 Burton-upon-Trent 3
Switchboard: 01283 568241, General Fax: 01283 517245

Burton-upon-Trent Magistrates' Court, The Court House, Horninglow Street, Burton-upon-Trent, Staffordshire, DE14 1NZ
Switchboard: 01785 223144, General Fax: 01785 258508

Bury County Court, Tenters Street, Bury, Greater Manchester, BL9 0HX
DX 702615 Bury 2
Switchboard: 0161 447 8699, General Fax: 0161 763 4995

Bury Magistrates' Court, The Courthouse, Tenters Street, Bury, Greater Manchester, BL9 0HX
DX 707370 Bury 4
Switchboard: 0161 447 8600, General Fax: 0161 447 8630

Bury St Edmunds County Court, Triton House, Entrance B, St Andrews Street (N), Bury St Edmunds, Suffolk, IP33 1TR
DX 97640 Bury St Edmunds 3
Switchboard: 01284 753254, General Fax: 01284 702687

Bury St Edmunds Crown Court, Shire Hall, Bury St Edmunds, Suffolk, IP33 1HF
Switchboard: 01473 228585, General Fax: 01473 228560

Bury St Edmunds Magistrates' Court, Shire Hall, Honey Hill, Bury St Edmunds, Suffolk, IP33 1HF
DX 741460 Bury St Edmunds 7
Switchboard: 01284 778000, General Fax: 01284 778020

Buxton Magistrates' Court, Peak Buildings, Terrace Road, Buxton, Derbyshire, SK17 6DY
DX 701980 Buxton 2
Switchboard: 01298 23951, General Fax: 01298 26031

Caernarfon County Court, The Court House, Llanberis Road, Caernarfon, Gwynedd, Wales, LL55 2DF
DX 702483 Caernarfon 2
Switchboard: 01286 684600, General Fax: 01286 678965

Caernarfon Crown Court, Caernarfon Criminal Justice Centre, Llanberis Road, Caernarfon, Gwynedd, Wales, LL55 2DF
DX 713562 Caernarfon 5
Switchboard: 01286 669700, General Fax: 01286 669798

Caernarfon Magistrates' Court, Caernarfon Criminal Justice Centre, Llanberis Road, Caernarfon, Gwynedd, Wales, LL55 2DF
DX 713562 Caernarfon 5
Switchboard: 01286 669700, Administration Fax: 01286 669798

Caernarfon Probate Sub-Registry, The Criminal Justice Centre, Llanberis Road, Caernarfon, Gwynedd, Wales, LL57 2DF
DX 744381 Caernarfon 6
Switchboard: 01286 669755, General Fax: 01286 671509

Caerphilly Magistrates' Court, The Court House, Mountain Road, Caerphilly, Glamorgan, Wales, CF83 1HG
Switchboard: 01633 645000, General Fax: 01633 645177

Camberwell Green Magistrates' Court, 15 D'Eynsford Road, Camberwell Green, London, SE5 7UP
DX 35305 Camberwell
Switchboard: 0845 601 3600, General Fax: 020 7805 9896

Camborne Magistrates' Court, The Bassett Centre, Bassett Road, Camborne, Cornwall, TR14 8SL
Switchboard: 01872 321900, General Fax: 01872 276227

Cambridge County Court, 197 East Road, Cambridge, Cambridgeshire, CB1 1BA
DX 97650 Cambridge 3
Switchboard: 01223 224500, General Fax: 01223 224590

Cambridge Crown Court, The Court House, 83 East Road, Cambridge, Cambridgeshire, CB1 1BT
DX 97365 Cambridge 2
Switchboard: 01223 488321, General Fax: 01223 488333

Cambridge Magistrates' Court, 12 St Andrews Street, Cambridge, Cambridgeshire, CB2 3AX
DX 131966 Cambridge 6
Switchboard: 0845 310 0575, General Fax: 01223 376094

Cannock Magistrates' Court, The Court House, Wolverhampton Road, Cannock, Staffordshire, WS11 1AT
Switchboard: 01785 223144, General Fax: 01785 258508

Canterbury Combined Court Centre, Canterbury Combined Court, The Law Courts, Chaucer Road, Canterbury, Kent, CT1 1ZA
DX 99710 Canterbury 3
Switchboard: 01227 819200, County Court Fax: 01227 819283, Crown Court Fax: 01227 819329

Canterbury Magistrates' Court, Broad Street, Canterbury, Kent, CT1 2UE
Switchboard: 01304 218600, General Fax: 01304 213819

Cardiff Civil Justice Centre, 2 Park Street, Cardiff, South Wales, Wales, CF10 1ET
DX 99500 Cardiff 6
Switchboard: 029 20376400, General Fax: 029 20376475

Cardiff Crown Court, The Law Courts, Cathays Park, Cardiff, South Wales, Wales, CF10 3PG
DX 99450 Cardiff 5
Switchboard: 02920 678730, General Fax: 02920 678732

Cardiff Magistrates' Court, Fitzalan Place, Cardiff, South Wales, Wales, CF24 0RZ
Switchboard: 029 2046 3040, General Fax: 029 2046 0264

Cardiff Probate Registry of Wales, Cardiff Probate Registry of Wales, 3rd Floor Cardiff Magistrates Court, Fitzalan Place, Cardiff, South Wales, Wales, CF24 0RZ
DX 743940 Cardiff 38
Switchboard: 02920 474373, General Fax: 02920 456411

Cardigan Magistrates' Court, Court House, Priory Street, Cardigan, Cardiganshire, Wales, SA43 1BZ
General Office: 01545 570886, General Fax: 01545 570295

Carlisle Combined Court Centre, Courts of Justice, Earl Street, Carlisle, Cumbria, CA1 1DJ
DX 65331 Carlisle 2
Fax: 01228 590588, County Court Switchboard: 01228 882140, Crown Court Office: 01228 882120

Carlisle Magistrates' Court, The Court House, Rickergate, Carlisle, Cumbria, CA3 8QH
DX 63018 Carlisle
Switchboard: 01228 518800, General Fax: 01228 518844

Carlisle Probate Sub-Registry, Courts of Justice, Earl Street, Carlisle, Cumbria, CA1 1DJ
DX 63034 Carlisle
Switchboard: 01228 521751

Carmarthen County Court, The Old Vicarage, Picton Terrace, Carmarthen, Carmarthenshire, Wales, SA31 1BJ
DX 99570 Carmarthen 2
Switchboard: 01267 228010, General Fax: 01267 221844

Carmarthen Crown Court, The Guildhall (hearing venue only), Guildhall Square, Carmarthen, Carmarthenshire, Wales, SA31 1PR
Switchboard: 01792 637000, General Fax: 01792 637049

Carmarthen Magistrates' Court, The Guildhall, Guildhall Square, Carmarthen, Carmarthenshire, Wales, SA31 1PR
Switchboard: 01554 757201, General Fax: 01554 759669

Carmarthen Probate Sub-Registry, 14 King Street, Carmarthen, Carmarthenshire, Wales, SA31 1BL
DX 51420 Carmarthen
Switchboard: 01267 242560, General Fax: 01267 229067

Central Accounting Office, PO Box 31093, London, SW1P 3WT
DX 120554 Victoria 6
Switchboard: 08459 400 111, General Fax: 020 7805 1892

Central Buckinghamshire Magistrates' Court, Walton Street, Aylesbury, Buckinghamshire, HP21 7QZ
Switchboard: 01296 554350

Central Criminal Court, Old Bailey, London, EC4M 7EH
DX 46700 Old Bailey
Switchboard: 020 7248 3277, General Fax: 020 7192 2671

Central London County Court, 13-14 Park Crescent, London, W1B 1HT
DX 97325 Regents Park 2
Switchboard: 020 7917 5000, General Fax: 020 7917 5014

Centralised Attachment of Earnings Payments (CAPS), 5th Floor, St Katharine's House, 21-27 St Katharine's Street, Northampton, Northamptonshire, NN1 2LH
DX 702885 Northampton 7
Switchboard: 0845 408 5312, General Fax: 0845 408 5315

Chancery Division, The Royal Courts of Justice, Strand, London, WC2A 2LL
Switchboard: 020 7947 6000

Chatham Magistrates' Court, The Court House, The Brook, Chatham, Kent, ME4 4JZ
Switchboard: 01634 830232, General Fax: 01634 847400

Chelmsford County & Family Proceedings Court, Priory Place, New London Road, Chelmsford, Essex, CM2 0PP
DX 97660 Chelmsford 4
Switchboard: 01245 264670, Fax: 01245 295395

Chelmsford Crown Court, PO Box 9, New Street, Chelmsford, Essex, CM1 1EL
DX 97375 Chelmsford 3
Switchboard: 01245 603000, General Fax: 01245 603011

Chelmsford Magistrates' Court, Shire Hall, Tindal Square, Chelmsford, Essex, CM1 1RA
Switchboard: 01245 313300, General Fax: 01245 313399

Cheltenham County Court, 1st Floor, Cheltenham Magistrates Court, St Georges Road, Cheltenham, Gloucester, Gloucestershire, GL50 3PF
Switchboard: 01452 834991, General Fax: 01452 834923

Cheltenham Magistrates' Court, Cheltenham Courthouse, St Georges Road, Cheltenham, Gloucestershire, GL50 3PF
DX 98665 Gloucester 5
Switchboard: 01452 420100, General Fax: 01452 833557

Cheshunt Magistrates' Court, King Arthur Court, Cheshunt, Hertfordshire, EN8 8LD
Switchboard: 01992 411040, General Fax: 01992 411047

Chester Civil Justice Centre, Trident House, Little St John Street, Chester, Cheshire, CH1 1SN
DX 702460 Chester 4
Enquiries: 01244 404200, Fax: 01244 404300

Chester Crown Court, The Castle, Chester, Cheshire, CH1 2AN
DX 702527 Chester 5
Switchboard: 01244 317606, General Fax: 01244 350773

Chester Probate Sub-Registry, Chester Civil Justice Centre, Trident House, Little John Street, Chester, Cheshire, CH1 1SN
DX 702470 Chester 18

Chester, Ellesmere Port & Neston Magistrates' Court, Grosvenor Street, Chester, Cheshire, CH1 2XA
Switchboard: 0870 162 6261, General Fax: 01244 405843

Chesterfield County Court, St Mary's Gate, Chesterfield, Derbyshire, S41 7TD
DX 703160 Chesterfield 3
Switchboard: 01246 501200, General Fax: 01246 501205

Chesterfield Magistrates' Court, Tapton Lane, Chesterfield, Derbyshire, S41 7TW
DX 742041 Chesterfield 7
Switchboard: 01246 224040, General Fax: 01246 246492

Chester-le-Street Magistrates' Court, Newcastle Road, Chester-le-Street, Co. Durham, DH3 3UA
DX 721663 Chester-le-Street 2
Switchboard: 0191 387 0700, General Fax: 0191 387 0746

Chichester Combined Court Centre, Southgate, Chichester, West Sussex, PO19 1SX
DX 97460 Chichester 2
County Court: Tel: 01243 520700, Fax: 01243 533756
Crown Court: Tel: 01243 520742, Fax: 01243 538252

Chichester Magistrates' Court, 6 Market Avenue, Chichester, West Sussex, PO19 1YE
DX 97463 Chichester 2
Switchboard: 01243 817000, General Fax: 01243 533655

Chippenham Magistrates' Court, North West Wiltshire Magistrates' Court, The Courthouse, Pewsham Way, Chippenham, Wiltshire, SN15 3BF
DX 34213 Chippenham
Switchboard: 01249 463473, General Fax: 01249 444319

Chorley County Court, 59 St Thomas's Road, Chorley, Lancashire, PR7 1JE
DX 702655 Chorley 3
Switchboard: 01257 262778, General Fax: 01257 232843

Chorley Magistrates' Court, The Court House, St Thomas's Square, Chorley, Lancashire, PR7 1DY
General Fax: 01257 261948, Switchboard: 01257 240500

Cirencester Magistrates' Court, Cirencester Courthouse, The Forum, Cirencester, Gloucestershire, GL7 2PL
DX 98665 Gloucester 5
Switchboard: 01452 420100, General Fax: 01452 833557

City of London Magistrates' Court, 1 Queen Victoria Street, London, EC4N 4XY
DX 98943 Cheapside 2
General Enquiries: 0845 0601 3600, General Fax: 020 7332 1493

City of Westminster Magistrates' Court, 70 Horseferry Road, London, SW1P 2AX
DX 120551 Victoria 6
Switchboard: 0845 601 3600, General Fax: 020 7805 1193

Claim Production Centre (CPC), 2nd Floor, St Katharine's House, 21-27 St Katharine's Street, Northampton, Northamptonshire, NN1 2LH
DX 702885 Northampton 7
Switchboard: 0845 408 5310, General Fax: 0845 408 5311

Clerkenwell & Shoreditch County Court, The Gee Street Courthouse, 29-41 Gee Street, London, EC1V 3RE
DX 121000 Shoreditch 2
General Office: 020 7250 7200, General Fax: 020 7250 7250

Coalville Magistrates' Court, The Courthouse, Vaughan Street, Coalville, Leicestershire, LE67 3DP
Switchboard: 01455 623000

Colchester County Court, Falkland House, 25 Southway, Colchester, Essex, CO3 3EG
DX 97670 Colchester 3
Switchboard: 01206 717200, Fax: 01206 717250

Colchester Magistrates' Court, Town Hall Square, High Street, Colchester, Essex, CO1 1FP
Switchboard: 01245 313300, General Fax: 01245 313399

Coleford Magistrates' Court, Coleford Courthouse, Gloucester Road, Coleford, Gloucestershire, GL16 8BQ
DX 98665 Gloucester 5
Switchboard: 01452 420100, General Fax: 01452 833557

Commercial Court, The Royal Courts of Justice, Strand, London, WC2A 2LL
Registry: 020 7947 6112, Listing Office: 020 7947 6826, Fax: 020 7947 7670

Companies Court, The Royal Courts of Justice, Strand, London, WC2A 2LL
Switchboard: 020 7947 6000

Consett County Court, Victoria Road, Consett, Co. Durham, DH8 5AU
DX 65106 Consett 2
Switchboard: 01207 502854, General Fax: 01207 582626

Consett Magistrates' Court, Ashdale Road, Consett, Co. Durham, DH8 6LY
Switchboard: 0191 387 0700, General Fax: 0191 387 0746

Conwy & Colwyn County Court, 36 Princes Drive, Colwyn Bay, Conwy, Wales, LL29 8LA
DX 702492 Colwyn Bay
Switchboard: 01492 530807, General Fax: 01492 533591

Corby Magistrates' Court, The Court House, Elizabeth Street, Corby, Northamptonshire, NN17 1SQ
DX 151720 Northampton 27
Switchboard: 01604 497000, General Fax: 01604 497010

County Court Bulk Centre (CCBC), 4th Floor, St Katharine's House, 21-27 St Katharine's Street, Northampton, Northamptonshire, NN1 2LH
DX 702885 Northampton 7
Switchboard: 0845 408 5302, General Fax: 0845 408 5304

Court of Appeal Civil Division, The Royal Courts of Justice, Strand, London, WC2A 2LL
Switchboard: 020 7947 6000

Court of Appeal Criminal Division, Criminal Appeal Office, The Royal Courts of Justice, Strand, London, WC2A 2LL
DX 44450 RCJ/Strand
Switchboard: 020 7947 6000

Court of Protection, Archway Tower, 2 Junction Road, London, N19 5SZ
DX 141150 Archway 2
Contact Centre: 0845 330 2900, Listing and Appeals Team: 020 7664 7178

Coventry Combined Court Centre, 140 Much Park Street, Coventry, West Midlands, CV1 2SN
DX 701580 Coventry 5
Switchboard: 024 7653 6166, General Fax: 024 7652 0443

Coventry Magistrates' Court, Little Park Street, Coventry, West Midlands, CV1 2SQ
DX 701583 Coventry 5
Switchboard: 02476 630 666, General Fax: 02476 500 699

Crawley Magistrates' Court, The Court House, County Buildings, Woodfield Road, Crawley, West Sussex, RH10 8BF
DX 135596 Haywards Heath 6
Switchboard: 01444 417611, General Fax: 01444 472639

Crewe County Court, The Law Courts, Civic Centre, Crewe, Cheshire, CW1 2DP
DX 702504 Crewe 2
Switchboard: 01270 539300, General Fax: 01270 216344

Cromer Magistrates' Court, The Courthouse, Holt Road, Cromer, Norfolk, NR27 9EB
Switchboard: 01493 849800, General Fax: 01263 511446

Croydon County Court, The Law Courts, Altyre Road, Croydon, Surrey, CR9 5AB
DX 97470 Croydon 6
Switchboard: 020 8410 4797, Fax: 020 8760 0432

Croydon Crown Court, The Law Courts, Altyre Road, Croydon, Surrey, CR9 5AB
DX 97473 Croydon 6
Switchboard: 0208 410 4700, Fax: 020 8781 1007

Croydon Magistrates' Court, Barclay Road, Croydon, Surrey, CR9 3NG
DX 97474 Croydon 6
Switchboard: 020 8686 8680, General Fax: 020 8680 9801

Cullompton Magistrates' Court, Court House, Exeter Hill, Cullompton, Devon, EX15 1DJ
Switchboard: 01392 415300, General Fax: 01392 415593

Cwmbran Magistrates' Court, Tudor Road, Cwmbran, Torfaen, Wales, NP44 3YA
Switchboard: 01633 645000, General Fax: 01633 645177

Darlington County Court, 4 Coniscliffe Road, Darlington, Co. Durham, DL3 7RL
DX 65109 Darlington 3
Switchboard: 01325 463224, General Fax: 01325 362829

Darlington Magistrates' Court, Parkgate, Darlington, Co. Durham, DL1 1ZD
Switchboard: 01325 318114, General Fax: 01325 327697

Dartford County Court, Home Gardens, Dartford, Kent, DA1 1DX
DX 98090 Dartford 2
Switchboard: 01322 627600, General Fax: 01322 270902

Dartford Magistrates' Court, Session House, Highfield Road, Dartford, Kent, DA1 2JW
Switchboard: 01634 830232, General Fax: 01634 847400

Daventry Magistrates' Court, The Court House, New Street, Daventry, Northamptonshire, NN11 4BS
DX 151720 Northampton 27
Switchboard: 01604 497000, General Fax: 01604 497010

Denbigh Magistrates' Court, Grove Road, Denbigh, Denbighshire, Wales, LL16 3UU
Switchboard: 01492 871333, General Fax: 01492 872321

Derby Combined Court Centre, Morledge, Derby, Derbyshire, DE1 2XE
DX 724060 Derby 21
Switchboard: 01332 622600, General Fax: 01332 622543

Southern Derbyshire Magistrates' Court, The Court House, St Mary's Gate, Derby, Derbyshire, DE1 3JR
DX 707570 Derby 8
Switchboard: 01332 362000, General Fax: 01332 333183

Devizes Magistrates' Court, The Courthouse, Northgate Gardens, off Northgate Street, Devizes, Wiltshire, SN10 1JN
Switchboard: 01722 333225, General Fax: 01722 413395

Devon & Cornwall Fixed Penalty Office, Fixed Penalty Office, PO Box 76, Plymouth, Devon, PL1 2YN
Switchboard: 01752 675444, General Fax: 01752 269492

Dewsbury County Court, County Court House, Eightlands Road, Dewsbury, West Yorkshire, WF13 2PE
DX 702086 Dewsbury 2
Switchboard: 01924 466135, General Fax: 01924 456419

Didcot Magistrates' Court, The Court House, Mereland Road, Didcot, Oxfordshire, OX11 8BG
Switchboard: 0870 241 2808, General Fax: 01865 448024

Dolgellau Crown Court, The County Hall, Dolgellau, Gwynedd, Wales
Switchboard: 01352 707340, General Fax: 01352 753874

Dolgellau Magistrates' Court, Courtroom, County Hall, Dolgellau, Gwynedd, Wales, LL40 1AU
Switchboard: 01286 669700, General Fax: 01286 669798

Doncaster County Court, 74 Waterdale, Doncaster, South Yorkshire, DN1 3BT
DX 702089 Doncaster 4
Switchboard: 01302 381730, General Fax: 01302 768090

Doncaster Crown Court, College Road, Doncaster, South Yorkshire, DN1 3HS
DX 703001 Doncaster 5
Switchboard: 01302 322211, General Fax: 01302 329471

Doncaster Magistrates' Court, PO Box 49, The Law Courts, College Road, Doncaster, South Yorkshire, DN1 3HT
DX 742840 Doncaster 20
Switchboard: 01302 366711, General Fax: 01302 347359

Dorchester Crown Court, County Hall, Colliston Park, Dorchester, Dorset, DT1 1XJ
Switchboard: 01305 752510, General Fax: 01305 788293

Dorking Magistrates' Court, London Road, Dorking, Surrey, RH4 1SX
DX 149260 Dorking 4
Switchboard: 01737 765581, General Fax: 01306 742194

Dover Magistrates' Court, Pencester Road, Dover, Kent, CT16 1BS
Switchboard: 01304 218600, General Fax: 01304 213819

Dudley Magistrates' Court, The Inhedge, Dudley, West Midlands, DY1 1RY
DX 12769 Dudley
Switchboard: 01384 211411, General Fax: 01384 211415

Durham County Court, Durham County Court, Civil & Family Justice Centre, Green Lane, Old Elvet, Durham, Co. Durham, DH1 3RG
DX 65115 Durham 5
Switchboard: 0191 375 1840, Fax: 0191 375 1844

Durham Crown Court, The Law Courts, Old Elvet, Durham, Co. Durham, DH1 3HW
DX 65112 Durham 4
Switchboard: 0191 386 6714, General Fax: 0191 383 0605

Durham Magistrates' Court, Old Elvet, Durham, Co. Durham, DH1 3HW
Switchboard: 0191 387 0700, General Fax: 0191 387 0746

Ealing Magistrates' Court, The Court House, Green Man Lane, Ealing, London, W13 0SD
DX 5166 Ealing
Switchboard: 0845 601 3600, General Fax: 020 8579 2985

East Berkshire Magistrates' Court, Bracknell, Court House, Town Square, Bracknell, Berkshire, RG12 1AE
Switchboard: 01753 232100, General Fax: 01753 232190

East Berkshire Magistrates' Court, Maidenhead, Bridge Road, Maidenhead, Berkshire, SL6 8PB
General Fax: 01753 232190, Switchboard: 01753 232100

East Berkshire Magistrates' Court, Slough, Law Courts, Chalvey Park, off Windsor Road, Slough, Berkshire, SL1 2HJ
DX 98033 Slough 3
Switchboard: 01753 232100, General Fax: 01753 232190

Eastbourne County Court, The Law Courts, Old Orchard Road, Eastbourne, East Sussex, BN21 4UN
DX 98110 Eastbourne 2
Switchboard: 01323 727518, General Fax: 01323 649372

Edmonton County Court, Court House, 59 Fore Street, Edmonton, London, N18 2TN
DX 136686 Edmonton 3
Civil direct line: 020 8884 6500, Civil Fax: 020 8803 0564, Family direct line: 020 8884 6560, Family Fax: 020 8887 0413

Ely Magistrates' Court, Sessions House, Lynn Road, Ely, Cambridgeshire, CB7 4EG
Switchboard: 0845 310 0575, General Fax: 01223 844980

Enfield Magistrates' Court, The Court House, Lordship Lane, Tottenham, London, N17 6RT
DX 134490 Tottenham 3
Switchboard: 0845 601 3600, General Fax: 020 8885 4343

Epping Magistrates' Court, The Court House, Epping, Essex, CM16 4AP
Switchboard: 01245 313300, General Fax: 01245 313399

Epsom County Court, Epsom Point, 84-90 East Street, Epsom, Surrey, KT17 1DN
DX 97850 Epsom 3
Switchboard: 01372 721801, General Fax: 01372 734229

Evesham County Court, 1st Floor, 87 High Street, Evesham, Worcestershire, WR11 4EE
DX 70910 Evesham 3
Switchboard: 01386 442287, General Fax: 01386 49203

Exeter Combined Court Centre, Southernhay Gardens, Exeter, Devon, EX1 1UH
DX 98440 Exeter 2
Switchboard: 01392 415300, General Fax: 01392 415642

Exeter Magistrates' Court, The Court House, Heavitree Road, Exeter, Devon, EX1 2LS
Switchboard: 01392 415300, General Fax: 01392 415593

Exeter Probate Sub-Registry, 1st Floor, Exeter Crown & County Courts, Southernhay Gardens, Exeter, Devon, EX1 1UH
DX 98442 Exeter 2
Switchboard: 01392 415370, General Fax: 01392 415608

Family Division, The Royal Courts of Justice, Strand, London, WC2A 2LL
Switchboard: 020 7947 6000

Fareham Magistrates' Court, The Court House, Trinity Street, Fareham, Hampshire, PO16 7SB
DX 98494 Portsmouth 5
Switchboard: 023 92 819421, General Fax: 023 92 293085

Feltham Magistrates' Court, Hanworth Road, Feltham, Middlesex, TW13 5AF
DX 133821 Feltham 3
Switchboard: 020 8917 3400, General Fax: 020 8917 3527

Fleetwood Magistrates' Court, The Esplanade, Fleetwood, Lancashire, FY7 6AT
Switchboard: 01253 757000, General Fax: 01253 757024

Flint Magistrates' Court, Court House, Chapel Street, Flint, Flintshire, Wales, CH6 5AY
Switchboard: 01978 310106, General Fax: 01978 358213

Folkestone Magistrates' Court, The Law Courts, Castle Hill Avenue, Folkestone, Kent, CT20 2DH
Switchboard: 01304 218600, General Fax: 01304 213819

Frome Magistrates' Court, The Court House, Oakfield Road, Frome, Somerset, BA11 4JG
General Admin: 01935 426281, General Fax: 01935 431022

Furness Magistrates' Court, Abbey Road, Barrow in Furness, Cumbria, LA14 5QX
DX 63909 Barrow in Furness
Switchboard: 01229 820161, General Fax: 01229 870287

Gainsborough Magistrates' Court, The Court House, Roseway, Gainsborough, Lincolnshire, DN21 2BB
Switchboard: 01522 528218, General Fax: 01522 525832

Gateshead County Court, Gateshead Law Courts, Warwick Street, Gateshead, Tyne & Wear, NE8 1DT
DX 742120 Gateshead 6
Switchboard: 0191 477 5821, General Fax: 0191 440 7209

Gateshead Magistrates' Court, PO Box 26, Warwick Street, Gateshead, Tyne & Wear, NE8 1DT
DX 742120 Gateshead 6
Switchboard: 0191 4775821, General Fax: 0191 4787825

Gloucester Crown Court, Gloucestershire Crown Courthouse, Longsmith Street, Gloucester, Gloucestershire, GL1 2TS
Switchboard: 01452 420100, General Fax: 01452 833557

Gloucester Magistrates' Court, Gloucester Courthouse, Barbican Way, Gloucester, Gloucestershire, GL1 2JH
DX 98665 Gloucester 5
Switchboard: 01452 420100, General Fax: 01452 833557

Gloucester Probate Sub-Registry, 2nd Floor, Combined Court Building, Kimbrose Way, Gloucester, Gloucestershire, GL1 2DG
DX 98663 Gloucester 5
Switchboard: 01452 834966, General Fax: 01452 834970

Gloucestershire Family & Civil Courts, Kimbrose Way, Gloucester, Gloucestershire, GL1 2DE
DX 98660 Gloucester 5
Switchboard: 01452 834900, Fax: 01452 834923, Family Proceedings: 01452 834924

Goole Caller Office, The Court House, Estcourt Terrace, Goole, East Yorkshire, DN14 5AE

Goole Magistrates' Court, The Court House, Estcourt Terrace, Goole, East Yorkshire, DN14 5AE
Switchboard: 01482 861607, General Fax: 01482 882004

Grantham County Court, Grantham County Court, Harlaxton Road, Grantham, Lincolnshire, NG31 7SB
DX 711100 Grantham 4
Switchboard: 01476 539030, General Fax: 01476 539040

Grantham Magistrates' Court, Harlaxton Road, Grantham, Lincolnshire, NG31 7SB
DX 711100 Grantham
Switchboard: 01476 563438, General Fax: 01476 567200

Grays Magistrates' Court, The Court House, Orsett Road, Grays, Essex, RM17 5DA
Switchboard: 01245 313300, General Fax: 01245 313399

Great Grimsby Combined Court Centre, Great Grimsby Combined Court, Town Hall Square, Grimsby, Lincolnshire, DN31 1HX
DX 702007 Grimsby 3
County Court: Tel: 01472 265200, Fax: 01472 265201
Crown Court: Tel: 01472 265250, Fax: 01472 265251

Great Yarmouth Magistrates' Court, Magistrates' Courthouse, North Quay, Great Yarmouth, Norfolk, NR30 1PW
DX 139400 Great Yarmouth 3
Switchboard: 01493 849800, General Fax: 01493 852169

Greenwich Magistrates' Court, 9 Blackheath Road, Greenwich, London, SE10 8PE
DX 156800 Bromley
General Fax: 020 8276 1399, Switchboard: 0845 6013600

Grimsby Magistrates' Court, Victoria Street, Grimsby, Lincolnshire, DN31 1NH
DX 707680 Grimsby 5
Switchboard: 01472 320444, General Fax: 01472 320440

Guildford County Court, The Law Courts, Mary Road, Guildford, Surrey, GU1 4PS
DX 97860 Guildford 5
Switchboard: 01483 405300, General Fax: 01483 300031

Guildford Crown Court, Bedford Road, Guildford, Surrey, GU1 4ST
DX 97862 Guildford 5
Switchboard: 01483 468500, General Fax: 01483 579545

Guildford Magistrates' Court, Mary Road, Guildford, Surrey, GU1 4PS
DX 97865 Guildford 5
Switchboard: 01483 405300, General Fax: 01483 449208

Halesowen Magistrates' Court, Laurel Lane, Halesowen, West Midlands, B63 3DA
Switchboard: 01384 211411, General Fax: 01384 211415

Halifax County Court, Prescott Street, Halifax, West Yorkshire, HX1 2JJ
DX 702095 Halifax 2
Switchboard: 01422 344700, General Fax: 01422 360132

Halifax Magistrates' Court, PO Box 32, Harrison Road, Halifax, West Yorkshire, HX1 2AF
Switchboard: 01422 360695, General Fax: 01422 347874

Hampshire & Isle of Wight Fixed Penalty Office, Fixed Penalty Office, PO Box 431, Winchester, Hampshire, SO23 7XF
Tel: 01962 814888, Fax: 01962 814884

Haringey Magistrates' Court, Highgate Court House, Bishops Road, Archway Road, Highgate, London, N6 4HS
DX 123550 Highgate 3
Switchboard: 0845 601 3600, General Fax: 020 8273 3838

Harlow County Court, Gate House, The High, Harlow, Essex, CM20 1UW
DX 97700 Harlow 2
Switchboard: 01279 443291, General Fax: 01279 451110

Harlow Magistrates' Court, The Court House, Harlow, Essex, CM20 1HH
Switchboard: 01245 313300, General Fax: 01245 313399

Harrogate County Court, 2 Victoria Avenue, Harrogate, North Yorkshire, HG1 1EL
DX 702098 Harrogate 3
Switchboard: 01423 503921, General Fax: 01423 528679

Harrogate Magistrates' Court, The Court House, Victoria Avenue, Harrogate, North Yorkshire, HG1 1LS
DX 742910 Harrogate 3
Switchboard: 01423 722 000, General Fax: 01423 722 001

Harrow Crown Court, Hailsham Drive, off Headstone Drive, Harrow, London, HA1 4TU
DX 97335 Harrow 5
Switchboard: 020 8424 2294, General Fax: 020 8424 2209

Harrow Magistrates' Court, The Court House, Rosslyn Crescent, Wealdstone, Harrow, London, HA1 2JY
DX 30451 Harrow 3
Switchboard: 020 8427 5146, General Fax: 020 8863 9518

Hartlepool County Court, The Law Courts, Victoria Road, Hartlepool, Cleveland, TS24 8BS
DX 65121 Hartlepool 2
Switchboard: 01429 268198, General Fax: 01429 862550

Hartlepool Magistrates' Court, The Law Courts, Victoria Road, Hartlepool, Cleveland, TS24 8AG
DX 68706 Hartlepool 2
Switchboard: 01429 271451, General Fax: 01429 866696

Harwich Magistrates' Court, 363 Main Road, Dovercourt, Harwich, Essex, CO12 4DN
Switchboard: 01245 313300, General Fax: 01245 313399

Hastings County Court, The Law Courts, Bohemia Road, Hastings, East Sussex, TN34 1QX
DX 98150 Hastings 2
Switchboard: 01424 710280, General Fax: 01424 421585

Hastings Magistrates' Court, The Law Courts, Horntye Park, Bohemia Road, Hastings, East Sussex, TN34 1ND
Switchboard: 01424 437644, General Fax: 01424 429878

Hatfield Magistrates' Court, Comet Way, Hatfield, Hertfordshire, London, AL10 9SJ
Switchboard: 01923 297500, General Fax: 01923 297528

Haverfordwest County Court, Penffynnon, Hawthorn Rise, Haverfordwest, Pembrokeshire, Wales, SA61 2AX
DX 99610 Haverfordwest 2
Switchboard: 01437 772060, General Fax: 01437 769222

Haverfordwest Magistrates' Court, Penffynnon, Hawthorn Rise, Haverfordwest, Dyfed, Wales, SA61 2AX
DX 98287 Haverfordwest
Switchboard: 01437 772090, General Fax: 01437 768662

Havering Magistrates' Court, Main Road, Romford, Essex, RM1 3BH
DX 743410 Romford 15
Switchboard: 0845 601 3600, Fax: 01708 794270

Haywards Heath Law Courts, The Law Courts, Bolnore Road, Haywards Heath, Sussex, RH16 4BA
DX 135596 Haywards Heath 6
Switchboard: 01444 417611, General Fax: 01444 472639, County Court: Fax: 01444 472637

Hemel Hempstead Magistrates' Court, Dacorum Way, Hemel Hempstead, Hertfordshire, HP1 1HF
Switchboard: 01923 297500, General Fax: 01923 297528

Hendon Magistrates' Court, The Court House, The Hyde, Hendon, London, NW9 7BY
DX 154720 Hendon 4
Switchboard: 020 8511 1200, General Fax: 020 8511 1347

Hereford County Court, 1st Floor, Barclays Bank Chambers, 1-3 Broad Street, Hereford, Herefordshire, HR4 9BA
DX 701904 Hereford 2
Switchboard: 01432 357233, General Fax: 01432 352593

Hereford Crown Court, The Shirehall, St Peter's Square, Hereford, Herefordshire, HR1 2HY
Switchboard: 01432 276118, General Fax: 01432 274350

Hereford Magistrates' Court, The Court House, Bath Street, Hereford, Herefordshire, HR1 2HE
Switchboard: 01562 514000, General Fax: 01562 514111

Hertford County Court, 4th Floor, Sovereign House, Hale Road, Hertford, Hertfordshire, SG13 8DY
DX 97710 Hertford 2
Switchboard: 01992 503954, General Fax: 01992 501274

Hertford Magistrates' Court, Shire Hall, Fore Street, Hertford, Hertfordshire, SG13 1DF
Switchboard: 01438 730412, General Fax: 01438 730413

High Peak Magistrates' Court, Peak Buildings, Terrace Road, Buxton, Derbyshire, SK17 6DY
DX 701980 Buxton 2
Switchboard: 01298 23951, General Fax: 01298 26031

High Wycombe County Court, The Law Courts, Ground Floor, Easton Street, High Wycombe, Buckinghamshire, HP11 1LR
DX 98010 Reading 6
Switchboard: 0118 987 0508, General Fax: 01494 651030

High Wycombe Magistrates' Court, Law Courts, Easton Street, High Wycombe, Buckinghamshire, HP11 1LR
DX 97883 High Wycombe 1
Switchboard: 01494 651017, General Fax: 01494 651030

Highbury Corner Magistrates' Court, 51 Holloway Road, London, N7 8JA
DX 51855Highbury
Switchboard: 0845 601 3600, General Fax: 020 7506 3191

Hinckley Magistrates' Court, The Courthouse, Upper Bond Street, Hinckley, Leicestershire, LE10 1NZ
DX 742580 Hinckley 5
Switchboard: 01455 623000

Hitchin County Court, Park House, 1-12 Old Park Road, Hitchin, Hertfordshire, SG5 2JR
DX 97720 Hitchin 2
Helpdesk: 0844 892 0550, General Fax: 01462 445444

Holyhead Magistrates' Court, Law Courts, Stanley Street, Holyhead, Isle of Anglsey, Wales, LL65 1HG
Switchboard: 01407 763906, General Fax: 01407 761047

Honiton Magistrates' Court, The Court House, Dowell Street, Honiton, Devon, EX14 1LZ
Switchboard: 01392 415300, General Fax: 01392 415593

Horsham County Court, The Law Courts, Hurst Road, Horsham, West Sussex, RH12 2EU
DX 98170 Horsham 2
Switchboard: 01403 252474, General Fax: 01403 258844

Horsham Magistrates' Court, The Law Courts, Hurst Road, Horsham, West Sussex, RH12 2ET
DX 135596 Haywards Heath 6
Switchboard: 01444 417611, General Fax: 01444 472639

Houghton-le-Spring Magistrates' Court, Dairy Lane, Houghton-le-Spring, Tyne & Wear, DH4 5BL
Switchboard: 0191 5141621, Fax: 0191 5658564

Hove Trial Centre, Hove Trial Centre, The Court House, Lansdowne Road, Hove, East Sussex, BN3 3BN
DX 99402 Hove 3
Switchboard: 01273 229200, General Fax: 01273 229229

Huddersfield County Court, Queensgate House, Queensgate, Huddersfield, West Yorkshire, HD1 2RR
DX 703013 Huddersfield 2
Switchboard: 01484 421043, General Fax: 01484 426366

Huddersfield Magistrates' Court, Court House, Civic Centre, Huddersfield, West Yorkshire, HD1 2NH
Switchboard: 01484 423552, General Fax: 01484 430085

Hull & Holderness Magistrates' Court, The Law Courts, Market Place, Kingston-upon-Hull, East Yorkshire, HU1 2AD
DX 742160 Hull 20
Switchboard: 01482 328914, General Fax: 01482 219790

Huntingdon Law Courts, Walden Road, Huntingdon, Cambridgeshire, PE29 3DW
Crown/County Court: Switchboard: 01733 349161, Fax: 01733 557348
Magistrates' Court: Switchboard: 0845 310 0575, Fax: 01733 313749

Ilford County Court, Buckingham Road, Ilford, Essex, IG1 1TP
DX 97510 Ilford 3
General Enquiries: 020 8477 1920, General Fax: 020 8553 2824

Ilkeston Magistrates' Court, The Court House, Pimlico, Ilkeston, Derbyshire, DE7 5HZ
Switchboard: 01332 362000, General Fax: 01332 333183

Inner London Crown Court, Sessions House, Newington Causeway, London, SE1 6AZ
DX 97345 Southwark 3
Switchboard: 020 7234 3100, General Fax: 020 7234 3287

Inner London Family Proceedings Court, 59-65 Wells Street, London, W1A 3AE
DX 89268 Soho Square
Switchboard: 020 7805 3400, General Fax: 020 7805 3490

Ipswich County Court, 8 Arcade Street, Ipswich, Suffolk, IP1 1EJ
DX 97730 Ipswich 3
Switchboard: 01473 214256, General Fax: 01473 251797

Ipswich Crown Court, The Courthouse, 1 Russell Road, Ipswich, Suffolk, IP1 2AG
DX 729480 Ipswich 19
Switchboard: 01473 228 585, General Fax: 01473 228 560

Ipswich District Probate Registry, Ground Floor, 8 Arcade Street, Ipswich, Suffolk, IP1 1EJ
DX 97733 Ipswich 3
Switchboard: 01473 284260, General Fax: 01473 231951

Ipswich Magistrates' Court, Elm Street, Ipswich, Suffolk, IP1 2AP
DX 3232 Ipswich
Switchboard: 01473 217261, General Fax: 01473 231249

Isles of Scilly Magistrates' Court, Old Wesleyan Chapel, Garrison Lane, St Mary's,
Isles of Scilly, Cornwall, TR21 0JD
Switchboard: 01872 321900, General Fax: 01872 276227

Isleworth Crown Court, 36 Ridgeway Road, Isleworth, London, TW7 5LP
DX 97420 Isleworth 1
Switchboard: 020 8380 4500, General Fax: 020 8568 5368

Keighley County Court, County Court House, North Street, Keighley, West Yorkshire,
BD21 3SH
Switchboard: 01535 602803, General Fax: 01535 610549

Keighley Magistrates' Court (Sitting at Bingley Magistrates' Court), The Court
House, Bradford Road, Bingley, West Yorkshire, BD16 1YA
DX 21106 Bingley 2
Switchboard: 01274 568411, General Fax: 01274 551289

Kendal County Court, The Court House, Burneside Road, Kendal, Cumbria,
LA9 4NF
DX 63450 Kendal 2
Switchboard: 01539 721218, General Fax: 01539 733840

Kendal Magistrates' Court, The Court House, Burneside Road, Kendal, Cumbria,
LA9 4TJ
Switchboard: 01229 820161, General Fax: 01229 870287

Kettering County Court, Dryland Street, Kettering, Northamptonshire, NN16 0BE
DX 701886 Kettering 2
Switchboard: 01536 512471, General Fax: 01536 416857

Kettering Magistrates' Court, The Court House, London Road, Kettering,
Northamptonshire, NN15 7QP
DX 151720 Northampton 27
Switchboard: 01604 497000, General Fax: 01604 497010

Kidderminster County Court, Comberton Place, Kidderminster, Worcestershire,
DY10 1QT
Switchboard: 01562 514 000, General Fax: 01562 514 084

Kidderminster Magistrates' Court, Comberton Place, Kidderminster, Worcestershire,
DY10 1QQ
Switchboard: 01562 514000, General Fax: 01562 514097

King's Lynn County Court, Chequer House, 12 King Street, King's Lynn, Norfolk,
PE30 1ES
DX 97740 King's Lynn 2
Switchboard: 01553 772067, General Fax: 01553 769824

King's Lynn Crown Court, The Court House, College Lane, King's Lynn, Norfolk,
PE30 1PQ
Switchboard: 01553 760847, General Fax: 01553 772873

King's Lynn Magistrates' Court, The Court House, College Lane, King's Lynn, Norfolk, PE30 1PQ
DX 743330 King's Lynn 6
Switchboard: 01553 770120, General Fax: 01553 775098

Kingston-upon-Hull Combined Court Centre, Kingston-upon-Hull Combined Court, Lowgate, Humberside, HU1 2EZ
DX 703010 Hull 5
Switchboard: 01482 586161, General Fax: 01482 588527

Kingston-upon-Hull Magistrates' Court, The Law Courts, Market Place, Kingston-upon-Hull, East Yorkshire, HU1 2AD
DX 742160 Hull 20
Switchboard: 01482 328914, General Fax: 01482 219790

Kingston-upon-Thames County Court, St James Road, Kingston-upon-Thames, Surrey, KT1 2AD
DX 97890 Kingston-Upon-Thames 3
Switchboard: 020 8972 8700, General Fax: 020 8547 1426

Kingston-upon-Thames Crown Court, 6-8 Penrhyn Road, Kingston-upon-Thames, Surrey, KT1 2BB
DX 97430 Kingston-Upon-Thames 2
Switchboard: 020 8240 2500, General Fax: 020 8240 2675

Kingston-upon-Thames Magistrates' Court, The Guildhall, Kingston-upon-Thames, Surrey, KT1 1EU
DX 97893 Kingston-upon-Thames 3
Switchboard: 020 8481 6565, General Fax: 020 8481 6556

Knowsley Magistrates' Court, Court House, Lathom Road, Huyton, Merseyside, L36 9XY
DX 19488 St Helens
Switchboard: 01744 620244, General Fax: 01744 20518

Knutsford Crown Court, Sessions House, Toft Road, Knutsford, Cheshire, WA16 0PB
Switchboard: 01565 624020, General Fax: 01565 624029

Lambeth County Court, Court House, Cleaver Street, Kennington Road, London, SE11 4DZ
DX 145020 Kennington 2
Switchboard: 020 7091 4410, General Fax: 020 7587 1951

Lanbaurgh Magistrates' Court, The Court House, Church Lane, Guisborough, Cleveland, TS14 6HX
Switchboard: 01642 240301, General Fax: 01642 224010

Lancaster County Court, 2nd Floor, Mitre House, Church Street, Lancaster, Lancashire, LA1 1UZ
DX 145880 Lancaster 2
Switchboard: 01524 68112, General Fax: 01524 846478

Lancaster Crown Court, Castle Hill, Lancaster, Lancashire, LA1 1YJ
Switchboard: 01524 32454

Lancaster Magistrates' Court, George Street, Lancaster, Lancashire, LA1 1XZ,
Tel: 01524 597000, General Fax: 01524 597024

Lancaster Probate Sub-Registry, Room 111, Mitre House, Church Street, Lancaster,
Lancashire, LA1 1HE
DX 145883 Lancaster 2
Switchboard: 01524 36625, General Fax: 01542 35561

Launceston Magistrates' Court, The Court House, Dunheved Road, Launceston,
Cornwall, PL15 9JE
Switchboard: 01208 262700, General Fax: 01208 77198

Leamington Spa Magistrates' Court, The Courthouse, 3 Newbold Terrace,
Leamington Spa, Warwickshire, CV32 4EA
DX 11874 Leamington Spa 1
Switchboard: 01926 429133, General Fax: 01926 426217

Leeds Combined Court Centre, The Court House, 1 Oxford Row, Leeds, West
Yorkshire, LS1 3BG
DX 703016 Leeds 6
Switchboard: 0113 306 2800

Leeds District Magistrates' Court, Westgate, Leeds, West Yorkshire, LS1 3JP
Switchboard: 0113 245 9653, General Fax: 0113 244 4700

Leeds District Probate Registry, Coronet House, 3rd Floor, Queen Street, Leeds,
West Yorkshire, LS1 2BA
DX 26451 Leeds Park Square
Switchboard: 0113 386 3540, General Fax: 0113 247 1893

Leicester County Court, 90 Wellington Street, Leicester, Leicestershire, LE1 6HG
DX 17401 Leicester 3
Switchboard: 0116 222 5700, General Fax: 0116 222 5763

Leicester Crown Court, 90 Wellington Street, Leicester, Leicestershire, LE1 6HG
DX 10880 Leicester 3
Switchboard: 0116 222 5800, General Fax: 0116 222 5888

Leicester Magistrates' Court, 15 Pocklingtons Walk, Leicester, Leicestershire,
LE1 6BT
DX 10828 Leicester 1
Switchboard: 0116 2553666, General Fax: 0116 2545851

Leicester Probate Sub Registry, Crown Court Building, 90 Wellington Street,
Leicester, Leicestershire, LE1 6HG
DX 17403 Leicester 3
Switchboard: 0116 285 3380

Leigh & Wigan Magistrates' Court, Darlington Street, Wigan, Greater Manchester,
WN1 1DW
Switchboard: 01942 405405, General Fax: 01942 405444

Leigh County Court, Darlington Street, Wigan, Greater Manchester, WN1 1DW
Switchboard: 01942 405405, Fax: 01942 405459

Lewes Combined Court Centre, The Law Courts, High Street, Lewes, East Sussex, BN7 1YB
DX 97395 Lewes 4
Switchboard: 01273 480400, General Fax: 01273 485269

Lewes Magistrates' Court, The Courthouse, Friars Walk, Lewes, East Sussex, BN7 2PG
Switchboard: 01273 670888, General Fax: 01273 811770

Lincoln County Court, 360 High Street, Lincoln, Lincolnshire, LN5 7PS
DX 703231 Lincoln 6
Switchboard: 01522 551500, General Fax: 01522 551551

Lincoln Crown Court, The Castle, Castle Hill, Lincoln, Lincolnshire, LN1 3GA
DX 722500 Lincoln 11
Switchboard: 01522 525222, General Fax: 01522 543962

Lincoln Magistrates' Court, The Court House, 358 High Street, Lincoln, Lincolnshire, LN5 7QA
DX 703232 Lincoln 6
Switchboard: 01522 528218, General Fax: 01522 525832

Lincoln Probate Sub-Registry, 360 High Street, Lincoln, Lincolnshire, LN5 7PS
DX 703233 Lincoln 6
Switchboard: 01522 523 648, General Fax: 01522 539 903

Liskeard Magistrates' Court, The Court House, Ground Floor, Trevecca, Liskeard, Cornwall, PL14 6RF
Switchboard: 01208 262700, General Fax: 01208 77198

Liverpool Civil & Family Court, 35 Vernon Street, Liverpool, Merseyside, L2 2BX
DX 702600 Liverpool 5
Switchboard: 0151 296 2200, General Fax: 0151 296 2201

Liverpool Crown Court, The Queen Elizabeth II Law Courts, Derby Square, Liverpool, Merseyside, L2 1XA
DX 740880 Liverpool 22
Switchboard: 0151 473 7373, General Fax: 0151 471 1000

Liverpool District Probate Registry, Queen Elizabeth II Law Courts, Derby Square, Liverpool, Merseyside, L2 1XA
DX 14246 Liverpool 1
Switchboard: 0151 236 8264, General Fax: 0151 227 4634

Liverpool Magistrates' Court, 107 Dale Street, Liverpool, Merseyside, L2 2JQ
DX 707900 Liverpool 8
Switchboard: 0151 243 5500, General Fax: 0151 243 5555

Liverpool Youth Court, The Queen Elizabeth II Law Courts, Derby Square, Liverpool, Merseyside, L2 1XA
DX 740880 Liverpool 22
Tel: 0151 471 1048, Fax: 0151 471 1053

Llandrindod Wells Magistrates' Court, High Street, LLandridod Wells, Powys, Wales, LD1 6BG
Brecon Admin Office: 01874622993, Welshpool Magistrates Court Office: 01938 555968

Llandudno Magistrates' Court, Conwy Road, Llandudno, Conwy, Wales, LL30 1GA
DX 11365 Llandudno
Switchboard: 01492 871333, General Fax: 01492 872321

Llanelli County Court, 2nd Floor, Court Buildings, Town Hall Square, Llanelli,
Carmarthenshire, Wales, SA15 3AL
DX 99510 Llanelli 2
General Office: 01554 757171, General Fax: 01554 758079

Llanelli Magistrates' Court, Town Hall Square, Llanelli, Carmarthenshire, Wales,
SA15 3AW
DX 99512 Llanelli 2
Switchboard: 01554 757 201, General Fax: 01554 759 669

Llangefni County Court, County Court Buildings, Llangefni, Glanhwfa Road,
Anglesey, Isle of Anglsey, Wales, LL77 7EN
DX 702480 Llangefni 2
Switchboard: 01248 750225, General Fax: 01248 750778

Llangefni Magistrates' Court, Shire Hall Street, Glanhwfa Road, Llangefni, Isle of
Anglsey, Wales, LL77 7TW
Switchboard: 01286 669700, General Fax: 01286 669798

Llwynypia Magistrates' Court, The Court House, Glyncornel, Llwynypia, Tonypandy,
Rhondda Cynon Taf, Wales, CF40 2ER
Switchboard: 01443 480750, General Fax: 01443 485472

London Mercantile Court, The Royal Courts of Justice, Strand, London, WC2A 2LL
Tel: 020 7947 6112

London Probate Department, PRFD, First Avenue House, 42-49 High Holborn,
Ground Floor, Holborn, London, WC1V 6NP
DX 941 London Chancery Lane
Probate Helpline: 0845 3020 900, General Fax: 020 7947 6946

Loughborough Court House, 60 Pinfold Gate, Loughborough, Leicestershire,
LE11 1AZ
DX 716116 Loughborough 4
Switchboard: 01509 215715, General Fax: 01509 261714

Lowestoft County Court, Old Nelson Street, Lowestoft, Suffolk, NR32 1HJ
DX 97750 Lowestoft 2
Switchboard: 01502 501060, General Fax: 01502 513875

Lowestoft Magistrates' Court, Old Nelson Street, Lowestoft, Suffolk, NR32 1HJ
DX 97750 Lowestoft 2
Switchboard: 01502 501060, General Fax: 01502 513875

Ludlow County Court, The Guildhall, Mill Street, Ludlow, Shropshire, SY8 1BB
DX 702013 Ludlow 2
Direct all enquiries to Telford County Court

Ludlow Magistrates' Court, The Guildhall, Mill Street, Ludlow, Shropshire, SY8 1AZ
Switchboard: 01952 204500, General Fax: 01952 204554

Luton & South Bedfordshire Magistrates' Court, Stuart Street, Luton, Bedfordshire, LU1 5BL
DX 151660 Luton 16
Switchboard: 01582 524200, General Fax: 01582 524252

Luton County Court, 2nd Floor, Cresta House, Alma Street, Luton, Bedfordshire, LU1 2PU
DX 97760 Luton 4
Switchboard: 01582 506700, General Fax: 01582 506701

Luton Crown Court, 7 George Street, Luton, Bedfordshire, LU1 2AA
DX 120500 Luton 6
Switchboard: 01582 522000, General Fax: 01582 522001

Lyndhurst Magistrates' Court, The Court House, Pike's Hill, Lyndhurst, Hampshire, SO43 7AY
Main Switchboard: 023 8038 4200, General Fax: 023 8038 4201

Macclesfield County Court, 2nd Floor, Silk House, Park Green, Macclesfield, Cheshire, SK11 7NA
DX 702498 Macclesfield 3
Switchboard: 01625 412800, General Fax: 01625 501262

Macclesfield Magistrates' Court, The Law Courts, 6-8 Hibel Road, Macclesfield, Cheshire, SK10 2AB
Switchboard: 0870 1626261, General Fax: 01606 48740

Maidstone Combined Court Centre, The Law Courts, Barker Road, Maidstone, Kent, ME16 8EQ
DX 130065 Maidstone 7
Switchboard: 01622 202000, Crown Court Fax: 01622 202001, County Court Fax: 01622 202002

Maidstone Magistrates' Court, The Courthouse, Palace Avenue, Maidstone, Kent, ME15 6LL
Switchboard: 01622 671041, General Fax: 01622 691800

Maidstone Probate Sub-Registry, The Law Courts, Barker Road, Maidstone, Kent, ME16 8EQ
DX 130066 Maidstone 7
Switchboard: 01622 202048

Manchester City Magistrates' Court, Crown Square, Manchester, Greater Manchester, M60 1PR
Switchboard: 0161 830 4200, General Fax: 0161 830 4208

Manchester County Court, Manchester Civil Justice Centre, 1 Bridge Street West, Manchester, Greater Manchester, M60 9DJ
DX 724783 Manchester 44
Switchboard: 0161 240 5000

Manchester Crown Court (Crown Square), Courts of Justice, Crown Square, Manchester, Greater Manchester, M3 3FL
DX 702538 Manchester 11
Switchboard: 0161 954 1800, General Fax: 0161 954 1705

Manchester Crown Court (Minshull Street), The Court House, Minshull Street, Manchester, Greater Manchester, M1 3FS
DX 724860 Manchester 43
Switchboard: 0161 954 7500, General Fax: 0161 954 7600

Manchester District Probate Registry, Manchester Civil Justice Centre, Ground Floor, 1 Bridge Street West, PO Box 4240, Manchester, Greater Manchester, M60 1WJ
DX 724784 Manchester 44
Switchboard: 0161 240 5700

Mansfield County Court, Beech House, 58 Commercial Gate, Mansfield, Nottinghamshire, NG18 1EU
DX 702180 Mansfield 3
Switchboard: 01623 656406, General Fax: 01623 626561

Mansfield Magistrates' Court, Rosemary Street, Mansfield, Nottinghamshire, NG19 6EE
DX 179560 Mansfield 9
Switchboard: 01623 451500, General Fax: 01623 451648

Margate Magistrates' Court, The Courthouse, Cecil Square, Margate, Kent, CT9 1RL
Switchboard: 01304 218600, General Fax: 01304 213819

Market Drayton Magistrates' Court, The Magistrates Court, Cheshire Street, Market Drayton, Shropshire, TF9 1PQ
Switchboard: 01743 458500, General Fax: 01743 458502

Market Harborough Magistrates' Court, Dodderidge Road, Market Harborough, Leicestershire, LE16 7NH
Switchboard: 0116 255 3666, Switchboard: 020 7506 3761

Mayor's & City of London Court, Guildhall Buildings, Basinghall Street, London, EC2V 5AR
DX 97520 Moorgate EC2
Switchboard: 020 7796 5400, General Fax: 020 7796 5424

Medway County Court, Anchorage House, 47-67 High Street, Chatham, Kent, ME4 4DW
DX 98180 Chatham 4
Switchboard: 01634 810720, General Fax: 01634 811332

Medway Magistrates' Court, The Court House, The Brook, Chatham, Kent, ME4 4JZ
Switchboard: 01634 830232, General Fax: 01634 847400

Melton Mowbray County Court, The Court House, Norman Way, Melton Mowbray, Leicestershire, LE13 1NH
DX 701937 Melton Mowbray 2
Switchboard: 01664 485100, General Fax: 01664 501869

Melton Mowbray Magistrates' Court, The Courthouse, Norman Way, Melton Mowbray, Leicestershire, LE13 1NH
Switchboard: 01509 215715

Mendip Magistrates' Court, North Parade Road, Bath, Somerset, BA1 5AF
DX 138142 Bath 5
Switchboard: 01225 463281, General Fax: 01225 420255

Merthyr Tydfil Combined Court Centre, The Law Courts, Glebeland Place, Merthyr Tydfil, South Wales, Wales, CF47 8BH
DX 99582 Merthyr Tydfil 2
Switchboard: 01685 727600, General Fax: 01685 727703

Middlesbrough County Court at Teesside Combined Court, The Law Courts, Russell Street, Middlesbrough, Cleveland, TS1 2AE
DX 65152 Middlesbrough 2
Switchboard: 01642 340000, General Fax: 01642 340002

Middlesbrough Probate Sub-Registry, Teesside Combined Court Centre, Russell Street, Middlesbrough, Cleveland, TS1 2AE
DX 60536 Middlesbrough
Switchboard: 01642 430001

Mildenhall Magistrates' Court, The Court House, Queensway, Mildenhall, Suffolk, IP28 7ER
Switchboard: 01284 778000, General Fax: 01284 778020

Milton Keynes County Court, 351 Silbury Boulevard (Rear), Witan Gate East, Central Milton Keynes, Buckinghamshire, MK9 2DT
DX 136266 Milton Keynes 6
General Fax: 01908 230063, Civil matters: 01908 302800, Family Matters: 01908 302801

Milton Keynes Magistrates' Court, 301 Silbury Boulevard, Witan Gate East, Milton Keynes, Buckinghamshire, MK9 2AJ
DX 136270 Milton Keynes 6
Switchboard: 01908 451145, General Fax: 01908 451146

Minehead Magistrates' Court, Townsend Road, Minehead, Somerset, TA24 5RJ
Switchboard: 01823 257084, General Fax: 01823 335195

Mold County Court, Law Courts, Civic Centre, Mold, Flintshire, Wales, CH7 1AE
DX 702521 Mold 2
Switchboard: 01352 707330, General Fax: 01352 707333

Mold Crown Court, The Law Courts, Civic Centre, Mold, Flintshire, Wales, CH7 1AE
Switchboard: 01352 707340, General Fax: 01352 753874

Mold Magistrates' Court, Magistrates' Clerks Office, County Civic Centre, Mold, Flintshire, Wales, CH7 1AE
Switchboard: 01352 707342/707381, General Fax: 01352 753551

Money Claim Online (MCOL), 4th Floor, St Katharine's House, 21-27 St Katharine's Street, Northampton, Northamptonshire, NN1 2LH
DX 702885 Northampton 7
Switchboard: 0845 601 5935, General Fax: 0845 601 5889

Morpeth & Berwick County Court, Fountain House, Newmarket, Morpeth, Northumberland, NE61 1LA
DX 65124 Morpeth 2
General Office: 01670 512221, General Fax: 01670 504188, Civil & Family enquiries: 01670 503015

Neath & Port Talbot County Court, Forster Road, Neath, South Wales, Wales,
SA11 3BN
DX 99550 Neath 2
Switchboard: 01639 642267, General Fax: 01639 633505

Neath Magistrates' Court, Fairfield Way, Neath, South Wales, Wales, SA11 1RF
Switchboard: 01639 765900, General Fax: 01639 765954

Nelson County Court, Phoenix Chambers, 9-13 Holme Street, Nelson, Lancashire,
BB9 9SU
DX 702560 Nelson 2
Switchboard: 01282 601177, General Fax: 01282 619557

Newark & Southwell Magistrates' Court, Magnus Street, Newark, Nottinghamshire,
NG24 1LD
DX 11836 Newark 2
Switchboard: 01636 688200, General Fax: 01636 688222

Newark County Court, Beech House, 58 Commercial Gate, Mansfield,
Nottinghamshire, NG18 1EU
DX 702180 Mansfield 3
Switchboard: 01623 656406

Newbury County Court, The Court House, Mill Lane, Newbury, Berkshire, RG14 5QS
DX 30816 Newbury 1
Switchboard: 01635 642210, General Fax: 01635 529580

Newcastle District Probate Registry, 1 Waterloo Square, Newcastle-upon-Tyne,
Tyne & Wear, NE1 4DR
DX 61081 Newcastle-upon-Tyne 14
Switchboard: 0191 211 2170, General Fax: 0191 211 2184

Newcastle under Lyme Magistrates' Court, The Court House, Ryecroft, Newcastle-
under-Lyme, Staffordshire, ST5 2DT
Switchboard: 01782 418300, General Fax: 01782 744782

Newcastle-upon-Tyne Magistrates' Court, PO Box 839, Market Street, Newcastle-
upon-Tyne, Tyne & Wear, NE99 1AU
DX 61098 Newcastle-upon-Tyne
Switchboard: 0191 232 7326, General Fax: 0191 221 0025

Newcastle-upon-Tyne Combined Court Centre, The Law Courts, The Quayside,
Newcastle-upon-Tyne, Tyne & Wear, NE1 3LA
DX 65127 Newcastle-upon-Tyne 2
Switchboard: 0191 201 2000, General Fax: 0191 201 2001

Newport (Gwent) County Court, Olympia House, 3rd Floor, Upper Dock Street,
Newport, Gwent, Wales, NP20 1PQ
DX 99480 Newport (South Wales) 4
Switchboard: 01633 227150, General Fax: 01633 263820

Newport (Isle of Wight) Crown & County Court, The Law Courts, 1 Quay Street,
Newport, Isle of Wight, PO30 5YT
DX 98460 Newport IW2
Switchboard: 01983 535 100, County Court Fax: 01983 821 039, Crown Court Fax:
01983 554 977

Newport (South Wales) Crown Court, Faulkner Road, Newport, Gwent, Wales, NP20 4PR
DX 99460 Newport 1/2
Switchboard: 01633 266211, General Fax: 01633 216824

Newport Magistrates' Court, Civic Centre, Faulkner Road, Newport, Gwent, Wales, NP20 4UR
Switchboard: 01633 645000, General Fax: 01633 645177

Newton Abbot Magistrates' Court, The Court House, Newfoundland Way, Newton Abbot, Devon, TQ12 1NG
DX 98740 Torquay 4
Switchboard: 01803 612211, General Fax: 01803 618618

Newton Aycliffe Magistrates' Court, Central Avenue, Newton Aycliffe, Co. Durham, DL5 5RT
DX 63808 Newton Aycliffe
Switchboard: 01325 318114, General Fax: 01325 327697

North Avon Magistrates' Court, Kennedy Way, Yate, Bristol, BS37 4PY
DX 743500 Yate 2
Switchboard: 01454 310505, General Fax: 01454 319404

North East Derbyshire & Dales Magistrates' Court, Magistrates' Court, Tapton Lane, Chesterfield, Derbyshire, S41 7TW
DX 742041 Chesterfield 7
Switchboard: 01246 224040, General Fax: 01246 246492

North Liverpool Community Justice Centre, Boundary Street, Liverpool, Merseyside, L5 2QD
DX 730120 Kirkdale
Switchboard: 0151 298 3600, Main Fax: 0151 298 3725

North Sefton Magistrates' Court, Albert Road, Southport, Merseyside, PR9 0LJ
Switchboard: 0151 933 6999, General Fax: 01704 500226

North Shields County Court, Kings Court, Earl Grey Way, Royal Quays, North Shields, Tyne & Wear, NE29 6AR
DX 65137 North Shields 2
Switchboard: 0191 2982339, General Fax: 0191 2982337

North Somerset Magistrates' Court, North Somerset Courthouse, The Hedges, St Georges, Weston-Super-Mare, Avon, BS22 7BB
DX 152361 Weston-Super-Mare 5
Switchboard: 01934 528 700, General Fax: 01934 528 599

North Tyneside Magistrates' Court, The Courthouse, Tynemouth Road, North Shields, Tyne & Wear, NE30 1AG
Switchboard: 0191 296 0099, General Fax: 0191 296 2478

North Yorkshire Magistrates' Courts Central Finance Unit, PO Box 87, Northallerton, North Yorkshire, DL7 8GF
DX 69143 Northallerton
Switchboard: 01609 783539, General Fax: 01609 760918

Northallerton Magistrates' Court, 3 Racecourse Lane, Northallerton, North Yorkshire, DL7 8QZ
DX 742420 Northallerton
Switchboard: 01609 788200, General Fax: 01609 783509

Northampton Combined Court, 85/87 Lady's Lane, Northampton, Northamptonshire, NN1 3HQ
DX 725380 Northampton 21
Switchboard: 01604 470400, General Fax: 01604 232398

Northampton County Court Bulk Centre, 4th Floor, St Katharine's House, 21-27 St Katharine's Street, Northampton, Northamptonshire, NN1 2LH
DX 702885 Northampton 7
County Court Bulk Centre: Tel: 0845 408 5302, Fax: 0845 408 5304
Money Claim Online: Tel: 0845 601 5935, Fax: 0845 601 5889

Northampton Magistrates' Court, Campbell Square, Northampton, Northamptonshire, NN1 3EB
DX 151720 Northampton 27
Switchboard: 01604 497000, General Fax: 01604 497010

Northampton Magistrates' Court Office, Regent's Pavilion, Summerhouse Road, Moulton Park, Northamptonshire, NN3 6AS
DX 151720 Northampton 27
Switchboard: 01604 497000, General Fax: 01604 497010

Northwich Magistrates' & County Court, The Court House, Chester Way, Northwich, Cheshire, CW9 5ES
Magistrates' Court: Switchboard: 0870 1626261, Fax: 01606 48740
County Court: Switchboard: 01606 338508, Fax: 01606 48740

Norwich Combined Court Centre, The Law Courts, Bishopgate, Norwich, Norfolk, NR3 1UR
DX 97385 Norwich 5
Switchboard: 01603 728200, General Fax: 01603 760863

Norwich Magistrates' Court, Bishopgate, Norwich, Norfolk, NR3 1UP
DX 97389 Norwich 5
Switchboard: 01603 679500, General Fax: 01603 663263

Norwich Probate Sub-Registry, Combined Court Building, The Law Courts, Bishopgate, Norwich, Norfolk, NR3 1UR
DX 97390 Norwich 5
Switchboard: 01603 728267, General Fax: 01603 627469

Nottingham County Court, 60 Canal Street, Nottingham, Nottinghamshire, NG1 7EJ
DX 702380 Nottingham 7
Switchboard: 0115 910 3500, General Fax: 0115 910 3510

Nottingham Crown Court, 60 Canal Street, Nottingham, Nottinghamshire, NG1 7EL
DX 702383 Nottingham 7
Switchboard: 0115 910 3551, General Fax: 0115 910 3599

Nottingham Magistrates' Court, Carrington Street, Nottingham, Nottinghamshire, NG2 1EE
DX 719030 Nottingham 32
Switchboard: 0115 955 8111, General Fax: 0115 9558139

Nottingham Probate Sub-Registry, Butt Dyke House, 33 Park Row, Nottingham, Nottinghamshire, NG1 6GR
DX 10055 Nottingham
Switchboard: 0115 941 4288, General Fax: 0115 950 3383

Nuneaton County Court, Warwickshire Justice Centre, PO Box 3878, Vicarage Street, Nuneaton, Warwickshire, CV11 4JU
DX 701940 Nuneaton 2
Switchboard: 02476 482970, General Fax: 02476 352835

Nuneaton Magistrates' Court, Warwickshire Justice Centre, Vicarage Street, Nuneaton, Warwickshire, CV11 4JU,
Criminal Enquiries: 01926 429133, Family Enquiries: 02476 342279, General Fax: 02476 352835

Oldham County Court, New Radcliffe Street, Oldham, Greater Manchester, OL1 1NL
DX 702595 Oldham 2
Switchboard: 0161 290 4200, General Fax: 0161 290 4222

Oldham Magistrates' Court, St Domingo Place, West Street, Oldham, Greater Manchester, OL1 1QE
Switchboard: 0161 620 2331, General Fax: 0161 652 0172

Ormskirk Magistrates' Court, Magistrates' Court, Derby Street, Ormskirk, Lancashire, L39 2BJ
General Fax: 01257 261948, Switchboard: 01257 240500

Oswestry County Court, The Court House, Holbache Road, Oswestry, Shropshire, SY11 1RP
DX 701958 Oswestry 2
Main Reception: 01691 652127, General Fax: 01691 658902

Oswestry Magistrates' Court, Holbache Road, Oswestry, Shropshire, SY11 1RP
Switchboard: 01743 458500, General Fax: 01743 458502

Oxford & Southern Oxfordshire Magistrates Court, The Court House, PO Box 37, Speedwell Street, Oxford, Oxfordshire, OX1 1RZ
DX 96452 Oxford 4
Switchboard: 0870 241 2808, General Fax: 01865 448024

Oxford Combined Court Centre, St Aldates, Oxford, Oxfordshire, OX1 1TL
DX 96450 Oxford 4
Switchboard: 01865 264200, Civil Fax: 01865 790773, Crown Court Fax: 01865 264253

Oxford District Probate Registry, Combined Court Building, St Aldates, Oxford, Oxfordshire, OX1 1LY
DX 96454 Oxford 4
Switchboard: 01865 793 050, General Fax: 01865 793 090

Patents Court, The Royal Courts of Justice, Strand, London, WC2A 2LL
Switchboard: 020 7947 6000

Penrith County Court, The Court House, Lowther Terrace, Penrith, Cumbria, CA11 7QL
DX 65207 Penrith
Switchboard: 01768 862535, General Fax: 01768 899700

Penrith Magistrates' Court, Court House, Lowther Terrace, Penrith, Cumbria, CA11 7QL
Switchboard: 01228 518800, General Fax: 01228 518844

Penzance County Court, Trevear, Alverton Terrace, Penzance, Cornwall, TR18 4GH
Switchboard: 01872 267460, General Fax: 01872 222348

Penzance Magistrates' Court, The Guildhall, St John's Hall, Penzance, Cornwall, TR18 2QD
Switchboard: 01872 321900, General Fax: 01872 276227

Peterborough Combined Court Centre, Crown Buildings, Rivergate, Peterborough, Cambridgeshire, PE1 1EJ
DX 702302 Peterborough 8
Switchboard: 01733 349161, General Fax: 01733 557348, Crown Court Fax: 01733 891563

Peterborough Magistrates' Court, The Court House, Bridge Street, Peterborough, Cambridgeshire, PE1 1ED
DX 742250 Peterborough 23
Switchboard: 0845 310 0575, General Fax: 0173 331 3749

Peterborough Probate Sub-Registry, 1st Floor, Crown Building, Rivergate, Peterborough, Cambridgeshire, PE1 1EJ
DX 702305 Peterborough 8
Switchboard: 01733 562 802, General Fax: 01733 313 016

Peterlee Magistrates' Court, St Aidans Way, Peterlee, Co. Durham, SR8 1QR
Switchboard: 0191 387 0700, General Fax: 0191 387 0746

Plymouth Combined Court, The Law Courts, 10 Armada Way, Plymouth, Devon, PL1 2ER
DX 98470 Plymouth 7
Switchboard: 01752 677400, County Court Fax: 01752 677455, Crown Court Fax: 01752 208292, Family Fax: 01752 208286

Plymouth Magistrates' Court, St Andrews Street, Plymouth, Devon, PL1 2DP
Switchboard: 01752 206200, General Fax: 01752 206194

Pontefract County Court, Horsefair House, Horsefair, Pontefract, West Yorkshire, WF8 1RJ
DX 703022 Pontefract 2
Switchboard: 01977 702357, General Fax: 01977 600204

Pontefract Magistrates' Court, The Court House, 2 Front Street, Pontefract, West Yorkshire, WF8 1BW
Switchboard: 01977 691600, General Fax: 01977 691610

Pontypool County Court, Park Road, Riverside, Pontypool, Torfaen, South Wales, Wales, NP4 6NZ
DX 117500 Pontypool 2
Switchboard: 01495 762248, General Fax: 01495 762467

Pontypridd County Court, The Courthouse, Courthouse Street, Pontypridd, Rhondda Cynon Taf, Wales, CF37 1JR
DX 99620 Pontypridd 2
Switchboard: 01443 490800, General Fax: 01443 480305

Pontypridd Magistrates' Court, Union Street, Pontypridd, Rhondda Cynon Taf, Wales, CF37 1SD
Switchboard: 01443 480750, General Fax: 01443 485472

Poole County Court, The Law Courts, Civic Centre, Park Road, Poole, Dorset, BH15 2NS
DX 98700 Poole 4
Switchboard: 01202 741150, General Fax: 01202 747245

Poole Magistrates' Court, The Law Courts, Park Road, Poole, Dorset, BH15 2NS
DX 98700 Poole 4
Switchboard: 01202 745309, General Fax: 01202 711886

Port Talbot Magistrates' Court, Cramic Way, Port Talbot, South Wales, Wales, SA13 1RU
Switchboard: 01639 765900, General Fax: 01639 765954

Portsmouth Combined Court Centre, The Courts of Justice, Winston Churchill Avenue, Portsmouth, Hampshire, PO1 2EB
DX 98490 Portsmouth 5
Switchboard: 02392 893000, General Fax: 02392 826385, Crown Court Fax: 02392 816859

Portsmouth Magistrates' Court, The Law Courts, Winston Churchill Avenue, Portsmouth, Hampshire, PO1 2DQ
DX 98494 Portsmouth 5
Switchboard: 023 9281 9421, Fax: 023 9229 3085

Prestatyn Magistrates' Court, Victoria Road, Prestatyn, Denbighshire, Wales, LL19 7TE
Switchboard: 01745 851916, General Fax: 01745 887046

Preston Combined Court Centre, The Law Courts, Ring Way, Preston, Lancashire, PR1 2LL
DX 702660 Preston 5
Switchboard: 01772 844700, County Court Fax: 01772 844710, Crown Court Fax: 01772 844759

Preston Magistrates' Court, PO Box 52, Lawson Street, Preston, Lancashire, PR1 2QT
Switchboard: 01772 208000, General Fax: 01772 208026

Principal Registry of the Family Division, First Avenue House, 42-49 High Holborn, London, WC1V 6NP
DX 396 London/Chancery Lane
Switchboard: 020 7947 6000

Pwllheli Magistrates' Court, Troed yr Allt, Pwllheli, Gwynedd, Wales, LL53 5ED
Switchboard: 01286 669700, General Fax: 01286 669798

Queen's Bench Division, The Royal Courts of Justice, Strand, London, WC2A 2LL
Switchboard: 020 7947 6000

Rawtenstall County Court, 1 Grange Street, Rawtenstall, Lancashire, BB4 7RT
DX 702565 Rawtenstall 2
Switchboard: 01706 214614, General Fax: 01706 219814

Rawtenstall Magistrates' Court, The Court House, Oakley Road, Rossendale, Rawtenstall, Lancashire, BB4 6RB
DX 741470 Burnley 7
Switchboard: 01282 610000, General Fax: 01282 610034

Reading County Court, 160-163 Friar Street, Reading, Berkshire, RG1 1HE
DX 98010 Reading 6
Switchboard: 0118 987 0500, General Fax: 0118 987 0555

Reading Crown Court, Old Shire Hall, The Forbury, Reading, Berkshire, RG1 3EH
DX 97440 Reading 5
Switchboard: 0118 967 4400, General Fax: 0118 967 4444

Reading Magistrates' Court, Civic Centre, Reading, Berkshire, RG1 7TQ
DX 151160 Reading 25
Switchboard: 0118 980 1800, Fax: 0118 980 1830

Redbridge Magistrates' Court, 850 Cranbrook Road, Barkingside, Ilford, Essex, IG6 1HW
DX 156842 Ilford 9
Switchboard: 084 5601 3600, General Fax: 020 8437 6561

Redditch County Court, 13 Church Road, Redditch, Worcestershire, B97 4AB
DX 701880 Redditch 2
Switchboard: 01527 67822, General Fax: 01527 65791

Redditch Magistrates' Court, Grove Street, Redditch, Worcestershire, B98 8DB
Switchboard: 01562 514000, General Fax: 01562 514323

Redhill Magistrates' Court, The Law Courts, Hatchlands Road, Redhill, Surrey, RH1 6DH
DX 98021 Redhill West
Switchboard: 01737 765581, General Fax: 01737 778372

Reedley Magistrates' Court, The Court House, PO Box 64, Colne Road, Reedley, Burnley, Lancashire, BB10 2NQ
DX 741470 Burnley 7
Switchboard: 01282 610000, General Fax: 01282 610034

Reigate County Court, The Law Courts, Hatchlends Road, Redhill, Surrey, RH1 6BL
DX 98020 Redhill West
Switchboard: 01737 763637, General Fax: 01737 766917

Retford Magistrates' Court, The Court House, Exchange Street, Retford, Nottinghamshire, DN22 6BL
Switchboard: 01909 486111, General Fax: 01909 473521

Rhyl County Court, The Courthouse, Clwyd Street, Rhyl, Denbighshire, Wales, LL18 3LA
DX 702489 Rhyl 2
Switchboard: 01745 352940, General Fax: 01745 336726

Richmond-upon-Thames Magistrates' Court, The Court House, Parkshot, Richmond, Surrey, TW9 2RF
DX 155810 Richmond 4
Switchboard: 020 8271 2300, General Fax: 020 8271 2330

Rochdale Magistrates' Court, The Courthouse, PO Box 8, Town Meadows, Rochdale, Lancashire, OL16 1AR
Switchboard: 01706 514800, General Fax: 01706 514850

Romford County Court, 2a Oaklands Avenue, Romford, Essex, RM1 4DP
DX 97530 Romford 2
Switchboard: 01708 775353, General Fax: 01708 756653

Rotherham County Court, Rotherham Law Courts, The Statutes, PO Box 15, Rotherham, South Yorkshire, S60 1YW
DX 703025 Rotherham 4
Switchboard: 01709 839339, Fax: 01709 370082

Rotherham Magistrates' Court, Rotherham Law Courts, The Statutes, off Main Street, Rotherham, South Yorkshire, S60 1YW
DX 703025 Rotherham 4
Switchboard: 01709 839339, General Fax: 01709 370082

Royal Courts of Justice, Strand, London, WC2A 2LL
Switchboard: 0207 947 6000

Rugby County Court, The New Courthouse, Newbold Road, Rugby, Warwickshire, Cv21 2LQ
DX 701934 Rugby 2
Switchboard: 01788 542543, General Fax: 01788 866004

Rugby Magistrates' Court, Newbold Road, Rugby, Warwickshire, CV21 2DH
Criminal Enquiries: 01926 429 133, Family Enquiries: 02476 342279, General Fax: 01926 426217

Runcorn (Halton) Magistrates' Court, The Court House, Halton Lea, Runcorn, Cheshire, WA7 2HA
DX 17793 Warrington 1
Switchboard: 0870 162 6261, General Fax: 01925 231284

Runcorn County Hearing Centre, The Court House, Halton Lea, Runcorn, Cheshire, WA7 2HA
DX 17793 Warrington 1

Salford County Court, Prince William House, Peel Cross Road (off Eccles New Road), Salford, Lancashire, Salford, Greater Manchester, M5 4RR
DX 702630 Salford 5
Switchboard: 0161 7457511, General Fax: 0161 7457202

Salford Magistrates' Court, Bexley Square, Salford, Greater Manchester, M3 6DJ
DX 708270 Salford 8
Switchboard: 0161 834 9457, General Fax: 0161 839 1806

Salisbury Law Courts, Salisbury Law Courts, Wilton Road, Salisbury, Wiltshire, SP2 7EP
DX 98500 Salisbury 2
Switchboard: 01722 345200, Fax: 01722 345201

Salisbury Magistrates' Court, The Guildhall, Market Square, Salisbury, Wiltshire, SP1 1JH
Switchboard: 01722 333225, General Fax: 01722 413395

Scarborough County Court, Pavilion House, Valley Bridge Road, Scarborough, North Yorkshire, YO11 2JS
DX 65140 Scarborough 2
Switchboard: 01723 366361, General Fax: 01723 501992

Scarborough Magistrates' Court, The Law Courts, Northway, Scarborough, North Yorkshire, YO12 7AE
DX 68893 Scarborough
Switchboard: 01723 505000, General Fax: 01723 353250

Scunthorpe County Court, Scunthorpe Court Centre, Laneham Street, Scunthorpe, Lincolnshire, DN15 6JY
DX 742212 Scunthorpe 10
Switchboard: 01724 281100, Fax: 01724 281890

Scunthorpe Magistrates' Court, Scunthorpe Court Centre, Laneham Street, Scunthorpe, Lincolnshire, DN15 6JY
Switchboard: 01724 281100, General Fax: 01724 281890

Sedgemoor Magistrates' Court, The Court House, Northgate, Bridgwater, Somerset, TA6 3YL
Switchboard: 01823 257084, General Fax: 01823 335195

Selby Magistrates' Court, Court House, New Lane, Selby, North Yorkshire, YO8 4QB
Switchboard: 01904 615200, General Fax: 01904 615201

Senior Courts Costs Office, Cliffords Inn, Fetter Lane, London, EC4A 1DQ
DX 44454 Strand
Switchboard: 020 7947 6000

Sevenoaks Magistrates' Court, The Courthouse, Morewood Close, London Road, Sevenoaks, Kent, TN13 2HU
Switchboard: 01622 671041, General Fax: 01622 691800

Sheffield Combined Court Centre, The Law Courts, 50 West Bar, Sheffield, South Yorkshire, S3 8PH
DX 703028 Sheffield 6
Switchboard: 0114 281 2400, General Fax: 0114 281 2425, Family Proceedings Fax: 0114 201 5130

Sheffield Magistrates' Court, Castle Street, Sheffield, South Yorkshire, S3 8LU
DX 10599 Sheffield 1
Switchboard: 0114 2760760, General Fax: 0114 2720129

Sheffield Probate Sub-Registry, PO Box 832, The Law Courts, 50 West Bar, Sheffield, South Yorkshire, S3 8YR
DX 742916 Sheffield 6
Switchboard: 0114 281 2596, General Fax: 0114 273 0848

Sherborne Magistrates' Court, The Court House, Digby Road, Sherborne, Dorset, DT9 3NL
Switchboard: 01305 783891, General Fax: 01305 761418

Shrewsbury County Court, 4th Floor, Cambrian Business Centre, Chester Street, Shrewsbury, Shropshire, SY1 1NA
DX 702047 Shrewsbury 3
Switchboard: 01743 289069, General Fax: 01743 237954

Shrewsbury Crown Court, The Shirehall, Abbey Foregate, Shrewsbury, Shropshire, SY2 6LU
DX 702022 Shrewsbury 2
Switchboard: 01743 260820, General Fax: 01743 244236

Shrewsbury Magistrates' Court, The Court House, Preston Street, Shrewsbury, Shropshire, SY2 5NX
Switchboard: 01743 458500, General Fax: 01743 458502

Sittingbourne Magistrates' Court, The Court House, 1 Park Road, Sittingbourne, Kent, ME10 1DR
Switchboard: 01622 671041, General Fax: 01622 691800

Skegness County Court, 55 Norfolk Street, Boston, Lincolnshire, PE21 6PE
DX 701922 Boston 2
Switchboard: 01205 366080, General Fax: 01205 311692

Skegness Magistrates' Court, The Court House, Park Avenue, Skegness, Lincolnshire, PE25 1BH
DX 743030 Skegness 3
Switchboard: 01754 898848, General Fax: 01754 767318

Skipton County Court, The Court House, Otley Street, Skipton, North Yorkshire, BD23 1RH
DX 703031 Skipton 2
Switchboard: 01756 692650, General Fax: 01756 692655

Skipton Magistrates' Court, The Court House, Otley Street, Skipton, North Yorkshire, BD23 1RQ
DX 703031 Skipton 2
Switchboard: 01756 692670, General Fax: 01756 701169

Sleaford Magistrates' Court, Market Place, Sleaford, Lincolnshire, NG34 7SH
Switchboard: 01476 563438, General Fax: 01476 567200

Slough County Court, The Law Courts, Windsor Road, Slough, Berkshire, SL1 2HE
DX 98030 Slough 3
Switchboard: 01753 690300, General Fax: 01753 575990

Snaresbrook Crown Court, 75 Hollybush Hill, Snaresbrook, London, E11 1QW
DX 98240 Wanstead 2
Switchboard: 020 8530 0000, General Fax: 020 8530 0072

Solihull Magistrates' Court, The Court House, Homer Road, Solihull, West Midlands, B91 3RD
DX 708350 Solihull 14
Switchboard: 0121 705 8101, General Fax: 0121 711 2045

South Cheshire Magistrates' Court, The Law Courts, Civic Centre, Crewe, Cheshire, CW1 2DT
Switchboard: 01270 655927, General Fax: 01270 589357

South East Northumberland Magistrates' Court, The Law Courts, Bedlington, Northumberland, NE22 7LX
DX 62705 Bedlington
Switchboard: 01670 531100, General Fax: 01670 820133

South Ribble Magistrates' Court, Lancastergate, Leyland, Lancashire, PR25 2EX
General Fax: 01257 261948, Switchboard: 01257 240500

South Sefton Magistrates' Court, Merton Road, Bootle, Merseyside, L20 3XX
DX 707620 Bootle 3
Switchboard: 0151 933 6999, General Fax: 0151 922 4285

South Shields County Court, Millbank, Secretan Way, South Shields, Tyne & Wear,
NE33 1RG
DX 65143 South Shields 3
Switchboard: 0191 4563343, General Fax: 0191 4279503

South Somerset & Mendip Magistrates' Court, The Law Courts, Petters Way,
Yeovil, Somerset, BA20 1SW
DX 100537 Yeovil
Switchboard: 01935 426281, General Fax: 01935 431022

South Tyneside Magistrates' Court, Millbank, Secretan Way, South Shields, Tyne &
Wear, NE33 1RG
DX 68670 South Shields 6
Switchboard: 0191 4558800, General Fax: 0191 4274499

South Wales Central Finance Unit, Cramic Way, Port Talbot, South Wales, Wales,
SA13 1RU
Switchboard: 01639 889494

South Western Magistrates' Court, 176a Lavender Hill, Battersea, London,
SW11 1JU
DX 58559 Clapham Junction
Switchboard: 0845 601 3600, General Fax: 020 7805 1448

South Worcestershire Magistrates' Court, Castle Street, Worcester, Worcestershire,
WR1 3QZ
Switchboard: 01905 743200, General Fax: 01905 743346

Southampton Combined Court Centre, The Courts of Justice, London Road,
Southampton, Hampshire, SO15 2XQ
DX 111000 Southampton 11
Main Switchboard: 02380 213200, County Court Fax: 02380 213222, Crown Court
Fax: 02380 213234

Southampton Magistrates' Court, 100 The Avenue, Southampton, Hampshire,
SO17 1EY
DX 135986 Southampton 32
Main Switchboard: 023 8038 4200, General Fax: 023 8038 4201

Southend County Court, Tylers House, Tylers Avenue, Southend, Essex, SS1 2AW
DX 97780 Southend on Sea 2
Switchboard: 01702 601991, General Fax: 01702 603090

Southend Crown Court, The Court House, Victoria Avenue, Southend-on-Sea,
Essex, SS2 6EG
Switchboard: 01268 458000, General Fax: 01268 458100

Southend Magistrates' Court, The Court House, 80 Victoria Avenue, Southend-on-
Sea, Essex, SS2 6EU
Switchboard: 01245 313300, General Fax: 01245 313399

Southern Derbyshire Magistrates' Court, The Court House, St Mary's Gate, Derby, Derbyshire, DE1 3JR
DX 707570 Derby 8
Switchboard: 01332 362000, General Fax: 01332 333183

Southport County Court, Dukes House, 34 Hoghton Street, Southport, Merseyside, PR9 0PU
DX 702580 Southport 2
Switchboard: 01704 531541, General Fax: 01704 542487

Southport Magistrates' Court, Law Courts, Albert Road, Southport, Merseyside, PR9 0LJ
DX 708200/1/2 Southport
Switchboard: 0151 933 6999, General Fax: 0151 922 4285

Southwark Crown Court, 1 English Grounds (off Battlebridge Lane), Southwark, London, SE1 2HU
DX 39913 London Bridge South
Switchboard: 020 7522 7200, General Fax: 020 7522 7300

Spalding Magistrates' Court, The Sessions House, Sheepmarket, Spalding, Lincolnshire, PE11 1BB
Switchboard: 01476 563438, General Fax: 01476 567200

St Albans County Court, The Court Building, Bricket Road, St Albans, Hertfordshire, AL13JW
DX 97770 St Albans 2
Helpdesk: 0844 892 0550, General Fax: 01727 753234

St Albans Crown Court, The Court Building, Bricket Road, St Albans, Hertfordshire, AL1 3JW
DX 99700 St Albans 3
Switchboard: 01727 753220, General Fax: 01727 753221

St Albans Magistrates' Court, The Civic Centre, St Peter's Street, St Albans, Hertfordshire, AL1 3LB
Switchboard: 01923 297500, General Fax: 01923 297528

St Helens County Court, 1st Floor, Rexmore House, Cotham Street, St Helens, Merseyside, WA10 1SE
DX 725020 St Helens 4
Switchboard: 01744 27544, General Fax: 01744 20484

St Helens Magistrates' Court, The Court House, Corporation Street, St Helens, Merseyside, WA10 1SZ
DX 19488 St Helens
Switchboard: 01744 620244, General Fax: 01744 627286

Stafford Combined Court Centre, Victoria Square, Stafford, Staffordshire, ST16 2QQ
DX 703190 Stafford 4
Switchboard: 01785 610730, General Fax: 01785 213250

Stafford Magistrates' Court, The Court House, South Walls, Stafford, Staffordshire, ST16 3DW
DX 14575 Stafford 1
Switchboard: 01785 223144, General Fax: 01785 258508

Staffs Central Finance & Enforcement Unit, The Court House, Bryans Lane, Rugeley, Staffordshire, WS15 2FX
Switchboard: 01889 503500

Staines County Court, The Law Courts, Knowle Green, Staines, Middlesex, TW18 1XH
DX 98040 Staines 2
Switchboard: 01784 459175, General Fax: 01784 460176

Staines Magistrates' Court, The Law Courts, Knowle Green, Staines, Middlesex, TW18 1XH
DX 98045 Staines 2
Switchboard: 01784 459261, General Fax: 01784 459826, Family Fax: 01784 462870

Stamford Magistrates' Court, Town Hall, St Mary's Hill, Stamford, Lincolnshire, PE9 2DR
Switchboard: 01476 563438, General Fax: 01476 567200

Stevenage Magistrates' Court, Danesgate, Stevenage, Hertfordshire, SG1 1JQ
Switchboard: 01438 730412, General Fax: 01438 730413

Stockport County Court, 5th Floor, Heron House, Wellington Street, Stockport, SK1 3DJ
DX 702620 Stockport 4
Customer Service Team: 0161 474 7707, Fax: 0161 476 3129

Stockport Magistrates' Court, The Courthouse, Edward Street, Stockport, SK1 3NF
Switchboard: 0161 477 2020, General Fax: 0161 474 1115

Stoke-on-Trent Combined Court, Bethesda Street, Hanley, Stoke-on-Trent, Staffordshire, ST1 3BP
DX 703360 Hanley 3
Switchboard: 01782 854000, Crown Court Fax: 01782 854021, County Court Fax: 01782 854046, Family Court Fax: 01782 854014

Stoke-on-Trent Magistrates' Court, The Court House, Baker Street, Fenton, Staffordshire, ST4 3BX
DX 700402 Fenton
Switchboard: 01782 845353, General Fax: 01782 744782

Stoke-on-Trent Probate Sub-Registry, Combined Court Centre, Bethesda Street, Hanley, Stoke-on-Trent, Staffordshire, ST1 3BP
DX 703363 Hanley 3
Switchboard: 01782 854 065, General Fax: 01782 274 916

Stourbridge County Court, 7 Hagley Road, Stourbridge, West Midlands, DY8 1QL
DX 701889 Stourbridge 2
Switchboard: 01384 394232, General Fax: 01384 441736

Stratford Magistrates' Court, The Court House, 389-397 High Street, London, E15 4SB
DX 5417 Stratford
Switchboard: 0845 601 3600, General Fax: 020 8437 6010

Stratford upon Avon County Court, 5 Elm Court, Arden Street, Stratford-upon-Avon, Warwickshire, CV37 6PA
DX 701998 Stratford-upon-Avon 3
Switchboard: 01789 293056, General Fax: 01789 414973

Stratford upon Avon Magistrates' Court, The Court House, Rother Street, Stratford-upon-Avon, Warwickshire, CV37 6AX
Criminal Enquiries: 01926 429133, Family Enquiries: 02476 342279, General Fax: 01926 426217

Stroud Magistrates' Court, Stroud Courthouse, Parliament Street, Stroud, Gloucestershire, GL5 1ET
DX 98665 Gloucester 5
Switchboard: 01452 420100, General Fax: 01452 833557

Sudbury Magistrates' Court, The Court House, Acton Lane, Sudbury, Suffolk, CO10 1QN
Switchboard: 01284 778000, General Fax: 01284 778020

Sunderland County Court, 44 John Street, Sunderland, Tyne & Wear, SR1 1RB
DX 65149 Sunderland 2
Switchboard: 0191 5680750, General Fax: 0191 5143028

Sunderland Magistrates' Court, Gillbridge Avenue, Sunderland, Tyne & Wear, SR1 3AP
DX 742740 Sunderland 17
Switchboard: 0191 5141621, General Fax: 0191 5658564

Surrey Fines & Enforcement Unit, PO Box 88, Law Courts, Mary Road, Guildford, Surrey, GU1 4GB
DX 97866 Guildford 5

Surrey Fixed Penalty Office, PO Box 470, Law Courts, Mary Road, Guildford, Surrey, GU1 4GB
DX 97866 Guildford 5

Sussex Fines & Enforcement Unit, Sussex Central Fines Unit, PO Box 2989, Brighton, Brighton, East Sussex, BN2 0TF
DX 153460 Brighton 17

Sutton Coldfield Magistrates' Court, Lichfield Road, Sutton Coldfield, West Midlands, B74 2NS
DX 708310 Sutton Coldfield 6
Switchboard: 0121 354 7777, General Fax: 0121 355 0547

Sutton Magistrates' Court, The Court House, Shotfield, Wallington, Surrey, SM6 0JA
DX 97474 Croydon 6
Switchboard: 020 8770 5950, General Fax: 020 8770 5977

Swaffham (Central Norfolk) Magistrates' Court, The Courthouse, Westacre Road, Swaffham, Norfolk, PE37 7NH
Switchboard: 01553 770120, General Fax: 01553 775098

Swansea Civil Justice Centre, Caravella House, Quay West, Quay Street, Swansea, South Wales, Wales, SA1 1SP
DX 99740 Swansea 5
Switchboard: 01792 485800, General Fax: 01792 485810

Swansea Crown Court, The Law Courts, St Helens Road, Swansea, South Wales, Wales, SA1 4PF
DX 99540 Swansea 4
Switchboard: 01792 637000, General Fax: 01792 637049

Swansea Magistrates' Court, Grove Place, Swansea, South Wales, Wales, SA1 5DB
Switchboard: 01792 478300, General Fax: 01792 651066

Swindon Combined Court, The Law Courts, Islington Street, Swindon, Wiltshire, SN1 2HG
DX 98430 Swindon 5
Switchboard: 01793 690500, General Fax: 01793 690555, County Court: 01793 690505, Family Court: 01793 690508, Crown Court: 01793 690530

Swindon Magistrates' Court, Princes Street, Swindon, Wiltshire, SN1 2JB
DX 118725 Swindon 7
Switchboard: 01793 699800, General Fax: 01793 433740

Tameside County Court, PO Box 166, Henry Square, Ashton-Under-Lyne, Lancashire, OL6 7TP
DX 702625 Ashton-Under-Llyme 2
Switchboard: 0161 331 5614, Fax: 0161 331 5649

Tameside Magistrates' Court, Henry Square, Ashton-Under-Lyne, Lancashire, OL6 7TP
Switchboard: 0161 330 2023, General Fax: 0161 343 1498

Tamworth County Court, The Court House, Spinning School Lane, Tamworth, Staffordshire, B79 7AN
DX 702016 Tamworth 2
Switchboard: 01827 305910, Fax: 01827 303823

Tamworth Magistrates' Court, The Court House, Spinning School Lane, Tamworth, Staffordshire, B79 7AR
Switchboard: 01785 223144

Taunton County Court, The Shire Hall, Taunton, Somerset, TA1 4EU
DX 98410 Taunton 2
Switchboard: 01823 281110, General Fax: 01823 351337

Taunton Crown Court, The Shire Hall, Shuttern, Taunton, Somerset, TA1 4EU
DX 98410 Taunton 2
Switchboard: 01823 281100, General Fax: 01823 322116

Technology & Construction Court, St Dunstan's House, 133-137 Fetter Lane, London, EC4A 1HD
DX 44450 Strand
Switchboard: 020 7947 6000

Teesside Combined Court Centre, Russell Street, Middlesbrough, Cleveland, TS1 2AE
DX 65152 Middlesbrough 2
Switchboard: 01642 340000, General Fax: 01642 340002

Teesside Magistrates' Court, Teesside Magsitrates' Courts, Victoria Square, Middlesbrough, Cleveland, TS1 2AS
DX 60562 Middlesbrough
Switchboard: 01642 240301, General Fax: 01642 224010

Telford County Court, Telford Square, Malinsgate, Town Centre, Telford, Shropshire, TF3 4JP
DX 701976 Telford 3
Switchboard: 01952 238280, General Fax: 01952 291601

Telford Magistrates' Court, Telford Square, Malinsgate, Telford, Shropshire, TF3 4HX
Switchboard: 01952 204500, General Fax: 01952 204554

Thames Magistrates' Court, 58 Bow Road, London, E3 4DJ
DX 55654 Bow
Switchboard: 0845 601 3600, General Fax: 020 8271 1251

Thanet County Court, The Court House, 2nd Floor, Cecil Square, Margate, Kent, CT9 1RL
DX 98210 Cliftonville 2
Switchboard: 01843 221722, General Fax: 01843 222730

Thetford (South Norfolk) Magistrates' Court, The Courthouse, Old Bury Road, Thetford, Norfolk, IP24 3AQ
Switchboard: 01553 770120, General Fax: 01553 775098

Torquay & Newton Abbot County Court, The Willows, Nicholson Road, Torquay, Devon, TQ2 7AZ
DX 98740 Torquay 4
Switchboard: 01803 616791, General Fax: 01803 616795

Torquay Magistrates' Court, The Court House, Union Street, Torquay, Devon, TQ1 4BP
DX 98740 Torquay 4
Switchboard: 01803 612211, General Fax: 01803 618618

Totnes Magistrates' Court, The Court House, Ashburton Road, Totnes, Devon, TQ9 5JY
DX 98740 Torquay 4
Switchboard: 01803 612211, General Fax: 01803 618618

Towcester Magistrates' Court, The Court House, Watling Street West, Towcester, Northamptonshire, NN12 6DE
DX 151720 Northampton 27
Switchboard: 01604 497000, General Fax: 01604 497010

Tower Bridge Magistrates' Court, 211 Tooley Street, London, SE1 2JY
Switchboard: 0845 601 3600, General Fax: 020 7805 6718

Traffic Enforcement Centre (TEC), 5th Floor, St Katharine's House, 21-27 St Katharine's Street, Northampton, Northamptonshire, NN1 2LH
DX 702885 Northampton 7
Switchboard: 0845 704 5007, General Fax: 0845 707 8607

Trafford Magistrates' Court, PO Box 13, Ashton Lane, Sale, Cheshire, M33 7NR
DX 708290 Sale 6
Switchboard: 0161 976 3333, General Fax: 0161 975 4673

Trowbridge County Court, Ground Floor, Clarks Mill, Stallard Street, Trowbridge, Wiltshire, BA14 8DB
DX 98750 Trowbridge 2
Switchboard: 01225 752101, General Fax: 01225 776638

Truro County Court, Courts of Justice, Edward Street, Truro, Cornwall, TR1 2PB
DX 135396 Truro 2
Switchboard: 01872 267460, General Fax: 01872 222348

Truro Crown Court, Courts of Justice, Edward Street, Truro, Cornwall, TR1 2PB
DX 135396 Truro 2
Switchboard: 01872 267420, General Fax: 01872 261550

Truro Magistrates' Court, The Court House, Tremorvah Wood Lane, Mitchell Hill, Truro, Cornwall, TR1 1HZ
Switchboard: 01872 321900, General Fax: 01872 276227

Tunbridge Wells County Court, Merevale House, 42-46 London Road, Tunbridge Wells, Kent, TN1 1DP
DX 98220 Tunbridge Wells 3
Switchboard: 01892 700150, General Fax: 01892 513676

Tynedale Magistrates' Court, The Law Courts, Abbey Buildings, Beaumont Street, Hexham, Northumberland, NE46 3NB
DX 68720 Hexham
Switchboard: 01434 603248, General Fax: 01434 609378

Uxbridge County Court, 501 Uxbridge Road, Hayes, Middlesex, UB4 8HL
DX 44658 Hayes (Middlesex)
Switchboard: 020 8756 3520, General Fax: 020 8561 2020

Uxbridge Magistrates' Court, The Court House, Harefield Road, Uxbridge, Middlesex, UB8 1PQ
DX 149720 Uxbridge 4
Switchboard: 01895 814646, General Fax: 01895 274280

Vale of Glamorgan Magistrates' Court, Thompson Street, Barry, Glamorgan, Wales, CF63 4SX
Switchboard: 01446 737491, General Fax: 01446 732743

Wakefield County Court, Crown House, 127 Kirkgate, Wakefield, West Yorkshire, WF1 1JW
DX 703040 Wakefield 3
Switchboard: 01924 370268, General Fax: 01924 200818

Wakefield Magistrates' Court, The Court House, Cliff Parade, Wakefield, West Yorkshire, WF1 2TW
Switchboard: 01924 231100, General Fax: 01924 231146

Walsall Hearing Centre - County Court, Bridge House, Bridge Street, Walsall, West Midlands, WS1 1JQ
DX 701943 Walsall 2
Switchboard: 01922 728855, General Fax: 01922 728891

Walsall Magistrates' Court, Stafford Street, Walsall, West Midlands, WS2 8HA
DX 12118 Walsall 1
Switchboard: 01922 638222, General Fax: 01922 635657

Waltham Forest Magistrates' Court, The Court House, 1 Farnan Avenue,
Walthamstow, London, E17 4NX
DX 156842 Ilford 9
Switchboard: 0845 601 3600, General Fax: 020 8527 9063

Wandsworth County Court, 76-78 Upper Richmond Road, Putney, London,
SW15 2SU
DX 97540 Putney 2
Switchboard: 020 8333 4351, General Fax: 020 8877 9854

Wantage Magistrates' Court, The Courthouse, Church Street, Wantage, Oxfordshire,
OX12 8EQ
Switchboard: 0870 241 2808, General Fax: 01865 448024

Wareham Magistrates' Court, The Court House, Worgret Road, Wareham, Dorset,
BH20 4PL
Switchboard: 01202 745309, General Fax: 01202 711999

Warley (Oldbury) Magistrates' Court, The Court House, Oldbury Ringway, Oldbury,
West Midlands, B69 4JN
DX 708330 Oldbury 3
Switchboard: 0121 511 2222, General Fax: 0121 544 8492

Warrington & Runcorn County Courts, Law Courts, Legh Street, Warrington,
Cheshire, WA1 1UR
DX 702501 Warrington 3
Switchboard: 01925 256700, General Fax: 01925 413335

Warrington Magistrates' Court, Arpley Street, Warrington, Cheshire, WA1 1LQ
Switchboard: 0870 162 6261, General Fax: 01925 231284

Warwick Combined Court Centre, Northgate South Side, Warwick, Warwickshire,
CV34 4RB
DX 701964 Warwick 2
Crown Court: Tel: 01926 495428, Fax: 01926 474227, County Court: Tel: 01926
492276, Fax: 01926 411855

Watford County Court, 3rd Floor, Cassiobury House, 11-19 Station Road, Watford,
Hertfordshire, WD17 1EZ
DX 122740 Watford 5
Switchboard: 01923 699400/699401, General Fax: 01923 251317

Watford Magistrates' Court, Clarendon Road, Watford, Hertfordshire, WD17 1ST
DX 51509 Watford 2
Switchboard: 01923 297500, General Fax: 01923 297528

Wellingborough County Court, Lothersdale House, West Villa Road,
Wellingborough, Northamptonshire, NN8 4NF
DX 701883 Wellingborough 2
Switchboard: 01933 226168, General Fax: 01933 272977

Wellingborough Magistrates' Court, The Court House, Midland Road,
Wellingborough, Northamptonshire, NN8 1HF
DX 151720 Northampton 27
Switchboard: 01604 497000, General Fax: 01604 497010

Wells Magistrates' Court, Town Hall, Wells, Somerset, BA5 2RB
Switchboard: 01935 426281, General Fax: 01935 431022

Welshpool & Newtown County Court, The Mansion House, 24 Severn Street,
Welshpool, Powys, Wales, SY21 7UX
DX 702524 Welshpool 2
Switchboard: 01938 552004, General Fax: 01938 555395

Welshpool Crown Court, Town Hall, Welshpool, Powys, Wales, SY2 7TQ
Switchboard: 01938 553144, General Fax: 01938 553144

Welshpool Magistrates' Court, Mansion House, 24 Severn Street, Welshpool,
Powys, Wales, SY21 7UX
DX 702535 Welshpool 2
General Office: 01938 555968, General Fax: 01938 554593

West Berkshire Magistrates' Court, Newbury, The Court House, Mill Lane,
Newbury, Berkshire, RG14 5QS
Switchboard: 0118 980 1800, General Fax: 0118 980 1873

West Bromwich Magistrates' Court, Law Courts, Lombard Street West, West
Bromwich, West Midlands, B70 8ED
Switchboard: 0121 511 2222, General Fax: 0121 544 8492

West London County Court, West London Courthouse, Magistrates, County & Youth
Courts, 181 Talgarth Road, Hammersmith, London, W6 8DN
DX 97550 Hammersmith 8
Switchboard: 020 8600 6868, General Fax: 020 8600 6860

West London Magistrates' Court, 181 Talgarth Road, London, W6 8DN
DX 124800 Hammersmith 8
Switchboard: 0845 601 3600, General Fax: 020 8700 9344

West Somerset Magistrates' Court, St John's Road, Taunton, Somerset, TA1 4AX
DX 122473 Taunton 7
Switchboard: 01823 257084, General Fax: 01823 335195

Weston-Super-Mare County Court, North Somerset Courthouse, The Hedges,
St Georges, Weston-Super-Mare, Avon, BS22 7BB
DX 152361 Weston-Super-Mare 5
General Enquiries: 01934 528686, General Fax: 01934 528594

Wetherby Magistrates' Court, PO Box 97, Westgate, Leeds, West Yorkshire,
LS1 3AP
Switchboard: 0113 2459653, General Fax: 0113 2444700

Weymouth & Dorchester Combined Court Centre, Westwey House, Westwey
Road, Weymouth, Dorset, DT4 8TE
DX 98820 Weymouth 3
Switchboard: 01305 752510, General Fax: 01305 788293

Weymouth Magistrates' Court, The Law Courts, Westwey Road, Weymouth, Dorset,
DT4 8BS
DX 98820 Weymouth 3
Switchboard: 01305 783891, General Fax: 01305 761418

Whitby Magistrates' Court, Law Courts, Waterstead Lane, Whitby, North Yorkshire, YO21 1PY
Switchboard: 01723 505000, General Fax: 01947 821620

Whitehaven County Court, Old Town Hall, Duke Street, Whitehaven, Cumbria, CA28 7NU
DX 63990 Whitehaven 2
Switchboard: 01946 67788, General Fax: 01946 691219

Whitehaven Magistrates' Court, Catherine Street, Whitehaven, Cumbria, CA28 7PA
Switchboard: 01900 62244, General Fax: 01900 68644

Widnes Magistrates' Court, The Court House, Kingsway, Widnes, Cheshire, WA8 7QL
Switchboard: 0870 162 6261, General Fax: 01925 231284

Wigan & Leigh Magistrates' Court, Wigan & Leigh Courthouse, Darlington Street, Wigan, Greater Manchester, WN1 1DW
DX 724820 Wigan 9
Switchboard: 01942 405405, General Fax: 01942 405444

Wigan County Court, Wigan & Leigh Courthouse, Darlington Street, Wigan, Greater Manchester, WN1 1DW
DX 724820 Wigan 9
Switchboard: 01942 405405, Fax: 01942 405499

Willesden County Court, 9 Acton Lane, Harlesden, London, NW10 8SB
DX 97560 Harlesden 2
Switchboard: 0208 963 8200, General Fax: 020 84530946

Wimbledon Magistrates' Court, The Court House, Alexandra Road, Wimbledon, London, SW19 7JP
DX 116610 Wimbledon 4
Switchboard: 020 8946 8622, General Fax: 020 8946 7030

Wimborne Magistrates' Court, The Law Courts, Hanham Road, Wimborne, Dorset, BH21 1JW
Switchboard: 01202 745309, General Fax: 01202 711999

Winchester Combined Court Centre, Winchester Combined Court, The Law Courts, Winchester, Hampshire, SO23 9EL
DX 98520 Winchester 3
Switchboard: 01962 814100, General Fax: 01962 853821, County Court Fax: 01962 814260, Crown Court Fax: 01962 853821

Winchester District Probate Registry, 4th Floor, Cromwell House, Andover Road, Winchester, Hampshire, SO23 7EW
DX 96900 Winchester 2
Enquiries: 01962 897024, General Fax: 01962 840796

Wirral Magistrates' Court, Chester Street, Birkenhead, Merseyside, CH41 5HW
DX 17888 Birkenhead
Switchboard: 0151 285 4100, General Fax: 0151 285 4111

Wisbech Magistrates' Court, The Court House, Lynn Road, Wisbech, Cambridgeshire, PE13 3DE
Switchboard: 0845 310 0575, General Fax: 01733 313749

Witham Magistrates' Court, The Court House, Newland Street, Witham, Essex, CM8 2AS
Switchboard: 01245 313300, General Fax: 01245 313399

Witney Magistrates' Court, The Court House, Welch Way, Witney, Oxfordshire, OX28 6JH
Switchboard: 01295 452000, General Fax: 01295 452050

Woking Magistrates' Court, The Court House, Station Approach, Woking, Surrey, GU22 7YL
DX 135090 Woking 5
Switchboard: 01483 714950, General Fax: 01483 712500

Wolverhampton Combined Court Centre, Pipers Row, Wolverhampton, West Midlands, WV1 3LQ
DX 702019 Wolverhampton 4
Switchboard: 01902 481000, General Fax: 01902 481001

Wolverhampton Magistrates' Court, The Law Courts, North Street, Wolverhampton, West Midlands, WV1 1RA
DX 10419 Wolverhampton
Switchboard: 01902 773151, General Fax: 01902 427875

Wood Green Crown Court, Woodall House, Lordship Lane, Wood Green, London, N22 5LF
DX 130346 Wood Green 3
Switchboard: 020 8826 4100

Woolwich County Court, 165 Powis Street, Woolwich, London, SE18 6JW
DX 123450 Woolwich 8
Switchboard: 020 8301 8700, General Fax: 020 8316 4842

Woolwich Crown Court, 2 Belmarsh Road, London, SE28 0EY
DX 117650 Woolwich 7
Switchboard: 020 8312 7000, General Fax: 020 8312 7078

Woolwich Magistrates' Court, Market Street, Woolwich, London, SE18 6QY
Switchboard: 0845 6013600, General Fax: 0208 276 1399

Worcester Combined Court, The Shirehall, Foregate Street, Worcester, Worcestershire, WR1 1EQ
DX 721120 Worcester 11
Tel: 01905 730800, Fax: 01905 730801

Worcester Magistrates' Court, Castle Street, Worcester, Worcestershire, WR1 3QZ
Switchboard: 01905 743200, General Fax: 01905 743346

Workington Magistrates' Court, Hall Park, Ramsey Brow, Workington, Cumbria, CA14 4AS
DX 743420 Workington 5
Switchboard: 01900 62244, General Fax: 01900 68644

Worksop & Retford Magistrates' Courts, The Court House, 30 Potter Street, Worksop, Nottinghamshire, S80 2AJ
DX 743240 Worksop 4
Switchboard: 01909 486111, General Fax: 01909 473521

Worksop County Court, The Court House, 30 Potter Street, Worksop,
Nottinghamshire, S80 2AJ
DX 743240 Worksop 4
Switchboard: 01623 656406, General Fax: 01623 626561

Worthing County Court, The Law Courts, Christchurch Road, Worthing, West
Sussex, BN11 1JD
DX 98230 Worthing 4
Switchboard: 01903 221920, General Fax: 01903 235559

Worthing Magistrates' Court, The Law Courts, Christchurch Road, Worthing, West
Sussex, BN11 1JE
DX 98233 Worthing 4
Switchboard: 01903 210981, General Fax: 01903 820746

Wrexham County Court, 2nd Floor, Crown Buildings, 31 Chester Street, Wrexham,
Denbighshire, Wales, LL13 8XN
DX 721921 Wrexham 4
Switchboard: 01978 296140, General Fax: 01978 290677

Wrexham Magistrates' Court, Bodhyfryd, Wrexham, Denbighshire, Wales, LL12 7BP
DX 721923 Wrexham 4
Switchboard: 01978 310106, General Fax: 01978 358213

Yeovil County Court, 22 Hendford, Yeovil, Somerset, BA20 2QD
DX 98830 Yeovil 2
Switchboard: 01935 382150, General Fax: 01935 410004

York County Court, Piccadilly House, 55 Piccadilly, York, North Yorkshire, YO1 9WL
DX 65165, York 4
Switchboard: 01904 688550, General Fax: 01904 679963

York Crown Court, The Castle, York, North Yorkshire, YO1 9WZ
DX 65162 York 3
Switchboard: 01904 645121, General Fax: 01904 611689

York Magistrates' Court, Law Courts, Clifford Street, York, North Yorkshire, YO1 9RE
DX 744330 York 41
Switchboard: 01904 615200, General Fax: 01904 615201

York Probate Sub-Registry, 1st Floor, Castle Chambers, 5 Clifford Street, York,
North Yorkshire, YO1 9RG
DX 720629 York 21
Switchboard: 01904 666777, General Fax: 01904 666 776

Courts in Scotland

Source: www.scotcourts.gov.uk

Aberdeen Annex & High Court, Mercatgate, Sheriff Court Annex & High Court of the Justiciary, 53 Castle Street, Aberdeen, AB11 5BB
DX AB361
Tel: 01224 572026, Fax: 01224 579274

Aberdeen JP Court, Sheriff Court House, Castle Street, Aberdeen, AB10 1WP
DX AB61 or LP 7
Tel: 01224 657200, Fax: 01224 657234

Aberdeen Sheriff Court, Sheriff Clerk's Office, Sheriff Court House, Castle Street, Aberdeen, AB10 1WP
DX AB61 or LP 7
Tel: 01224 657200, Fax: 01224 657234

Airdrie Sheriff Court, Sheriff Clerk's Office, Sheriff Court House, Graham Street, Airdrie, ML6 6EE
DX 570416
Tel: 01236 751121, Fax: 01236 747497

Alloa JP Court, Sheriff Clerk's Office, Sheriff Court House, Mar Street, Alloa, FK10 1HR
DX 560433
Tel: 01259 722734, Fax: 01259 219470

Alloa Sheriff Court, Sheriff Clerk's Office, Sheriff Court House, Mar Street, Alloa, FK10 1HR
DX 560433
Tel: 01259 722734, Fax: 01259 219470

Arbroath JP Court, Sheriff Clerk's Office, Sheriff Court House, Town House, 88 High Street, Arbroath, DD11 1HL
DX 442
Tel: 01241 876600, Fax: 01241 874413

Arbroath Sheriff Court, Sheriff Clerk's Office, Sheriff Court House, Town House, 88 High Street, Arbroath, DD11 1HL
DX 442
Tel: 01241 876600, Fax: 01241 874413

Ayr Sheriff Court, Sheriff Clerk's Office, Sheriff Court House, Wellington Square, Ayr, KA7 1EE
DX AY16
Tel: 01292 268474, Fax: 01292 292249

Banff JP Court, Sheriff Court House, Low Street, Banff, AB45 1AU
DX 1325
Tel: 01261 812140, Fax: 01261 818394

Banff Sheriff Court, Sheriff Clerk's Office, Sheriff Court House, Low Street, Banff, AB45 1AU
DX 521325
Tel: 01261 812140, Fax: 01261 818394

Campbeltown Sheriff Court, Sheriff Clerk's Office, Sheriff Court House, Castlehill, Campbeltown, PA28 6AN
Tel: 01586 552503, Fax: 01586 554967

Court of Session, Parliament House, Parliament Square, Edinburgh, EH1 1RQ
DX 549306 Edinburgh 36
Tel: 0131 225 2595, Fax: 0131 240 6755

Cupar JP Court, Sheriff Clerk's Office, Sheriff Court House, County Buildings, St Catherine Street, Cupar, KY15 4LX
DX 560545
Tel: 01334 652121, Fax: 01334 656807

Cupar Sheriff Court, Sheriff Clerk's Office, Sheriff Court House, County Buildings, St Catherine Street, Cupar, KY15 4LX
DX 560545
Tel: 01334 652121, Fax: 01334 656807

Dingwall JP Court, Sheriff Court House, Ferry Road, Dingwall, IV15 9QX
DX 520584
Tel: 01349 863153, Fax: 01349 863153

Dingwall Sheriff Court, Sheriff Clerk's Office, Sheriff Court House, Ferry Road, Dingwall, IV15 9QX
DX 520584
Tel: 01349 863153, Fax: 01349 863153

Dornoch JP Court, Sheriff Court House, Castle Street, Dornoch, IV25 3FD
Tel: 01862 810224, Fax: 01862 810224

Dornoch Sheriff Court, Sheriff Court House, Castle Street, Dornoch, IV25 3SD
LP 2 Dornoch
Tel: 01862 810224, Fax: 01862 810224

Dumbarton Sheriff Court, Sheriff Clerk's Office, Sheriff Court House, Church Street, Dumbarton, G82 1QR
DX 500 597
Tel: 01389 763266, Fax: 01389 764085

Dumfries Sheriff Court, Sheriff Clerk's Office, Sheriff Court House, Buccleuch Street, Dumfries, DG1 2AN
DX 580617
Tel: 01387 262334, Fax: 01387 262357

Dundee JP Court, Sheriff Clerk's Office, Sheriff Court House, 6 West Bell Street, Dundee, DD1 9AD
DX DD33
Tel: 01382 229961, Fax: 01382 318262

Dundee Sheriff Court, Sheriff Clerk's Office, Sheriff Court House, 6 West Bell Street, Dundee, DD1 9AD
DX DD33
Tel: 01382 229961, Fax: 01382 318222

Dunfermline JP Court, Sheriff Clerk's Office, Sheriff Court House, 1/6 Carnegie Drive, Dunfermline, KY12 7HJ
DX DF17
Tel: 01383 724666, Fax: 01383 621205

Dunfermline Sheriff Court, Sheriff Clerk's Office, Sheriff Court House, 1/6 Carnegie Drive, Dunfermline, KY12 7HJ
DX DF17
Tel: 01383 724666, Fax: 01383 621205

Dunoon Sheriff Court, Sheriff Clerk's Office, Sheriff Court House, George Street, Dunoon, PA23 8BQ
DX 591655/LP 2 Dunoon
Tel: 01369 704166, Fax: 01369 702191

Duns JP Court, Sheriff Court House, 8 Newtown Street, Duns, TD11 3DU
DX 581222 Jedburgh
Tel: 01835 863231, Fax: 01835 864110

Duns Sheriff Court, Sheriff Court House, 8 Newtown Street, Duns, TD11 3DU
DX 581222 Jedburgh
Tel: 01835 863231, Fax: 01835 864110

Edinburgh JP Court, Sheriff Court House, Chambers Street, Edinburgh, EH1 1LB
DX ED308
Tel: 0131 2252525, Fax: 0131 2254422

Edinburgh Sheriff Court, Sheriff Court House, 27 Chambers Street, Edinburgh, EH1 1LB
DX ED 550 308
Tel: 0131 2252525, Fax: 0131 2254422

Elgin JP Court, Sheriff Court House, High Street, Elgin, IV30 1BU
DX 520652/LP 8
Tel: 01343 542505, Fax: 01343 559517

Elgin Sheriff Court, Sheriff Clerk's Office, Sheriff Court House, High Street, Elgin, IV30 1BU
DX 520652/LP 8
Tel: 01343 542505, Fax: 01343 559517

Falkirk JP Court, Sheriff Clerk's Office, Sheriff Court House, Main Street, Camelon, Falkirk, FK1 4AR
DX 55207 Falkirk 4
Tel: 01324 620822, Fax: 01324 678238

Falkirk Sheriff Court, Sheriff Clerk's Office, Sheriff Court House, Main Street, Camelon, Falkirk, FK1 4AR
DX 55207 Falkirk 4
Tel: 01324 620822, Fax: 01324 678238

Forfar JP Court, Sheriff Clerk's Office, Sheriff Court House, Market Street, Forfar, DD8 3LA
DX 503674
Tel: 01307 462186, Fax: 01307 462268

Forfar Sheriff Court, Sheriff Clerk's Office, Sheriff Court House, Market Street, Forfar, DD8 3LA
DX 503674
Tel: 01307 462186, Fax: 01307 462268

Fort William JP Court, Sheriff Court House, High Street, Fort William, PH33 6EE
DX 531405
Tel: 01397 702087, Fax: 01397 706214

Fort William Sheriff Court, Sheriff Clerk's Office, Sheriff Court House, High Street, Fort William, PH33 6EE
DX 531405
Tel: 01397 702087, Fax: 01397 706214

Glasgow JP Court, 21 St Andrews Street, Glasgow, G1 5PQ
Tel: 0141 429 8888

Glasgow Sheriff Court, Sheriff Clerk's Office, Sheriff Court of Glasgow & Strathkelvin, PO Box 23, 1 Carlton Place, Glasgow, G5 9DA
DX 551020
Tel: 0141 4298888, Fax: Civil 0141 4185248

Greenock Sheriff Court, Sheriff Clerk's Office, Sheriff Court House, 1 Nelson Street, Greenock, PA15 1TR
DX GR16
Tel: 01475 787073, Fax: 01475 729746

Haddington JP Court, Sheriff Clerk's Office, Sheriff Court House, Court Street, Haddington, EH41 3HN
DX 540732
Tel: 01620 822936, Fax: 01620 826350

Haddington Sheriff Court, Sheriff Clerk's Office, Sheriff Court House, Court Street, Haddington, EH41 3HN
DX 540732
Tel: 01620 822936, Fax: 01620 826350

Hamilton Sheriff Court Civil Department, Birnie House, Caird Park, Hamilton Business Park, Caird Street, Hamilton, ML3 0AL
DX HA 16/LP 4
Tel: 01698 282957, Fax: 01698 284870

Hamilton Sheriff Court, Sheriff Clerk's Office, Sheriff Court House, 4 Beckford Street, Hamilton, ML3 0BT
DX HA2 Hamilton 2/LP 15
Tel: 01698 282957, Fax: 01698 201365

High Court of Justiciary - Edinburgh, High Court of Justiciary, Lawnmarket, Edinburgh, EH1 2NS
DX 549307 Edinburgh 36
Tel: 0131 225 2595, Fax: 0131 240 6915

High Court of Justiciary - Glasgow, Justiciary Buildings, Saltmarket, Glasgow, G1 5JU
DX 501556
Tel: 0141 552 3795, Fax: 0141 559 4519

Inverness JP Court, Sheriff Court House, The Castle, Inverness, IV2 3EG
DX IN25
Tel: 01463 230782, Fax: 01463 710602

Inverness Sheriff Court, Sheriff Clerk's Office, Sheriff Court House, The Castle,
Inverness, IV2 3EG
DX IN25
Tel: 01463 230782, Fax: 01463 710602

Jedburgh JP Court, Sheriff Clerk's Office, Sheriff Court House, Castlegate, Jedburgh,
TD8 6AR
DX 581222
Tel: 01835 863231, Fax: 01835 864110

Jedburgh Sheriff Court, Sheriff Clerk's Office, Sheriff Court House, Castlegate,
Jedburgh, TD8 6AR
DX 581222
Tel: 01835 863231, Fax: 01835 864110

Kilmarnock Sheriff Court, Sheriff Clerk's Office, Sheriff Court House, St Marnock
Street, Kilmarnock, KA1 1ED
DX KK20
Tel: 01563 550024, Fax: 01563 543568

Kirkcaldy JP Court, Sheriff Clerk's Office, Sheriff Court House, Whytescauseway,
Kirkcaldy, KY1 1XQ
DX KY17
Tel: 01592 260171, Fax: 01592 642361

Kirkcaldy Sheriff Court, Sheriff Clerk's Office, Sheriff Court House,
Whytescauseway, Kirkcaldy, KY1 1XQ
DX KY17
Tel: 01592 260171, Fax: 01592 642361

Kirkcudbright Sheriff Court, Sheriff Clerk's Office, Sheriff Court House, High Street,
Kirkcudbright, DG6 4JW
DX 580812
Tel: 01557 330574. Fax: 01557 331764

Kirkwall Sheriff Court, Sheriff Clerk's Office, Sheriff Court House, Watergate,
Kirkwall, KW15 1PD
Tel: 01856 872110, Fax: 01856 874835

Lanark Sheriff Court, Sheriff Clerk's Office, Sheriff Court House, 24 Hope Street,
Lanark, ML11 7NE
DX 570832
Tel: 01555 661531, Fax: 01555 664319

Lerwick Sheriff Court Sheriff Court, Sheriff Clerk's Office, Sheriff Court House, King
Erik Street, Lerwick, ZE1 0HD
Tel: 01595 693914, Fax: 01595 693340

Linlithgow Sheriff Court, Sheriff Clerk's Office, Sheriff Court House, High Street,
Linlithgow, EH49 7EQ
DX 540881
Tel: 01506 842922, Fax: 01506 848457

Livingston JP Court, Livingston Sheriff Court, Sheriff Court House, The Civic Centre, Howden South Road, Livingston, EH54 6FF
Tel: 01506 402 400, Fax: 01506 415 262

Livingston Sheriff Court, Sheriff Court House, The Civic Centre, Howden South Road, Livingston, EH54 6FF
Tel: 01506 402 400, Fax: 01506 415 262

Lochmaddy Sheriff Court, Sheriff Clerk's Office, Sheriff Court House, Lochmaddy, HS6 5AE
Tel: 01876 500340 or 01478 612191, Fax: 08445613015

Oban Sheriff Court, Sheriff Clerk's Office, Sheriff Court House, Albany Street, Oban, PA34 4AL
DX OB8
Tel: 01631 562414, Fax: 01631 562037

Office of the Accountant of Court, 1st Floor, Hadrian House, Callendar Business Park, Callendar Road, Falkirk, FK1 1XR
DX 550361 Falkirk 3
Tel: 01324 677740, Fax: 01324 678365

Office of the Public Guardian, Hadrian House, Callendar Business Park, Callendar Road, Falkirk, FK1 1XR
DX 550360 Falkirk 3
Tel: 01324 678 300, Fax: 01324 678 301

Paisley Sheriff Court, Sheriff Clerk's Office, Sheriff Court House, St James Street, Paisley, PA3 2HW
DX PA48
Tel: 0141 8875291, Fax: 0141 8876702

Peebles JP Court, Sheriff Clerk's Office, Council Buildings, Rosetta Road, Peebles Correspondence address:, Heather Johnston, Sheriff Clerk Depute for Peebles Sheriff Court, c/o The Commissary Office, Sheriff Courthouse, 27 Chambers Street, Peebles, EH1 1LB
DX 540971
Tel: 01721 720204

Peebles Sheriff Court, Sheriff Clerk's Office, Ettrick Terrace, Selkirk
DX 581011 Selkirk/LP 2 Selkirk
Tel: 01750 721269

Perth JP Court, Sheriff Clerk's Office, Sheriff Court House, Tay Street, Perth, PH2 8NL
DX PE20
Tel: 01738 620546, Fax: 01738 623601

Perth Sheriff Court, Sheriff Clerk's Office, Sheriff Court House, Tay Street, Perth, PH2 8NL
DX PE20
Tel: 01738 620546, Fax: 01738 623601

Peterhead JP Court, Queen Street, Peterhead, AB42 1TP
DX 521376
Tel: 01779 476676, Fax: 01779 472435

Peterhead Sheriff Court, Queen Street, Peterhead, AB42 1TP
DX 521376
Tel: 01779 476676, Fax: 01779 472435

Portree JP Court, Sheriff Court House, Somerled Square, Portree, IV51 9EH
Tel: 01478 612191, Fax: 01478 613203

Portree Sheriff Court, Sheriff Clerk's Office, Sheriff Court House, Somerled Square,
Portree, IV51 9EH
Tel: 01478 612191, Fax: 01478 613203

Rothesay Sheriff Court, Eaglesham House, Mountpleasant Road, Rothesay, Isle of
Bute, PA20 9HQ
DX 590655
Tel: 01700 502982, Fax: 01700 504112

Scottish Court Service Headquarters, Hayweight House, 23 Lauriston Street,
Edinburgh, EH3 9DQ
DX 545309 Edinburgh 39
Tel: 0131 229 9200, Fax: 0131 221 6895

Selkirk JP Court, Sheriff Clerk's Office, Sheriff Court House, Ettrick Terrace, Selkirk,
TD7 4LE
DX 581011
Tel: 01750 21269, Fax: 01750 22884

Selkirk Sheriff Court, Sheriff Clerk's Office, Sheriff Court House, Ettrick Terrace,
Selkirk, TD7 4LE
DX 581011
Tel: 01750 21269, Fax: 01750 22884

Stirling JP Court, Sheriff Clerk's Office, Sheriff Court House, Viewfield Place, Stirling,
FK8 1NH, Sheriff Clerk: Mrs Maureen McLean
DX ST15/LP 6
Tel: 01786 462191, Fax: 01786 470456

Stirling Sheriff Court, Sheriff Clerk's Office, Sheriff Court House, Viewfield Place,
Stirling, FK8 1NH
DX ST15/LP 6
Tel: 01786 462191, Fax: 01786 470456

Stonehaven JP Court, Sheriff Clerk's Office, Sheriff Court House, Dunnottar Avenue,
Stonehaven, AB39 2JH
DX 521023
Tel: 01569 762758, Fax: 01569 762132

Stonehaven Sheriff Court, Sheriff Clerk's Office, Sheriff Court House, Dunnottar
Avenue, Stonehaven, AB39 2JH
DX 521023
Tel: 01569 762758, Fax: 01569 762132

Stornoway JP Court, Sheriff Clerk's Offic, Sheriff Court House, Lewis Street,
Stornoway, HS1 2JF
Tel: 01851 702231, Fax: 01851 704296

Stornoway Sheriff Court, Sheriff Clerk's Offic, Sheriff Court House, Lewis Street, Stornoway, HS1 2JF
Tel: 01851 702231, Fax: 01851 704296

Stranraer Sheriff Court, Sheriff Clerk's Office, Sheriff Court House, Lewis Street, Stranraer, DG9 7AA
DX 581261
Tel: 01776 702138/706135, Fax: 01776 706792

Tain JP Court, Sheriff Clerk's Office, Sheriff Court House, High Street, Tain, IV19 1AB
Tel: 01862 892518, Fax: 01862 892518

Tain Sheriff Court, Sheriff Clerk's Office, Sheriff & JP Court, High Street, Tain, IV19 1AB
LP 2 Tain
Tel: 01862 892518, Fax: 01862 892518

Wick JP Court, Sheriff Clerk's Office, Sheriff Court House, Bridge Street, Wick, KW1 4AJ
Tel: 01955 602846, Fax: 01955 602846

Wick Sheriff Court, Sheriff Clerk's Office, Sheriff Court House, Bridge Street, Wick, KW1 4AJ
Tel: 01955 602846, Fax: 01955 602846

Courts in Northern Ireland

Source: www.courtsni.gov.uk

Antrim Court Office, The Courthouse, 30 Castle Way, Antrim, BT41 4AQ
DX 3452 NR
Tel: 028 9446 2661, Fax: 028 9446 3301

Armagh Court Office, The Courthouse, The Mall, Armagh, BT61 9DJ
DX 2791 NR
Tel: 028 3752 2816, Fax: 028 3752 8194

Ballymena Court Office, The Courthouse, Albert Place, Ballymena, BT43 5BS
DX 3202 NR
Tel: 028 2564 9416, Fax: 028 2565 5371

Bangor Court Office, The Courthouse, 6 Quay Street, Bangor, BT20 5EA
DX 2507 NR
Tel: 028 9147 2626, Fax: 028 9127 2667

Belfast Combined Courts

Laganside Courts, Oxford Street, Belfast, BT1 3LL
DX 461 NR
Tel: 02890 328594, Fax: 028 9031 0227

Old Townhall Building, 80 Victoria Street, Belfast, BT1 3GL
DX 461 NR
Tel: 02890 328594, Fax: 028 9072 4555

Royal Courts of Justice, Chichester Street, Belfast, BT1 3JF
DX 456 NR
Tel: 02890 325111, Fax: 028 9031 3508

Coleraine Court Office, The Courthouse, 46A Mountsandel Road, Coleraine,
BT52 1NY
DX 3411 NR
Tel: 028 7034 3437, Fax: 028 7032 0156

Craigavon Court Office, The Courthouse, Central Way, Craigavon, BT64 1AP
DX 3762 NR
Tel: 028 3834 1324, Fax: 028 3834 1243

Downpatrick Court Office, The Courthouse, English Street, Downpatrick, BT30 6AB
DX 2971 NR
Tel: 028 4461 4621, Fax: 028 4461 3969

Dungannon Court Office, The Courthouse, 46 Killyman Road, Dungannon, BT71 DE
DX 3052 NR
Tel: 028 8772 2992, Fax: 028 8772 8169

Enniskillen Court Office, The Courthouse, East Bridge Street, Enniskillen,
BT74 7BW
DX 3553 NR
Tel: 028 6632 2356, Fax: 028 6632 3636

Larne Court Office, The Courthouse, Victoria Road, Larne, BT40 1RN
DX 2206 NR
Tel: 028 2827 2927, Fax: 028 2827 6414

Limavady Court Office, The Courthouse, Main Street, Limavady, BT49 0EY
DX 3504 NR
Tel: 028 7772 2688, Fax: 028 7776 8794

Lisburn Court Office, The Courthouse, Railway Street, Lisburn, BT28 1XR
DX 3383 NR
Tel: 028 9267 5336, Fax: 028 9260 4107

Londonderry Court Office, The Courthouse, Bishop Street, Londonderry, BT48 6PQ
DX 3151 NR
Tel: 028 7136 3448, Fax: 028 7137 2059

Magherafelt Court Office, The Courthouse, Hospital Road, Magherafelt, BT45 5DG
DX 3302 NR
Tel: 028 7963 2121, Fax: 028 7963 4063

Newry Court Office, The Courthouse, 23 New Street, Newry, BT35 6AD
DX 2068 NR
Tel: 028 3025 2040, Fax: 028 3026 9830

Newtownards Court Office, The Courthouse, Regent Street, Newtownards, BT23 4LP
DX 2602 NR
Tel: 028 9181 4343, Fax: 028 9181 8024

Omagh Court Office, The Courthouse, High Street, Omagh, BT78 1DU
DX 3602 NR
Tel: 028 8224 2056, Fax: 028 8225 1198

Strabane Court Office, The Courthouse, Derry Road, Strabane, BT82 8DT
DX 3312 NR
Tel: 028 7138 2544, Fax: 028 7138 3209

Crown Prosecution Service

Source: www.cps.gov.uk

CPS Avon & Somerset Area Office, 2nd Floor, Froomsgate House, Rupert Street, Bristol, BS1 2QJ
DX 78120 Bristol
Tel: 0117 930 2800, Fax: 0117 930 2810

CPS Bedfordshire Area Office, Sceptre House, 7-9 Castle Street, Luton, Bedfordshire, LU1 3AJ
DX 120503 Luton 6
Tel: 01582 816600, Fax: 01582 816678

CPS Cambridgeshire Area Office, Justinian House, Spitfire Close, Ermine Business Park, Huntingdon, Cambridgeshire, PE29 6XY
DX 123223 Huntingdon 5
Tel: 01480 825200, Fax: 01480 825205

CPS Cheshire Area Office, 2nd Floor, Windsor House, Pepper Street, Chester, Cheshire, CH1 1TD
DX 20019 Chester
Tel: 01244 408600, Fax: 01244 408658

CPS Cleveland Area Office, 1 Hudson Quay, The Halyard, Middlehaven, Middlesbrough, Cleveland, TS3 6RT
DX 60551 Middlesbrough 12
Tel: 01642 204500, Fax: 01642 204504

CPS Cumbria Area Office, 1st Floor, Stocklund House, Castle Street, Carlisle, Cumbria, CA3 8SY
DX 63032 Carlisle
Tel: 01228 882900, Fax: 01228 882910

CPS Derbyshire Area Office, 7th Floor, St Peter's House, Gower Street, Derby, Derbyshire, DE1 1SB
DX 725818 Derby 22
Tel: 01332 614000, Fax: 01332 614009

CPS Devon & Cornwall Area Office, Hawkins House, Pynes Hill, Rydon Lane, Exeter, Devon, EX2 5SS
DX 135606 Exeter 16
Tel: 01392 288000, Fax: 01392 288008

CPS Dorset Area Office, Ground Floor, Oxford House, Oxford Road, Bournemouth, Dorset, BH8 8HA
DX 7699 Bournemouth
Tel: 01202 498700, Fax: 01202 498860

CPS Durham Area Office, Elvet House, Hallgarth Street, Durham, Co. Durham, DH1 3AT
DX 60227 Durham
Tel: 0191 383 5800, Fax: 0191 383 5801

CPS Dyfed Powys Area Office, Heol Penlanffos, Tanerdy, Carmarthen, Dyfed,
Wales, SA31 2EZ
DX 51411 Carmarthen
Tel: 01267 242100, Fax: 01267 242111

CPS Essex Area Office, County House, 100 New London Road, Chelmsford, Essex,
CM2 0RG
DX 139160 Chelmsford 11
Tel: 01245 455800, Fax: 01245 455964

CPS Gloucestershire Area Office, 2 Kimbrose Way, Gloucester, Gloucestershire,
GL1 2DB
DX 7544 Gloucester
Tel: 01452 872400, Fax: 01452 872406

CPS Greater Manchester Area Office, PO Box 237, 8th Floor, Sunlight House, Quay
Street, Manchester, M60 3PS
DX 744372 Manchester 53
Tel: 0161 827 4700

CPS Gwent Area Office, Vantage Point, Ty Coch Way, Cwmbran, Wales, NP44 7XX
DX 743270 Cwmbran 4
Tel: 01633 261101, Fax: 01633 261106

CPS Hampshire Area Office, 3rd Floor, Black Horse House, 8-10 Leigh Road,
Eastleigh, Hampshire, SO50 9FH
DX 148580 Eastleigh 4
Tel: 023 80673800, Fax: 023 80673854

CPS Hertfordshire Area Office, Queen's House, 58 Victoria Street, St Albans,
Hertfordshire, AL1 3HZ
DX 120650 St Albans 7
Tel: 01727 798700, Fax: 01727 798795

CPS Humberside Area Office, Citadel House, 58 High Street, Kingston-upon-Hull,
Humberside, HU1 1QD
DX 11922 Hull
Tel: 01482 621000, Fax: 01482 621002

CPS Kent Area Office, Priory Gate, 29 Union Street, Maidstone, Kent, ME14 1PT
DX 4830 Maidstone
Tel: 01622 356300, Fax: 01622 356370

CPS Lancashire Area Office, 2nd Floor Podium, The Unicentre, Lords Walk, Preston,
Lancashire, PR1 1DH
DX 723740 Preston 20
Tel: 01772 208100, Fax: 01772 208144

CPS Leicestershire Area Office, Princes Court, 34 York Road, Leicester,
Leicestershire, LE1 5TU
DX 10899 Leicester 1
Tel: 0116 204 6700, Fax: 0116 204 6799

CPS Lincolnshire Area Office, The Regatta, Henley Office Park, Doddington Road,
Lincoln, LN6 3QR
DX 15562 Lincoln 4
Tel: 01522 585900, Fax: 01522 585969

CPS London Area Office, 7th Floor, 50 Ludgate Hill, London, EC4M 7EX
DX 300850 Ludgate EC4
Tel: 020 7796 8000, Fax: 020 7710 3447

CPS Merseyside Area Office, 7th Floor (South), Royal Liver Building, Pier Head,
Liverpool, Merseyside, L3 1HN
DX 700596 Liverpool 4
Tel: 0151 239 6400

CPS Norfolk Area Office, Carmelite House, St James Court, Whitefriars, Norwich,
Norfolk, NR3 1SL
DX 5299 Norwich
Tel: 01603 693000, Fax: 01603 693001

CPS North Wales Area Office, Bromfield House, Ellice Way, Wrexham, Wales,
LL13 7YW
DX 26684 Wrexham
Tel: 01978 346000, Fax: 01978 346001

CPS North Yorkshire Area Office, Athena House, Kettlestring Lane, Clifton Moor,
York, North Yorkshire, YO30 4XF
DX 729960 York 29
Tel: 01904 731700, Fax: 01904 731764

CPS Northamptonshire Area Office, Beaumont House, Cliftonville, Northampton,
Northamptonshire, NN1 5BE
DX 18512 Northampton
Tel: 01604 823600, Fax: 01604 823651

CPS Northumbria Area Office, St Ann's Quay, 122 Quayside, Newcastle-upon-Tyne,
Tyne & Wear, NE1 3BD
DX 61006 Newcastle-upon-Tyne
Tel: 0191 260 4200, Fax: 0191 260 4240

CPS Nottinghamshire Area Office, 2 King Edward Court, King Edward Street,
Nottingham, Nottinghamshire, NG1 1EL
DX 729100 Nottingham 48
Tel: 0115 852 3300, Fax: 0115 852 3314

CPS South Wales Area Office, 20th Floor, Capital Tower, Greyfriars Road, Cardiff,
Wales, CF10 3PL
DX 33056 Cardiff 1
Tel: 02920 803 902, Fax: 02920 803 906

CPS South Yorkshire Area Office, Greenfield House, 32 Scotland Street, Sheffield,
South Yorkshire, S3 7DQ
DX 711830 Sheffield 18
Tel: 0114 229 8600, Fax: 0114 229 8607

CPS Staffordshire Area Office, Building 3, Etruria Valley Office Village, Etruria,
Stoke-on-Trent, Staffordshire, ST1 5RU
DX 701706 Hanley2
Tel: 01782 664500, Fax: 01782 664555

CPS Suffolk Area Office, St Vincent's House, 9th Floor, 1 Cutler Street, Ipswich, Suffolk, IP1 1UL
DX 3266 Ipswich
Tel: 01473 282100, Fax: 01473 282101

CPS Surrey Area Office, Gateway, 31 Power Close, Guildford, Surrey, GU1 1EJ
DX 122041 Guildford 10
Tel: 01483 468200, Fax: 01483 468282

CPS Sussex Area Office, City Gates, 185 Dyke Road, Hove, East Sussex, BN3 1TL
DX 149840 Hove 6
Tel: 01273 765600, Fax: 01273 765606

CPS Thames Valley Area Office, Eaton Court, 112 Oxford Road, Reading, Berkshire, RG1 7LL
DX 40104 Reading
Tel: 01189 513600, Fax: 01189 513666

CPS Warwickshire Area Office, Rossmore House, 10 Newbold Terrace, Leamington Spa, Warwickshire, CV32 4EA
DX 11881 Leamington Spa
Tel: 01926 455000, Fax: 01926 455003

CPS West Mercia Area Office, Artillery House, Heritage Way, Droitwich, Worcester, Worcestershire, WR9 8YB
DX 179491 Droitwich 4
Tel: 01905 825000, Fax: 01905 825103

CPS West Midlands Area Office, 14th Floor, Colmore Gate, 2 Colmore Row, Birmingham, West Midlands, B3 2QA
DX 719540 Birmingham 45
Tel: 0121 262 1300, Fax: 0121 262 1500

CPS West Yorkshire Area Office, 27 Park Place, Leeds, LS1 2SZ
DX 26435 Leeds Park Square
Tel: 0113 290 2700, Fax: 0113 290 2707

CPS Wiltshire Area Office, Fox Talbot House, Bellinger Close, Malmesbury Road, Chippenham, Wiltshire SN15 1BN
DX 98644 Chippenham 2
Tel: 01249 766100, Fax: 01249 766101

Legal Services Commission

Source: www.legalservices.gov.uk

London Region

Legal Services Commission, Exchange Tower, 2 Harbour Exchange Square, London, E14 9GE
DX 100170 Docklands 2
Switchboard: 020 7718 8466

Midlands Region

Birmingham Office (including the Public Defender Service Business Team)
Legal Services Commission, 1st Floor, Cannon House, 18 The Priory Queensway, Birmingham, West Midlands, B4 6BS
DX 13041 Birmingham 1
Tel: 0121 232 5500, Fax: 0121 232 5695

Cambridge Office
Legal Services Commission, 62-68 Hills Road, Cambridge, Cambridgeshire, CB2 1LA
DX 5803 Cambridge 1
Tel: 01223 417991

Nottingham Office
Legal Services Commission, Fothergill House, 2nd Floor, 16 King Street, Nottingham, Nottinghamshire, NG1 2AS
DX 10035 Nottingham 1
Tel: 01159 084200, Fax: 01159 084399

Northern Region

Chester Office
Legal Services Commission, Pepper House, Pepper Row, Chester, Cheshire, CH1 1DW
DX 19981 Chester
Tel: 01244 404 500, Fax: 01244 404 691

Leeds Office
Legal Services Commission, Harcourt House, Chancellor Court, 21 The Calls, Leeds, LS2 7EH
DX 12068 Leeds
Tel: 0113 390 7300

Liverpool Office
Legal Services Commission, Cavern Walks, 8 Mathew Street, Liverpool, Merseyside, L2 6RE
DX 14208 Liverpool 1
Switchboard: 0151 242 5200

Manchester Office
Legal Services Commission, 2nd Floor Lee House, 90 Great Bridgewater Street, Manchester, M1 5JW
DX 14343 Manchester 1
Customer Advice Team: 0845 602 1400

South Tyneside Office
Legal Services Commission, Berkley Way, Viking Business Park, Jarrow, Tyne & Wear, NE31 1SF
DX 742350 Jarrow 2
Tel: 0191 428 3600

Southern Region

Bristol Office
Legal Services Commission, South Western Regional Office, 33-35 Queen Square, Bristol, BS1 4LU
DX 7852 Bristol 1
Tel: 0117 302 3000, Fax: 0117 302 3198

Reading Office
Legal Services Commission, Dukesbridge House, 23 Duke Street, Reading, RG1 4SA
DX 4050 Reading
Tel: 0118 955 8600, Fax: 0118 955 8612

Brighton Office
Legal Services Commission, 3rd & 4th Floors, Invicta House, Trafalgar Place, Brighton, West Sussex, BN1 4FR
DX 2752 Brighton 1
Tel: 01273 878800

Wales

Cardiff Office
Marland House, Central Square, Cardiff, Wales, CF10 1PF
DX 33006 Cardiff 1
Tel: 0845 608 7070, Fax: 02920 647173

Other organisations

Academy of Experts
3 Gray's Inn Square, London, WC1R 5AH
Tel: 020 7430 0333, Fax: 020 7430 0666

Bond Solon
Paulton House, 8 Shepherdess Walk, London, N1 7LB
Tel: 020 7549 2549, Fax: 020 7549 2505

Children & Family Court Advisory Support Service – CAFCASS
CAFCASS National Office, 6th Floor, Sanctuary Buildings, Great Smith Street, London, SW1P 3BT
Tel: 0844 353 3350, Fax: 0844 353 3351

Civil Justice Council
Room E214, Royal Courts of Justice, Strand, London, WC2A 2LL
e-mail: cjc@judiciary.gsi.gov.uk

Expert Witness Institute
7 Warwick Court, London, WC1R 5DJ
Tel: 0870 366 6367, Fax: 0870 411 2470

Forensic Science Regulator
21st Floor, Alpha Tower, Suffolk Street, Queensway, Birmingham, B1 1TT

J S Publications
11 Kings Court, Willie Snaith Road, Newmarket, Suffolk, CB8 7SG
Tel: 01638 561590, Fax: 01638 560924

Judicial Studies Board
Steel House, 11 Tothill Street, London, SW1H 9LJ
Fax: 020 3334 0789

Ministry of Justice
102 Petty France, London, SW1H 9AJ
DX 152380 Westminster 8
Tel: 020 3334 3555, Fax: 020 3334 4455

Professional Solutions
7 Warwick Court, London, WC1R 5DJ
Tel: 0800 781 2021

Society of Expert Witnesses
PO Box 345, Newmarket, Suffolk, CB8 7TU
Tel: 01638 660684, Fax: 01638 668656

UK Register of Expert Witnesses
11 Kings Court, Willie Snaith Road, Newmarket, Suffolk, CB8 7SG
Tel: 01638 561590, Fax: 01638 560924

7

Calendars

Year-to-view

January 2010

S	M	T	W	T	F	S
					1	2
3	4	5	6	7	8	9
10	11	12	13	14	15	16
17	18	19	20	21	22	23
24	25	26	27	28	29	30
31						

February 2010

S	M	T	W	T	F	S
1	2	3	4	5	6	
7	8	9	10	11	12	13
14	15	16	17	18	19	20
21	22	23	24	25	26	27
28						

March 2010

S	M	T	W	T	F	S
	1	2	3	4	5	6
7	8	9	10	11	12	13
14	15	16	17	18	19	20
21	22	23	24	25	26	27
28	29	30	31			

April 2010

S	M	T	W	T	F	S
				1	2	3
4	5	6	7	8	9	10
11	12	13	14	15	16	17
18	19	20	21	22	23	24
25	26	27	28	29	30	

May 2010

S	M	T	W	T	F	S
						1
2	3	4	5	6	7	8
9	10	11	12	13	14	15
16	17	18	19	20	21	22
23	24	25	26	27	28	29
30	31					

June 2010

S	M	T	W	T	F	S
		1	2	3	4	5
6	7	8	9	10	11	12
13	14	15	16	17	18	19
20	21	22	23	24	25	26
27	28	29	30			

July 2010

S	M	T	W	T	F	S
				1	2	3
4	5	6	7	8	9	10
11	12	13	14	15	16	17
18	19	20	21	22	23	24
25	26	27	28	29	30	31

August 2010

S	M	T	W	T	F	S
1	2	3	4	5	6	7
8	8	10	11	12	13	14
15	16	17	18	19	20	21
22	23	24	25	26	27	28
29	30	31				

September 2010

S	M	T	W	T	F	S
			1	2	3	4
5	6	7	8	9	10	11
12	13	14	15	16	17	18
19	20	21	22	23	24	25
26	27	28	29	30		

October 2010

S	M	T	W	T	F	S
					1	2
3	4	5	6	7	8	9
10	11	12	13	14	15	16
17	18	19	20	21	22	23
24	25	26	27	28	29	30
31						

November 2010

S	M	T	W	T	F	S
	1	2	3	4	5	6
7	8	9	10	11	12	13
14	15	16	17	18	19	20
21	22	23	24	25	26	27
28	29	30				

December 2010

S	M	T	W	T	F	S
			1	2	3	4
5	6	7	8	9	10	11
12	13	14	15	16	17	18
19	20	21	22	23	24	25
26	27	28	29	30	31	

January 2011

S	M	T	W	T	F	S
						1
2	3	4	5	6	7	8
9	10	11	12	13	14	15
16	17	18	19	20	21	22
23	24	25	26	27	28	29
30	31					

February 2011

S	M	T	W	T	F	S
		1	2	3	4	5
6	7	8	9	10	11	12
13	14	15	16	17	18	19
20	21	22	23	24	25	26
27	28					

March 2011

S	M	T	W	T	F	S
		1	2	3	4	5
6	7	8	9	10	11	12
13	14	15	16	17	18	19
20	21	22	23	24	25	26
27	28	29	30	31		

April 2011

S	M	T	W	T	F	S
					1	2
3	4	5	6	7	8	9
10	11	12	13	14	15	16
17	18	19	20	21	22	23
24	25	26	27	28	29	30

May 2011

S	M	T	W	T	F	S
1	2	3	4	5	6	7
8	9	10	11	12	13	14
15	16	17	18	19	20	21
22	23	24	25	26	27	28
29	30	31				

June 2011

S	M	T	W	T	F	S
			1	2	3	4
5	6	7	8	9	10	11
12	13	14	15	16	17	18
19	20	21	22	23	24	25
26	27	28	29	30		

July 2011

S	M	T	W	T	F	S
					1	2
3	4	5	6	7	8	9
10	11	12	13	14	15	16
17	18	19	20	21	22	23
24	25	26	27	28	29	30
31						

August 2011

S	M	T	W	T	F	S
	1	2	3	4	5	6
7	8	9	10	11	12	13
14	15	16	17	18	19	20
21	22	23	24	25	26	27
28	29	30	31			

September 2011

S	M	T	W	T	F	S
				1	2	3
4	5	6	7	8	9	10
11	12	13	14	15	16	17
18	19	20	21	22	23	24
25	26	27	28	29	30	

October 2011

S	M	T	W	T	F	S
						1
2	3	4	5	6	7	8
9	10	11	12	13	14	15
16	17	18	19	20	21	22
23	24	25	26	27	28	29
30	31					

November 2011

S	M	T	W	T	F	S
		1	2	3	4	5
6	7	8	9	10	11	12
13	14	15	16	17	18	19
20	21	22	23	24	25	26
27	28	29	30			

December 2011

S	M	T	W	T	F	S
				1	2	3
4	5	6	7	8	9	10
11	12	13	14	15	16	17
18	19	20	21	22	23	24
25	26	27	28	29	30	31

Month-to-view

Sun	Mon	Tue	Wed	Thu	Fri	Sat
					January 2010	
					1 Bank Holiday	2
3	4 Bank Holiday in Scotland	5	6	7	8	9
10	11	12	13	14	15	16
17	18	19	20	21	22	23
24	25	26	27	28	29	30
31						

February 2010						
Sun	Mon	Tue	Wed	Thu	Fri	Sat
	1	2	3	4	5	6
7	8	9	10	11	12	13
14	15	16	17	18	19	20
21	22	23	24	25	26	27
28						

March 2010

Sun	Mon	Tue	Wed	Thu	Fri	Sat
	1	2	3	4	5	6
7	8	9	10	11	12	13
14	15	16	17 Bank Holiday in Northern Ireland	18	19	20
21	22	23	24	25	26	27
28	29	30	31			

April 2010

Sun	Mon	Tue	Wed	Thu	Fri	Sat
				1	2 Bank Holiday	3
4)	5 Bank Holiday (not in Scotland	6	7	8	9	10
11	12	13	14	15	16	17
18	19	20	21	22	23	24
25	26	27	28	29	30	

May 2010

Sun	Mon	Tue	Wed	Thu	Fri	Sat
						1
2	3 Bank Holiday	4	5	6	7	8
9	10	11	12	13	14	15
16	17	18	19	20	21	22
23	24	25	26	27	28	29
30	31 Bank Holiday					

			June 2010			
Sun	**Mon**	**Tue**	**Wed**	**Thu**	**Fri**	**Sat**
		1	2	3	4	5
6	7	8	9	10	11	12
13	14	15	16	17	18	19
20	21	22	23	24	25	26
27	28	29	30			

July 2010						
Sun	Mon	Tue	Wed	Thu	Fri	Sat
				1	2	3
4	5	6	7	8	9	10
11	12 Bank Holiday in Northern Ireland	13	14	15	16	17
18	19	20	21	22	23	24
25	26	27	28	29	30	31

August 2010						
Sun	Mon	Tue	Wed	Thu	Fri	Sat
1	2 Bank Holiday in Scotland	3	4	5	6	7
8	9	10	11	12	13	14
15	16	17	18	19	20	21
22	23	24	25	26	27	28
29	30 Bank Holiday (not in Scotland	31				

September 2010

Sun	Mon	Tue	Wed	Thu	Fri	Sat
			1	2	3	4
5	6	7	8	9	10	11
12	13	14	15	16	17	18
19	20	21	22	23	24	25
26	27	28	29	30		

October 2010						
Sun	Mon	Tue	Wed	Thu	Fri	Sat
					1	2
3	4	5	6	7	8	9
10	11	12	13	14	15	16
17	18	19	20	21	22	23
24	25	26	27	28	29	30
31						

November 2010

Sun	Mon	Tue	Wed	Thu	Fri	Sat
	1	2	3	4	5	6
7	8	9	10	11	12	13
14	15	16	17	18	19	20
21	22	23	24	25	26	27
28	29	30 Bank Holiday in Scotland				

December 2010						
Sun	**Mon**	**Tue**	**Wed**	**Thu**	**Fri**	**Sat**
			1	2	3	4
5	6	7	8	9	10	11
12	13	14	15	16	17	18
19	20	21	22	23	24	25
26	27 Bank Holiday	28 Bank Holiday	29	30	31	

Expert Witness Year Book 2010

January 2011

Sun	Mon	Tue	Wed	Thu	Fri	Sat
						1
2	3 Bank Holiday	4 Bank Holiday in Scotland	5	6	7	8
9	10	11	12	13	14	15
16	17	18	19	20	21	22
23	24	25	26	27	28	29
30	31					

February 2011

Sun	Mon	Tue	Wed	Thu	Fri	Sat
		1	2	3	4	5
6	7	8	9	10	11	12
13	14	15	16	17	18	19
20	21	22	23	24	25	26
27	28					

March 2011						
Sun	Mon	Tue	Wed	Thu	Fri	Sat
		1	2	3	4	5
6	7	8	9	10	11`	12
13	14	15	16	17 Bank Holiday in Northern Ireland	18	19
20	21	22	23	24	25	26
27	28	29	30	31		

April 2011						
Sun	Mon	Tue	Wed	Thu	Fri	Sat
					1	2
3	4	5	6	7	8	9
10	11	12	13	14	15	16
17	18	19	20	21	22 Bank Holiday	23
24	25 Bank Holiday (not in Scotland)	26	27	28	29	30

Bank Holidays

Country	Holiday	2010	2011
UK	New Year's Day	1 Jan	3 Jan
Scotland	'2nd January' Holiday	4 Jan	4 Jan
Northern Ireland	St Patrick's Day	17 Mar	17 Mar
UK	Good Friday	2 Apr	22 Apr
Not Scotland	Easter Monday	5 Apr	25 Apr
UK	May Bank Holiday	3 May	2 May
UK	Spring Bank Holiday	31 May	30 May
Northern Ireland	Orangemen's Day	12 July	12 July
Scotland	Summer Bank Holiday	2 Aug	1 Aug
Not Scotland	Summer Bank Holiday	30 Aug	29 Aug
Scotland	St Andrew's Day	30 Nov	30 Nov
UK	Christmas Day	27 Dec	26 Dec
UK	Boxing Day	28 Dec	27 Dec